a year of
scrapbooking

a year of
scrapbooking

Debbie Janasak & Anna Swinney

Photography by David Kelly Crow

TIME
LIFE
BOOKS

TIME® LIFE BOOKS

Time-Life Books is a division of Time Life Inc.

TIME LIFE INC.

President and CEO: George Artandi
Executive Vice President: Lawrence J. Marmon

TIME-LIFE CUSTOM PUBLISHING

Vice President and Publisher	Neil Levin
Director of Acquisitions and Editorial Resources	Jennifer Pearce
Editor	Linda Bellamy
Director of Creative Services	Laura McNeill
Technical Specialist	Monika Lynde
Production Manager	Carolyn Bounds
Quality Assurance Manager	James D. King

Produced by The Philip Lief Group, Inc.

Design by Stephanie Tevonian, Tevonian Design and
Diane Collins, Design Director, Universal Communications, Inc.
Cover Design by Diane Collins, Design Director, Universal Communications, Inc.
Photography by David Kelly Crow

Additional Photo Credits
David Kelly Crow: In addition to full-page photography, pages 6, 21, 33, 47, 60,
61, 74, 87, 99, 112, 125, 139, 152, 153, 165
Andrea Kane: Page 66
John Tannock: Page 67
Neni Panourgiá: Page 113
Bernadette Hamilton: Page 149
Locations for full-page photography: EverMay on the Delaware, Erwinna, PA;
The Woolverton Inn, Stockton, NJ
Styling by Chris Cahill

First printing. Printed in U.S.A.

Pre-Press Services, Time-Life Imaging Center

TIME-LIFE is a trademark of Time Warner Inc. U.S.A.

Library of Congress Cataloging-in-Publication Data
Janasak, Debbie.
    A Year of Scrapbooking/written by Debbie Janasak and Anna Swinney;
    photography by David Kelly Crow.
        p.   cm.
    ISBN 0-7370-0049-X (hardcover). –ISBN 0-7370-0064-3 (softcover)
    1. Photograph albums. 2. Photographs–Conservation and
restoration. 3. Scrapbooks.   I. Swinney, Anna.   II. Title.
TR465.J36 1999
745-593–dc21   99-23429
                                                       CIP

Books produced by Time-Life Custom Publishing are available at a special bulk discount
for promotional and premium use. Custom adaptations can also be created to meet your
specific marketing goals. Call 1-800-323-5255.

dedication

To our parents and grandparents, who passed down stories and photographs to connect us to our heritage.

To our children, to whom we pass down stories and photographs to connect them to their heritage.

acknowledgments

Our husbands, David and Keith, who have encouraged us along the way and who have given us the freedom to spend countless hours working on this book.

Our children, Kara, Jenna, Nathan, and Jared, who responded with patience and understanding when we had to tell them "Give me just a minute more, honey," and who are a constant reminder of why we make scrapbooks.

Our editors at The Philip Lief Group, Inc., Jamie Saxon and Diane Rhodes, and our editor at Time-Life, Linda Bellamy, who had the confidence that we were the right people to write this book and who continually encouraged us to tap our inner resources to come up with unique ideas from the first page to the last.

All our friends who shared their photographs and memories with us for many of the layouts in this book, especially Evelyn Bridges, John Burke, Lorraine Calautti, Thien Dao, Sylvia Garza, Larry and Kathy Hall, Steve and Leslee Herling, Carlene Heschke, Lisa Hsiang, Kevin Janasak, Patricia Juricek, Karen Knoch, Alison Lee, Kim Martin, Susan Sheehan, Tinsley Silcox, Deborah Terasaki, and Mary Yarbrough.

The staff at Stamp Asylum, Mary Kaye Seckler and Donna Goss, who were always willing to take the time to demonstrate techniques to us.

Carol McBroom, who constantly encourages us to make progress on our own family albums, and the Friday night crowd who shares our joys as we gather to crop together.

The readers of our web site, www.gracefulbee.com, many of whom have written to us asking, "Why don't you write a book?"

contents

contents

contents

the art ofscrapbooking

There is, in all of us, the desire to record the events of our lives in precious photos and mementos so that the details, emotions, and significance are not dimmed by memory. People have been making scrapbooks even longer than they have been taking photographs. Today, scrapbooking has been elevated to a true art form.

THE ART OF SCRAPBOOKING

In addition to photographs and memorabilia, sophisticated scrapbookers use creative themes, motifs, and decorative elements, such as handmade papers, borders, and photo mats, as well as journaling and creative lettering.

Scrapbookers share four significant goals. First and foremost is the desire to get existing photographs out of boxes and into albums where they can be enjoyed and easily shared with others. Second, there is a concern for the longevity and safety of the photographs themselves. Third is creating scrapbook pages in which photos are integrated with memorabilia: a scrap of antique lace from grandmother's trunk, a lock of hair, a cherished letter, a delicate sketch, a button that came from a first love's coat. Fourth is developing an artistic eye for beauty, grace, and style—and even a sense of charm and wit—to create the perfect "story" that preserves your memories for all time. It is at this point that the scrapbooker becomes an artist, challenged to make her pages more innovative and captivating.

SOPHISTICATED SCRAPBOOKING

Explore the multitude of supplies and tools

While the sheer variety may seem overwhelming at first, familiarize yourself with new products by visiting art and craft stores, subscribing to scrapbooking mag-

FOUR SEASONS

Trees are a natural way to show the changing seasons.
1. Stamp each tree and leaves in seasonal colors onto white cardstock and heat emboss with clear embossing powder (to learn the technique for heat embossing, see May, page 70). **2.** Mat each tree with black cardstock. **3.** Using a leaf-shaped stamp, stamp leaves onto a thin sheet of cork and heat emboss with verdigris embossing powder. **4.** Mount the four trees on the stamped piece of cork with glue. **5.** On a piece of black paper, cut slightly larger than the piece of cork, attach a sheet of torn handmade paper. **6.** Mount the cork onto the torn paper with glue.

azines, or visiting a scrapbooking web site, such as ours—www.gracefulbee.com.

Broaden your sources

Don't limit your sources to scrapbooking magazines and books. Try scouring other magazines for ideas; good ones to try are those that focus on other crafts, architecture, fashion, home decorating, and cooking. Theme ideas can come from anywhere: a walk in a neighbor's garden, a trip to an art gallery or historic home, or even a rainy afternoon spent antiquing.

Keep several irons in the fire

Sophisticated scrapbookers keep several scrapbooks underway simultaneously: theme albums, such as a gardening album or a theater album; an album to keep favorite photos, menus, and wine labels; albums for different family members; or chronological albums of parties and holidays.

Album styles

A fixed-size album comes with a specific number of pages bound into a blank album. Although spiral-bound albums are the most readily available fixed-size albums, you can also find such albums with a sewn binding. Adjustable albums are another option. Like fixed-size albums, these come in a variety of bindings, including three-ring binders, post-bindings, and strap-bindings. These albums, however, share the ability to add, remove, and move pages.

COUSINS MAKE THE FINEST FRIENDS

Ribbons and bows accentuate these playful photos of cousins. **1.** Using a corner rounder, round the corners of your photographs. **2.** Mat your photographs in coordinating colors. Make at least one mat for each photograph ¼" larger than the photo in each direction. **3.** Using a ⅛" hole punch, punch holes around each photograph at even intervals through the wider mat. Use an even number of holes across the top to allow you to center the bow. **4.** Lace satin ribbon through the holes. Tie a bow at the center top. **5.** Add another contrasting mat behind the laced mat if you wish. **6.** Mount the matted photographs on the page. **7.** Add creative lettering.

Alex And Jenna

Cousins Make the Finest Friends

a word about

safe homes for photos

These conditions can cause your photographs to deteriorate over time:

- **Heat.** Heat speeds up chemical processes, which cause paper to deteriorate more quickly. Store photographs and albums in the rooms of your home kept at normal temperatures. Avoid the temperature extremes of attics and garages, and even kitchens or rooms with fireplaces.

- **Light.** Keep photographs away from direct sunlight to avoid the fading effects caused by the ultraviolet radiation in light.

- **Moisture and humidity.** Moisture and humidity can damage photographs by promoting mold growth.

- **Dust, dirt, and pollution.** All dirt is an irritant and can scratch your photographs when you attempt to wipe it off. Use camera lens tissue in order to avoid scratches.

- **Improper handling.** Fingerprints can contain an invisible residue of oil or dirt—use page protectors on completed album pages to guard against damage.

- **Acid.** Acid is a chemical substance that can weaken paper, causing it to turn brown and brittle. Its presence is measured by a pH factor on a scale of 0 to 14. Use acid-free products, those with a pH of 7.0 or higher.

- **Lignin.** Lignin is a substance found naturally in the cell walls of plants. While lignin is responsible for the rigidity and strength of plants, its presence in paper contributes to the deterioration of paper over time. Look for papers that have had all the lignin removed.

getting started

Following is just a sampling of some of the tools and supplies, techniques, and materials discussed in this book.

Tools and Supplies

Acid-free cardstock

Calligraphic pens

Circle cutter, oval cutter

Clip art

Corner rounder

Corrugator

Craft knife

Decorative inks

Decorative rulers

Decorative scissors, straight scissors

Die-cut shapes

Hole punches

Hot-glue gun

Light box

Markers

Paper adhesive

Personal trimmer

pH testing pen

Photo-safe, archival quality pens

Photo-safe adhesives

Stencils

Stylus

Templates and stencils

Watercolors

Techniques

Collage

Cornering

Creative lettering

Dry embossing

Embroidery

Heat embossing

Painting

Papercutting

Paper folding

Paper piercing

Paper tearing

Paper weaving

Pop-up pages

Pressing botanicals

Punch art

Rubber stamping

Sponging

Spritzing

Tinting photographs

Watercolor

Materials

Buttons

Candy wrappers

Children's artwork

Fabric

Lace

Menus

Ribbon

Sand

String, hemp, cording

Tiny shells

Unusual papers (corrugated, foil, handmade, parchment, vellum)

Wallpaper swatches

Wine labels

Wrapping paper

Try different materials

No place is off limits when you are looking for wonderful, unique materials with which to fashion your pages—art supply stores, antique shops, flea markets, sewing stores, and more. When searching for unusual materials for your scrapbooks, however, watch out for unsafe items, such as those with a high acid content. A pH testing pen is a must since materials are not always marked with regard to their acid content.

ENJOYING YOUR ART

As you learn more advanced techniques for scrapbooking, there may be a temptation to embellish your pages heavily. Remember that the mark of a true artist is knowing when to stop. Remember, too, that your photographs, memorabilia, and journaling are the most important items on your album pages. Consider choosing understated colors, or changing the size or placement of your embellishments, to allow them to support, rather than overwhelm, your photographs and focal pieces.

Also, take this tip on "artistic imperfection" from the Navajo Indians, who purposely wove one thread imperfectly in their beautiful handmade rugs so as not to insult the spirits. Don't be self-critical, or think that your work isn't "good enough." Life itself has many wonderful inconsistencies. If you find joy in the process, that is what is most important.

USING THIS BOOK

We've organized this book by the months of the year. In each chapter, you'll find techniques to try as well as thematic ideas on special ways to capture the spirit of the month on your album pages. Each chapter is divided into seven sections:

Memories to Capture

We offer seasonal ideas inspired by the special days and traditions of the month. This section is a "must read" as you contemplate unique ways to celebrate the special moments every month has to offer.

Album Idea

We discuss ideas for theme albums, including baby books, family heritage, and seasonal albums, and gift albums for friends and family. Included are wonderful tips and ideas to keep you focused on your goal and to present photos and memorabilia in magnificent settings.

ARIZONA CACTUS

Torn paper mats and natural colors add a "desert setting" to these photographs of native Arizona cacti. For a creative title, use slot lettering. **1.** Draw wide block letters in pencil on cardstock. **2.** Use a craft knife to cut slots in the cardstock at each side of the letter strokes. Be sure to leave an area in the center uncut to allow the letters to keep their form. **3.** Weave a strip of contrasting paper through the slots to highlight the lettering.

PARIS BY NIGHT

The black and gold in this layout highlight the contrast between the dark sky and illuminated monuments. **1.** Draw your own Eiffel Tower with a pencil and ruler, adding details from a photograph or illustration on a brochure or postcard. **2.** Using a needle, punch a hole at each "intersection" of the lines of your drawing. **3.** Use the holes to guide your stitching with gold lamé thread, taking care to be consistent in the direction of the stitches as you "build" your tower. **4.** Add your lettering in gold to complete the look.

Design Concept

We highlight one particular element of design in each chapter. Each principle can be used on its own, but remember, they work in concert to give you a complete portfolio of design knowledge to inspire your layouts.

Technique to Try

We also present a new technique every month, illustrated with sample scrapbook pages to give you a feel for the effects that you can create.

Journaling

Each chapter recognizes that your photos are of more value when accompanied by the stories that go with them. Journaling can be as simple as the addition of labels or a sentence or two of explanation, or as detailed as a full-page narrative reflecting on an unforgettable experience. Topics range from subjects to write about to creative ways to gather information.

Outside the Lines

To inspire a sense of fun and novelty, we explore unconventional techniques and materials for creating scrapbook pages—borrowed from the classical arts as well as stitchery and papercrafts. It is our hope that this section will be a launching point to explore your own skills and talents "outside the lines."

Photo Tip

Photographs are the heart and soul of scrapbooks and memory albums. The goal of each photo tip is to help you become a more experienced, confident, and creative photographer.

It is our hope that you will return to this book month after month and year after year. Remember, scrapbooks are a celebration of all that is dearest to your heart. Treasure the process of scrapbooking and take pride in your finished work. Check the Resources appendix for supplies and materials used in the scrapbook layouts throughout the book.

PHOTO TIP

The Photo Tip section in each chapter helps train your "photographer's eye" for seeking out, composing, and shooting wonderful, creative photographs that will serve to inspire new scrapbook layouts.

Philadelphia Museum of Art
Donna & Debra
Debra strikes that traditional "Rocky" pose on the steps to the Philadelphia Art Museum.

DAY AT THE ART MUSEUM

Memorabilia from a day trip to the Philadelphia Museum of Art inspired the selection of scrapbook materials for this two-page layout. **1.** Choose papers to complement the natural tones of the gift store bag, and then mount the bag as a background for other mementos. **2.** Create lettering with a computer font that matches the letter style found in the museum literature. **3.** Fashion a vellum paper pocket for tucking away the museum map by folding the sides of vellum paper under about 1" and gluing it to the page. Punch a half circle in the top of the pocket to allow items to be accessed more easily. **4.** Add a grouping of art postcards of your favorite paintings held together by a gold tassel.

january

January ushers in the New Year with the promise of change, fresh starts, and renewed commitments. The weather won't seem so dreary when you are making plans for a year even more fulfilling than the last one. Shut out the cold, clear your work area, open a new journal or notebook, uncap your favorite pen—then plan some ways to capture your *joie de vivre* in new, themed scrapbooks or new additions to scrapbooks in progress.

MEMORIES TO CAPTURE

January is the natural starting point for launching a year of scrapbooking memories. New Year's parties give way to resolutions and a clear look at the 12 months to come. But all too soon we get caught up in our day-to-day activities and lose sight of the promises of the coming year. This January, make a point to plan some creative photographs, and learn new techniques to include your favorite mementos of places, events, and loved ones in specially-designed pages in your memory album.

COUNTDOWN TO THE NEW YEAR

A "Past and Present" New Year's Eve

Host a party and on your invitations, ask guests to bring a photograph of themselves from earlier in the year; then take a color photograph of each guest ringing in the New Year. You might consider using a combination of black-and-white and color photos to add visual dimension. Draw on the idea of time as a theme—perhaps use paper imprinted with images of clocks as a background, and create a layout using the two photographs of each person. This layout becomes a wonderful tribute to the relationships that have meant the most to you in the past 12 months.

PINE CONES

These pine cones were created using a rubber stamp with a single pine cone design. **1.** Ink the stamp and stamp on Post-it paper. Cut out the design close to the edges and set aside. **2.** Color the rubber stamp with brown and green markers and stamp onto "snowy paper." **3.** Let dry about 10 minutes. **4.** Cover the stamped design with the Post-it pine cone (see May, page 71). **5.** Recolor the rubber stamp and stamp a second pine cone, partially overlapping the Post-it pine cone (called masking). **6.** Remove the Post-it pine cone. **7.** Cut the snowy paper into a small square and mount on a square of green paper at an angle.

A special children's New Year

Find ways to include your children in your New Year's plans. If your children are too young to stay up until midnight, consider sending them to bed early so that they can be awakened at 11:45 p.m. to help you celebrate. Or celebrate with them at breakfast on New Year's Day—decorate your table with streamers and confetti and take pictures of a festive family breakfast.

Bring on the bells

"Ringing in the New Year" makes a great title for a scrapbook. Did you know that people once rang bells and beat sticks to help physically bring in the New Year? Take photographs of your family ringing bells and use the pictures to create a delightful opener for your family's annual album.

IT'S A NEW YEAR

Personal goals and promises

Use journaling to create a page in your scrapbook about your resolutions or your aspirations for the New Year. Have each family member write his or her own page. Remember to use archival quality pens—be creative and decorate your page with elegant lettering.

Traditions are forever

Do you have any traditional New Year's Day rituals, such as serving black-eyed peas for good luck? Including the recipe for your favorite black-eyed pea dish, or a written description of what your favorite tradition means and how it came into your family, is an artistic and practical way to preserve your family's special rituals for future generations.

WINTER WONDERS

The beauty of snow

Don't wait until the snow has stopped falling before venturing outside. Bundle up in your warm woolen mittens and brightly colored scarves. Take photo-

SKI MEMORIES

This layout features handmade "snow."

To make snowy banks: **1.** Tear three strips of white cardstock about 2" in width by slowing "rocking" the paper back and forth from side to side as you tear it, to split the paper. **2.** With a cosmetic sponge, dab white pigment ink from a rubber stamp pad onto the torn edge of each strip. **3.** Sprinkle iridescent embossing powder over the white ink and heat emboss. (Tip: Use a clipboard to hold the paper in place when heat embossing small elements.) **4.** Layer the three strips across the bottom of dark blue paper.

To make snow falling background: **1.** Position a plastic template of small dots on top of the dark blue paper at the far right edge. (Note: Plastic template is not large enough to fill the entire dark blue paper, so you'll need to work in small sections.) **2.** With a cosmetic sponge, dab white pigment ink from a rubber stamp pad over the dots of the plastic template. **3.** Remove the plastic template carefully and slide it over, lining up the dots on the plastic template with a row of completed white dots. (Be very careful not to smear the white dots.) **4.** Dab the next row of dots with white pigment ink. **5.** Repeat until the dark blue paper is filled with snow.

To make trees: **1.** Press a snowy tree rubber stamp onto a white pigment ink pad and stamp onto pine green paper. Heat emboss with white embossing powder. **2.** Stamp another tree onto a snowy-patterned paper. Heat emboss with white embossing powder. **3.** Cut out both trees.

To finish layout: **1.** Cut letters to make the word SKI using an alphabet stencil and dark blue paper. Gently press the cut letters against a white pigment ink pad. Sprinkle letters with white embossing powder and heat emboss. **2.** Mat photographs with snowy-patterned paper and dark blue paper. **3.** Mount matted photographs, tucking them between the layers of the snowy banks. **4.** Mount the trees, positioning one behind the other **5.** Mount the SKI letters sticking out of one of the snow banks.

graphs while it is snowing. Capture the snow piled high on the tree branches. Be sure to include the deepest snowfall of the winter season so that you can remember it in years to come. Relish the muffled quiet of a snowy day. Jot down your impressions of the day to include as journaling on your scrapbook page.

Everyone loves a snowman

Create a scrapbook page describing and documenting all the steps of creating the perfect snowman from the carrot nose to the red scarf wrapped around his neck. Try making a unique snowman—perhaps one designed to look like a favorite movie star—complete with trademark attire.

Warm winters

Even if you live in a warmer climate, or have a year without snow, you can still take wonderful winter photographs. For a whimsical spread, don your favorite sweater for a professional photograph and ask the photographer for a "winter scene" backdrop. Or do it yourself—dress up for sledding, drag your sled out to a grassy hill, then make an exaggerated sad "no snow today" face and have a friend snap a picture.

Be a sport

Sledding down hills on a fancy toboggan or a dimestore sled is fun for the kid in all of us. Love to hit the slopes? Skiing offers many possibilities for picture taking: getting on the lift, swooshing down the slopes, and for some of us, falling at the bottom. In warmer regions, pack a bag with mittens and scarves and head for the local indoor ice skating rink. Even if it's 80 degrees outside, you can enjoy the thrill of ice

skating. To top off your outing, stop off at a local café for a cup of hot chocolate on your way home. Don't forget your camera.

OTHER NOTABLE EVENTS

Take time out for tea

Celebrate National Hot Tea Month with a tea party complete with vintage clothing and real china. If you like, visit antique shops to look for old-fashioned tea strainers or other tableware or linens to complement your table. Hold the party in a tearoom or quaint restaurant or host your own tea party at home. An afternoon tea is a great opportunity to use your best china to entertain a few friends. Young girls love a tea party (see layout on the next page).

Pooh for a day

Celebrate the January birthday of A. A. Milne, creator of Winnie the Pooh, by taking your family for a nature walk in your own neighborhood "Hundred Acre Wood" or a local park or nature center. Use soft colors and Pooh paraphernalia in the classic Pooh style to make an album page about your adventure.

ALBUM IDEA: FAMILY CHRONOLOGY

Whether you have a family of one or 10, it's incredibly rewarding to create a family chronological album. You'll be able to revisit an entire year (or a block of years, maybe three to five), capturing how your children have grown, how styles have changed, and how special occasions have been celebrated.

The task of collecting the assorted photos and memorabilia, much of which may be scattered or tucked away, may seem daunting. But creating a chronological album does not require as major a sorting effort as you might imagine. You need only sort your photographs and memorabilia by date, then you're ready to get started. One word of caution: you'll probably find it most rewarding to work backwards. If you start with your oldest family photographs (circa 1985 or 1972 or whenever), you'll never feel "caught up." Starting with the current year, and also working on the previous year as time allows, gives you a faster sense of accomplishment. Also, you're likely to remember more information about the recent photographs, allowing you to be more complete with your journaling.

My husband, Keith, and I met on a ski trip to Taos, New Mexico. Recently, while sorting and organizing photographs stuffed in boxes in my closet, I found pictures taken during this ski trip. I actually found two sets of photographs: ones I took and also ones that Keith took. Even though we had just met, we are both prominent in each other's photos.

— Debbie

TEA PARTY

Celebrate National Hot Tea Month with a Victorian tea party. **1.** On a handmade invitation (we used a dry embossed teapot and lettering on ours), invite the young ladies to wear their best party dresses or vintage dresses and fancy hats. **2.** Take lots of photos and save a tea bag, doilies, and other decorations. **3.** Cut an acid-free square paper doily and arrange it into the corners of a piece of pale blue cardstock.

4. Stamp a teacup rubber stamp onto vellum paper and heat emboss with gold embossing powder. **5.** Cut out the stamped cup and mount onto the page with an actual tea bag (first slit the bottom of the teabag with a craft knife and remove the tea) peeking over the rim of the cup. **6.** Mat your photographs in contrasting colors and mount along with the invitation and other mementos.

PLANO BALLOON FESTIVAL

Paper-pierced balloons add an extra dimension to these colorful photographs of a family day trip. **1.** By freehand, draw two balloon shapes and cut them out. We have found that a heart template or die cut makes a good beginning for a balloon—just round out the top and cut off the bottom. **2.** On the back of each balloon, draw in pencil the design you want to pierce. Designs can be inspired by your photographs—or use your own imagination. **3.** Using a piercing technique (see this chapter, page 18), pierce your balloon designs. **4.** By freehand, cut a basket for each balloon out of brown cardstock. **5.** Cut three short pieces of twine for each balloon (six in total). **6.** Tape the pieces of twine to the back of each balloon and basket with acid-free tape. **7.** Mat your photographs and attach to the page. Attach the balloons to the page, but allow the baskets to swing freely. **8.** Use fancy lettering for your page title.

Include a broad selection of pictures in your chronological album—wonderful photographs taken of your family playing in the snow in January or in a patch of wildflowers in the spring. Other pictures might include photographs from your family vacation, a trip to a local museum or historic site, or a religious holiday celebration.

Whether you put an entire year's or multiple years' worth of pictures in a single album, you'll probably want a cover page or title page for each year (see September, page 120). Take this into consideration when planning whether to start your first page on the left or the right side.

Chronological albums provide a coherent sense of the passage of time, for example, how a child changes over time, showing growth and development. Many scrapbookers create multiple types of chronology theme albums, such as a vacation album, a baby book, a holiday album, and so on. You may wish to showcase some of the best pictures in more than one book.

DESIGN CONCEPT: FOCAL POINT

Most of us create scrapbooks with the intention of highlighting and safeguarding precious photographs and memorabilia. When the two are combined on a scrapbook page, a very personal story is retold. Design techniques, such as color, patterns, and placement, should be chosen carefully to enhance and complement your story. In designing a scrapbook page, success begins with selecting a focal point. By choosing a particular photograph, group of photographs, or memory to emphasize, you can control the mood or theme of your layout.

A few good photos

Begin by editing your photographs and memorabilia down to the very best. Select photographs that are in focus, well composed, and have simple backgrounds. Visual clutter, poor composition, or telephone poles growing out of heads are out. Also for the cutting room floor are "mistakes," like photographs of people with closed eyes or unattractive expressions.

Resist the urge to use all 30 photographs of feeding pigeons in St. Mark's Square in Venice. Instead choose the two or three photographs that best capture the moment, setting, or event. As a rule of thumb, choose two to four photographs for a scrapbook layout (unless you are doing a collage design). Pick various poses and angles, different expressions and sequences, and contrasting viewpoints, being careful not to edit too much because of limited/restricted space. When in doubt, plan to create more than one page of a particular occasion.

Adding emphasis

One way to make a focal point out of a photograph is to have an enlargement made so it will dominate other elements on the page. Consider making a 5" x 7" enlargement of your focal picture and setting it off with complementary 4" x 6" shots. As an alternative to making an enlargement, you can also "enlarge" the size of a photograph by adding mats (see February, page 27).

Placing your focal point

Placement of your focal point on the page can influence its importance relative to the entire design. A photograph placed in the center of a page automatically serves as a centerpiece around which other design elements are placed. Or place your most important photograph at the end of a linear sequence, or path of movement—for instance, a series of photographs highlighting all the steps of building the perfect snowman. As your eyes take in each step as the snowman is built, you cannot help but notice the final photograph—the finished snowman.

TECHNIQUE TO TRY: CROPPING

Many new scrapbookers are hesitant to cut, or crop, their photographs. While cutting photographs may be intimidating at first, artful and effective trimming techniques can help create a great deal of visual appeal. Even professional photographers crop in the darkroom. Aside from the creative side of cropping your photographs, there are many practical reasons to do so.

FOCAL POINT

The focus of this layout is the giant redwood trees seen during a trip to California's northern shore. We chose a single photograph for a focal point to illustrate just how tall these trees really are. **1.** Measure rust-colored paper to mat your focal point photograph with a 1" border. Use a crimper (see July, page 96) to add texture to your rust-colored mat. **2.** Mount your focal point photograph to the rust-colored mat and mat again onto green paper. **3.** Cut a small triangle from the rust–colored paper and mount in the lower left corner of your tan background. **4.** Create journaling on your computer and print directly onto green paper. Mat the journaling with rust-colored paper. **5.** Mount your matted focal point photograph in the top right corner of your layout. **6.** Mount your remaining photographs. **7.** Mount journaling.

Most of us are not professional photographers

We've all taken a picture where the people look too small against the background or someone's arm is cut off and there's space on the other side. Cropping lets you zoom in on the best part of the picture.

Composition mistakes

Most point-and-shoot cameras allow the photographer to look through a hole that is close to the lens, but not through the lens. That means that your eye does not see exactly what the camera "sees," and what you see, unfortunately, may not be what you get. Cropping lets you take out what you don't like.

Director's chair

Sometimes you may be required to stand farther away from your subject than you would like, leaving you with a smaller subject and excess background "clutter" in your photograph. A zoom lens can help but does not always eliminate the problem. Unless you want to infuriate the other proud parents at a ballet recital, you may have to resign yourself to standing in an awkward location, such as far off to one side. Capture the memory. Cropping will help you later.

Not all subjects are rectangular

A standard 35-mm print will be 3½" x 5" or 4" x 6". What if your subject is square or round? There may be a fair amount of wasted space on your photograph that can be eliminated with creative cropping.

California Redwoods

During our vacation to San Francisco, we drove north to see the California Redwoods. We were amazed at how tall these trees grew. The giant redwoods of Northern California grow as high as 370 feet. Each tree begins as a seed no bigger than a tomato seed.

CROPPING

(TOP TO BOTTOM) **1.** Trimming away excess landscape can improve the composition of the photograph. **2.** An oval cutter can help salvage a crooked shot and add an elegant touch. **3.** With a sharp pair of straight scissors, you can trim very close to the edge of the subject of your photograph, removing the background and producing a silhouette.

We've all heard those famous six words so important in newspaper journalism: who, what, when, where, why, and how. Use these as a guideline for what information to include on your scrapbook page.

Who

Have you ever looked at a friend's album and wondered who the people were? Or, have you ever wondered exactly who you were looking at in one of your own photo albums from 10 or 20 years ago? Whereas you might eventually figure out the family relationships, you might never figure out that the girl in the red dress lived next door to you when you were in the second grade. You can help solve that problem by always remembering to include names and relationships in your journal entries.

Consider the approach that novelists take. The first time they introduce a character, they give him a name and describe his relationship to other characters in the story. Later in the story they may add details by referring to him by his name, a nickname, or a special feat he achieved.

You can use a similar approach in your albums. The first time a person appears in the album, "introduce" him or her. You may give a person several titles: Pearl Habich, Nanny, Nanny Pearl, David's grandmother, Joan's mother. You can include as many titles as you may wish to use later in the album. Then, on subsequent pages, use the title that seems most appropriate. For instance, if you include a photograph of David with his grandmother, it's natural to label it "David with Nanny."

An even more detailed approach is to use the familiar labels throughout the album, but include a reference list in the back of the album, perhaps with a small photograph of each significant person, and include pertinent information such as his or her name, nicknames, and relationships.

What

Include information about what is happening in the photographs. It may not be as obvious in 10 years as it is now. Sometimes the "what" will be obvious from the title you give a page, such as "Ashley's First Haircut." Other times it will not be as clear; these are the photographs that benefit from additional journaling.

METAL "QUILTING"

A metal "quilted" zebra sets off this page, capturing the classic family zoo outing. **1.** With a rubber stamp, stamp an image onto a paper thin piece of metal—in this case, a zebra stamp and copper were used. **2.** To create the "quilted" zebra, use a stylus or knitting needle to press firmly on the metal along all the lines of the stamped image of the zebra. **3.** Cut the zebra out with deckle-edged scissors, leaving ½" or more around all edges. **4.** Using a larger stylus or knitting needle, tap lightly in the background area (between the zebra and deckled edge) to create a "distressed" look.

making the perfect cut

As a scrapbooker, you have a number of tools available to help you achieve clean, professional cropping. Paper cutters and trimmers come in a variety of styles and sizes.

- **Standard paper cutters use a lever action to cut paper up to 12" or 15" in length and should be used for long, straight cuts, not for fine detail.**

- **Personal trimmers are like standard paper cutters but smaller. A lever-style personal trimmer will cut paper or photographs up to 6" or 7" in length. The smaller size enables more precise cutting.**

- **Sliding-blade trimmers, originally used in photography shops to crop enlargements, are now readily available to consumers. They vary in size, allowing cuts up to 8" or 12" in common models, and provide great precision in your cuts. One advantage unique to sliding-blade trimmers is the fact that you can raise the blade at any point during the cut, allowing you to cut intricate shapes.**

- **Rotary trimmers use an interchangeable circular blade to cut through your paper or photographs. The round blade gives a continuous clean cut. The interchangeable blades, which come in plain and decorative styles, give a variety of looks.**

- **Circle cutters work on the same principle as a compass. With a post in the middle, you slide a blade around the pivot point. With a circle cutter, you can make perfect circles in sizes that range from 1" to 8" in diameter.**

- **Oval cutters work similarly to circle cutters except with different geometrical mechanics to create an elliptical shape. Some oval cutters can also cut circles, thus filling two niches.**

Sophisticated scrapbookers use journaling that extends beyond simple label or caption techniques. You can achieve great results by penning one or several paragraphs to narrate what is happening. For an elegant touch, write on handmade paper or elegant stationery and cut out the written area to fit on your scrapbook page. Overlapping the photos on the written area is also very effective.

When

If you have more than a few years' worth of photographs, it is easy to forget when many were taken. Dating pictures helps add a sense of order. Not only can dates help with the sequencing of events, but they can also help by connecting the events depicted in your photo album to those in the outside world.

The precision of the dates you will want to record in your albums will vary greatly. The most common way is to include the month and year or the holiday and the year: July 1975, Christmas 1997. However, your journaling can be more or less specific. With older photographs, you may not know the exact date. You might choose "Winter 1955-1956" or "The mid-1950s." On the other end of the spectrum, when working with recent photographs, you might want to include not only the exact date but also the time of day. Imagine a three-year-old's birthday with captions like these: 10 a.m.—Anticipation; Noon—The center of attention; 3 p.m.—All this loot is mine; 7 p.m.—The lights are out, the party's over.

There are other ways to impart a sense of time in your album. One way involves using the ages of the people in the photographs. Rather than writing "October 1996," achieve a more individualized approach by substituting something like "Katie, Age 5." Depending on the situation, one approach may seem more appropriate than the other.

Another way to convey a sense of time is to document the relationship between events in your life and those in contemporary history. For example, your journaling could say "Hannah was born on July 11," or it could say "there was a solar eclipse the day that Hannah was born—July 11, 1991."

Where

It is at least as easy to forget where pictures were taken as it is to forget when. And, just like dates, the precision of how closely you want to document where a picture was taken will vary with the situation.

When documenting pictures taken on a trip to the zoo, you will of course want to mention what zoo you visited. Refrain from stating the obvious; it is probably

I recently had the opportunity to rummage through some old photographs that belonged to my husband's grandmother. I found many photographs carefully inscribed on the back with information about the people in the pictures and where they were taken. I was delighted. The most mysterious pictures, however, just had the date 10-21-50 written on the back. No one in the family knew the significance of that date.

— Anna

I cried when they took you away right after you were born.

The delivery room was filled with people: doctors, nurses, anesthetists, and specialists from Neonatal Intensive Care. Everyone was concerned because they were afraid that you might have ingested meconium. They let me say goodbye as they hurried you off to the NICU but I didn't get to touch you.

Hours later, when I came to visit you, several doctors and nurses were still working on you. It wasn't until the next morning that they let me hold you. You were still hooked up to wires and monitors, but I didn't care. Just to hold you and know that you were mine, my firstborn daughter, was my greatest joy.

not necessary to note that a particular picture was taken in front of the monkey exhibit, especially if the monkeys are visible in the picture. When writing about a trip across the country, mention your most memorable sightseeing adventures.

Recording where pictures were taken is especially important with vacation shots. You'll want to make notes as soon as you return, and have your film developed promptly to make sure that you don't forget the name of that cathedral and whether it was in Venice or Florence. In fact, you might even want to document vacation photos in a small notebook when you take them: #7-#17, Versailles; #18-#36, The Louvre. (A well-documented album is a treasure chest of information when you decide to make a return trip to the same place five, even 10, years later, or if you want to make recommendations to a friend who is planning a trip.)

Another helpful tip when traveling is to keep mementos with addresses and locations on them—restaurant bills, museum tickets, hotel note paper. Simply cut out the address portion and incorporate it into your scrapbook page.

Why

Some of the most interesting journaling in albums often describes the "whys" of a group of pictures. Have you ever asked yourself, "Why did I take this picture?"

FIRST IMPRESSIONS

While photographs of newborn babies are guaranteed to result in a chorus of oohs and aahs, the emotions that come with giving birth are most dramatically captured in a layout that incorporates journaling. **1.** Compose journaling on your computer and print directly onto cardstock. Cut to size. **2.** Using creative lettering (see April, page 56), draw the title on a curved line in a fancy lettering style. Alternatively, compose the title in a publishing program on your computer and add special effects to achieve the curve. **3.** Mat the title, journaling, and photograph with coordinating colors using a combination of straight edges and edges made with decorative scissors. Mount on the page. **4.** Create a decorative rattle with a combination of circles in various sizes (cut with a circle cutter or a circle punch, depending on the size), a small rabbit punch, and a ¼" star-shaped punch. Layer the pieces and glue together. **5.** As a final touch, add a satin ribbon bow to the rattle before attaching it to the page.

If you don't remember why you took it, others probably won't appreciate it either.

Consider some of these "why" questions to answer in your journaling:

■ Why is she smiling? (Or crying)

■ Why was this group of people together?

■ Why did this event take place?

■ Why is someone important missing from some of the pictures?

How

Answering the question "how" in your album can often fill in the gaps of the story between the pictures. "How" stories that document a sequence of events can be very entertaining, such as the steps required to make a gingerbread house. You might want to include the recipe for the spiced apple cider that the people at the holiday party are drinking, or the steps for a popular dance alongside the pictures of your friends tearing up the dance floor. Also, write about senses that can't be captured in photographs, such as how something smelled or sounded.

OUTSIDE THE LINES: PAPER PIERCING

By piercing a series of small dots with a sharp needle, you can create beautiful raised patterns and designs on paper. This technique is known as paper piercing. The designs you create can be as simple as piercing dots around the outside of a heart or as elaborate as fashioning a beautiful border.

The tools needed for this technique are probably already around your home: a sharp needle or corsage pin and a folded towel. (We like to use a corsage pin because it has a large head, which means we don't have to use a thimble.) Papers of medium weight will work best. You can also pierce paper die cuts for layering on your scrapbook page, or create your own cut-paper element, such as hearts, stars, hands, doves, snowflakes, and flowers.

Pierced paper designs can be mounted directly onto scrapbook pages for a wonderful look that adds visual texture to the page. Mounting a contrasting color paper behind your pierced element will make your design really stand out.

PHOTO TIP: EQUIPMENT

Point-and-shoot and 35-mm cameras are the most popular among scrapbookers and are also the easiest to use. We advise you to spend as much as you can afford on your camera—it's a worthwhile investment in your artistry.

PAPER PIERCING

Paper piercing lends an exquisite, delicate touch.
1. Decide what type of design you want and lightly trace it with a pencil onto the back side of your paper. Piercing can be used to emphasize or embellish a particular design element; for instance, consider using a hand-shaped pattern around a handmade paper valentine heart, to make it look like it's being held. You can also use piercing to actually create a design, for example, stars, moons, or flowers on small squares of paper that are then mounted on your page. **2.** Place your paper on a folded towel and use a sharp needle or corsage pin to pierce through the paper as indicated on your design. Keeping the needle straight up and down as you work will help you achieve evenly spaced and sized holes.

Once you have a good piece of equipment, you'll want to do the following:

Read your manual

The starting point for getting the most out of your camera equipment is to read the manual. It sounds so simple, but you'd be surprised how many people never read the manual or only read a very small portion of it. If you don't read the manual, you are probably missing out on some features of your camera that could help you produce higher quality photographs.

Practice! Practice! Practice!

When you purchase a new camera or begin experimenting with a new feature on your camera, you will want to practice first. Take a roll of "unimportant" pictures and carefully document the settings you used as well as specific information about lighting and your distance from the subject. When your photographs are developed and printed, carefully analyze the results in relation to the settings used. Take note of the techniques that worked and the ones that didn't.

Practice preventive maintenance

Assuming that you've read your manual and are taking advantage of most of the features of your camera, you'll also want to maintain the camera in the best possible condition. Protect your camera from dust, dirt, dampness, rain, and excessive heat. Avoid touching the lens. When the lens needs cleaning, use a soft lint-free lens tissue or cloth. Avoid opening your camera to change film in a dirty or windy location; dirt from the environment can seriously damage the interior mechanics and cause a need for professional cleaning or repair. Invest in a sensible camera case.

Keep your bases loaded

Your camera will be useless to you if the battery is dead or you run out of film. The cost of keeping an extra battery and extra film on hand is far less than the cost of missing a once-in-a-lifetime photograph. Watch the dates on film and batteries, however. While a battery that is past its expiration date will probably work, it may not last long. Film that has passed its expiration date may not yield the quality of pictures that you are accustomed to. Keep extras on hand, but not so many that the product will expire before you have the opportunity to use it.

FILM CHOICE

Over the years, there have been several types of print film

BABY'S FIRST HAIRCUT

Capture this important "first" with a colorful layout. **1.** Cut wide mats for your photographs, and embellish them with contrasting spiral punches to give the impression of locks of hair. **2.** Preserve a lock of your baby's hair by placing it between the layers of a page protector. **3.** Machine or hand stitch around the hair, leaving a sealed pouch; trim the excess plastic away. **4.** To cover up the stitching, create a frame like this one by cutting concentric circles with a circle cutter. **5.** Embellish the frame as you did the photograph mats, using contrasting spiral punches. **6.** Be sure to include the date and the name of the salon on your page.

available to consumers: 35-mm, APS, 110, 126, disc. Some have come and gone, but 35-mm seems here to stay. Your choice of film type will depend on the kind of film your camera uses. Beyond that, your film choices will revolve around the speed of the film and the color.

Consumer print films come in various speeds: 100, 200, 400, 800—with 100 ASA film being a "slow" film and 800 ASA being a "fast" film.

OLD-FASHIONED WEDDING

A one-hour photo lab can create a negative from an original print. **1.** Using a pair of deckle-edged scissors, cut a piece of plum cardstock in appropriate dimensions to mat your photograph. **2.** Using a stylus, dry emboss a thin piece of vellum with a stenciled leaf design (see April, page 55). **3.** Using a sharp needle or corsage pin, pierce the vellum in a pattern that comple-ments the dry embossed design (piercing is discussed on page 18). **4.** Mount the vellum atop a sheet of plum cardstock the size of the scrapbook pages that fit your album, then mount the matted photograph in the center of the vellum. **5.** Use an embossing pen to journal the couple's name and wedding date, and then heat emboss with gold embossing powder.

FILM SPEED

(TOP) This candid photo was taken with 400 ASA film, a high-speed film, because the indoor café lighting was low. A high-speed film quickly picks up what available light there is. (BOTTOM) This casual portrait of four friends was taken with 100 ASA film, a slow-speed film. This type of film is preferable for outdoor, sunny environments because the grain structure is tighter and the contrast between light and dark areas will not be as severe.

Slow film

Slower speed films, most often used in the bright outdoors, are less sensitive to light and produce sharper prints, with less grain, which is helpful if you intend to have enlargements made. Slow film forces you to use a wider aperture, which in turn gives you a smaller depth-of-field, in effect keeping your subject in keen focus while allowing the background to recede and blur.

Fast film

Since they are more sensitive to light, fast films can produce grainier prints, especially on enlargements. Nevertheless, fast films are helpful for low light conditions and excellent for sports photography and other situations where you want to freeze the action.

Ideally, you would choose the best film for every unique situation, sometimes choosing a fast film and others a slow one. However, for most people, the best alternative is to choose a medium-speed film, such as 200, which will be adequate for most situations.

Film color

Kodak Gold film and Fuji films are excellent for color print photography. There are variations, however, in the color hues between the two brands as well as within different films from the same company. Some films show more vivid warm colors, such as reds and yellows. Other films are more vibrant in their cool blues and greens. You will want to experiment with the different manufacturers as well as different films to determine the ones that suit you best. For a different look, try XP2 film—it can be processed in any regular lab and renders great looking sepia toned photos that will add a nice touch to your pages.

Don't forget about black-and-white film as an option. Black-and-white photographs can be quite striking, especially for portraits. You can now buy black-and-white films that can be developed at color labs, even one-hour processing labs, but for better results, use a custom lab (see August, page 111, for more about black-and-white photography).

CHOOSING A LAB

There are three basic types of photo labs that you may use to process your film and print your photographs:

Commercial labs

Commercial labs are large operations that process film from a variety of sources. Most discount stores, supermarkets, and drugstores send their processing to commercial labs. Mail-order labs also fall in this category. In these labs, your film is processed on a computer controlled assembly line.

Custom labs

In a custom lab, your film is processed in-house by a person you can consult with about the effects you wish to see in your finished photographs. This is where professional photographers have their film developed if they don't do it themselves. While custom labs charge higher prices than commercial labs, under some circumstances the additional cost is well worthwhile because of the personal attention given to each roll of film.

One-hour labs

It seems that every street corner now has a one-hour lab. They are convenient, but they are limited in the services they provide. Most can develop and print in 3½" x 5", 4" x 6", and possibly 5" x 7" sizes. If you need other services, such as prints from slides, your work may still need to be sent to a commercial or custom lab.

february

Nestled between January's dawn of a new year and March's warming temperatures and blustery winds are the cold days and gray skies of February. But despite the weather, February is rich with natural themes and holidays to inspire new scrapbook pages. Cozy up with a warm comforter and a cup of hot chocolate—and steep yourself in these ideas to chase away the winter blues while celebrating loved ones near and far.

MEMORIES TO CAPTURE

Valentine's Day provides the best excuse for exchanging cards, flowers, jewelry, and other gifts with our sweethearts, loved ones, and dear friends. But when the chocolates have been eaten, the flowers have wilted, and the cards have been tucked away, how quickly we forget the tender emotions that motivated these gifts. Why not take some extra steps to capture some of your special Valentine's Day memories this year?

LOVE FOR FAMILY

Pucker up

It's fun to take staged photographs of family members "spontaneously" expressing their love for each other with big hugs and kisses. For extra festive pictures, ask everyone to wear their favorite red outfit. It is also very effective to create a backdrop of beautiful red flowers or heart-shaped balloons.

Surprising the children

If you have young children, and Valentine gifts are part of your family tradition, have their gifts ready and waiting for them at the breakfast table. Use a cookie cutter to make heart-shaped breakfast toast. Be ready to take their pictures when they find the gifts—try bright red gloves, mittens, or socks for

WOVEN VALENTINE

Embellish a valentine layout with this intricate design element. **1.** Following the directions on page 30 for weaving a design, glue woven strips of paper together with Perfect Paper adhesive. **2.** Once the weaving is dry, cut the heart design from the woven base. You can also use this technique to make other designs, such as circles and flowers.

boys, or barrettes, hairbands, or earrings decorated with hearts for girls.

Making flowers last forever

Put the camera in someone else's hands to get photographs of Dad giving flowers to Mom. If you are unable to get a picture of the actual gift giving, stage a photograph while the flowers are at their best. You may even want to press the flowers for an exquisite addition to your memory album (see May, page 72).

LOVE FOR FRIENDS

Handcrafted gifts

What better gift is there to give a dear friend than one you made yourself? Decorate a frame with dried or silk flowers, and put a photograph of yourself with your friend in the frame. Capture the gift giving on film, then decorate your scrapbook page with the photo plus some of the same flowers you used to decorate the frame. Other ideas: decorate a basket, embroider a border on a set of pillowcases, or make a pillow in an elegant fabric like velvet. See Not Just Albums, page 166 for hand-made gift ideas that use scrapbooking techniques.

Reminiscences with an old friend

As adults, we often lose touch with our closest friends. Home, family, and work consume so much of our time that we rarely have time even to pick up the phone and chat. Pull out some old photographs of yourself with your best friend. Find the time to get together to catch up on life and look at the photos—and have someone take your picture while you're together again. Scrapbook layouts don't have to stay in your book. Create a mini-layout or collage of "best friend" pictures that can be displayed in a frame or given as a gift.

Children's valentines

Young children love to exchange valentines with friends, and all children are proud when they learn how to write their names. Valentines—hand-signed in the trademark, crooked penmanship of a youngster are priceless. If your child is too young to write his name, buy a rubber stamp of his name, and let him "sign" each card using the stamp. Save the valentines your child receives to use for scrapbook pages.

SEND ROSES

On Valentine's Day, create a centerpiece by wrapping a large gift box and leaving the box open. Place a small gift for each family member in the box. Tie a length of ribbon to each gift, and attach a heart-shaped, gold-embossed name tag to the other end of each ribbon (the ribbons must be long enough to reach from the box to the place settings). After dinner, the family members gently pull on their ribbons to retrieve their special Valentine's Day gift. (Pictured here are all of Debbie's family: Debbie, her husband Keith, and children Kara and Nathan.)

To create the layout: **1.** On tan background paper, stamp a vine pattern rubber stamp down the outside edge of both pages with tan pigment ink. Heat emboss with verdigris embossing powder. **2.** Tear raspberry-colored mulberry paper by wetting the paper and gently pulling the paper apart. **3.** Create two fancy mats by stamping a small rubber stamp pattern on tan paper with tan pigment ink and heat embossing with verdigris embossing powder. Mount photographs on mats. **4.** Mount photographs on the layout. Layer mulberry paper behind some of the photographs. **5.** Mount rose bouquet card on center of layout. **6.** Use your computer to create fancy lettering. Trace the lettering with an embossing pen. Heat emboss with claret embossing powder.

ROMANTIC LOVE

An elegant evening out

Choose a fine restaurant to dine with your spouse or partner. Stay at the honeymoon suite of a hotel near the restaurant. Be sure to write about this special date for a journaling section on your scrapbook page. Collect keepsakes of the evening—ribbons and gift wrap from gifts you exchanged, a wine label, a restaurant matchbook cover, flowers from the table, even the menu, if possible—to use in your scrapbook layout.

A romantic portrait

All too often a couple has their picture taken together only a few times over the course of many years. Schedule an appointment with a photographer to have romantic photographs taken. Try a black-and-white portrait to evoke a softer, quieter mood. Create a scrapbook page using the portrait surrounded by smaller photos of the two of you enjoying special moments, such as holidays or common interests together.

OTHER NOTABLE EVENTS

National Black History Month

Plan a family day trip relating to black history in your area, such as a museum exhibit or historic site near your home, and be sure to take the camera along. Create a theme page in your scrapbook using decorative elements, such as an African-inspired border.

Mardi Gras

For an especially festive layout, host your own Mardi Gras party! Offer your guests traditional Mardi Gras costumes, such as decorated masks and beaded necklaces. Serve plenty of decadent foods "N' Awlins" style, such as Cajun dishes and the exotically-flavored daiquiris Bourbon Street is famous for. Wrap up the party with beignets (French doughnuts rolled in powdered sugar) and Creole coffee flavored with chicory.

National Cherry Month

Bake an old fashioned cherry pie with your family. Create a scrapbook page with pictures of the pie-making event. Use appealing cherry designs—on stickers, stamps, paper, or hand-drawn art. Don't forget to include the recipe.

ALBUM IDEA: BABY BOOK

A baby book is an invaluable keepsake and an expression of love between a parent and child. Give your child the chance—through photography and journaling—to share the many milestones and emotions of a time in her life before her earliest memories. While preprinted baby books can be beautiful and prompt you to document many important events, a handmade baby book is a very personal gift you can create for your child.

Some people choose to include only the baby's first year, others choose to include everything up to the beginning of the school-age years, and still others choose something in-between. Another option is to make the baby book just the first installment in an open-ended series of albums that span the child's lifetime.

Decide whether you want to create a chronological account of your child's life or a thematic one. You might make an album of the highlights of his life from birth to age five. Or, you could create an album dedicated entirely to Halloween or birthdays. Be sure to leave room for photographs and mementos on the same theme for future years.

You may want to use a common theme for your overall design throughout the baby book. Carrying a motif through each page of the book can result in a lovely design. Consider using a common border on every page or spread. Another option is

I am privileged to have my mother's baby book, which is over 70 years old. The binding is frayed and damaged, but the pages are in decent shape. Unfortunately, the journaling is barely readable because the ink has faded. I can make out a few gems, however. Among the gifts was a "pillow from great-great-grandmother's feather bed" from Grandma Prince.

—Anna

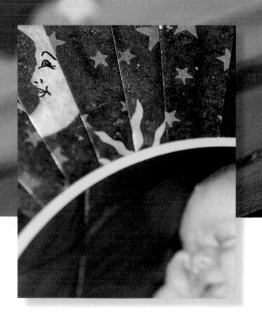

HANDMADE BABY ANNOUNCEMENT

A handmade baby announcement makes a compelling introduction to a scrapbook-style baby book. **1.** Choose an unusual theme, such as this celestial one, for added interest. **2.** Crop your baby's photo into a full moon. **3.** Shape and mount over fantails folded from stars-and-moons tissue paper. Use gold ink for hand lettering for a dramatic look. **4.** Using specially-shaped craft punches, finish your layout with a sun, a moon, and stars punched from metallic papers.

Scrapbook layout text visible:

ate of Baptism

Nathan Daniel
Was baptized in Dallas, Texas
on the 13th day of June
in the year of our Lord 1993

Baby's Hanky Bonnet

I'm just a little hanky,
as square as square can be,
there a stitch or two,
make a bonnet out of me.
Worn from the hospital
to the Baptismal Day,
a very special place,
carefully packed away...

BAPTISM

This heirloom handkerchief baptism bonnet will be kept safe for generations. **1.** Tuck the bonnet between two layers of a clear plastic page protector, and stitch together with ribbon. **2.** Embellish the layout with an elegant border, a stamped and heat embossed Celtic cross, and matted photographs. **3.** Mount the actual baptism certificate with photo corners so that it can be easily removed for reading.

to select a theme, then use different but consistent images relating to the theme on each page. For example, if you use Noah's Ark as your theme, you can include a different pair of animals on each layout. Consider using the decor of your baby's room as a theme for her baby album. Whether your decor is Winnie the Pooh, Beatrix Potter, or choo-choo trains, the theme can easily be incorporated into artwork for your scrapbook pages. Include swatches of wallpaper and fabric, or copy design elements from the fabric or wallpaper using a light box or opaque projector (see April, page 54).

DESIGN CONCEPT: BALANCE

Technically speaking, balance is the visual equilibrium achieved by handling proportions in an aesthetically pleasing way. Proportion is the relationship of one part to the whole. Every element on a scrapbook page has specific characteristics of form, size, shape, color, and texture. These characteristics, along with the factors of placement and orientation, determine each element's "visual weight"—how much attention it attracts on the overall page.

Keep in mind the following principles of design when you are trying to increase the visual weight of a particular element:

- Larger shapes naturally attract more attention than smaller shapes.

- Freeform shapes have greater visual weight than geometric shapes.

- Warm and bright colors have greater visual weight than cool and dull colors.

- Rough or busy textures and patterns seem heavier than smooth or plain ones. (A pattern attracts your attention more than a solid color, even if the basic color is the same.)

- Diagonal lines demand more attention than horizontal or vertical lines.

THREE FORMS OF BALANCE

Radial balance

A circular arrangement of elements around a central point produces a composition that draws the eye to the middle of the layout. Radial balance is ideal in a layout where you want to draw attention to a perfect photograph mounted in the center of the page.

Symmetrical balance

The arrangement of identical elements—corresponding in shape, size, and relative position—around a dominant element is symmetrical balance. This form of balance helps achieve a formal feeling.

Asymmetrical balance

There are two ways to achieve asymmetrical balance on a scrapbook page. One is to arrange different photographs and embellishments with similar visual weight at equal distances from a dominant point. Another is to place dissimilar elements with different visual weights at unequal distances from the dominant point, usually placing the "heavier" element closer to the center. Asymmetrical balance is often more visually dynamic than symmetrical balance. It can effectively express change, action, and even exuberance.

The next time you are working with a layout that feels "off balance," ask yourself: Could I substitute a "heavier" color for a mat or other detail in one area? Could I add some texture or pattern? Would a border help elements look more balanced on the page?

TECHNIQUE TO TRY: MATTING

When you look at photo albums and scrapbooks from the early 1900s, most of the pages are black, all of the photographs are black-and-white, and most of the journaling is written in white ink. The photographs are printed with a white border, making them stand out against the black pages. We can take a lesson from vintage scrapbooks and add distinctive mats to our photographs.

Creative matting can make all the difference in the presentation of photographs on a scrapbook page. Use matting to:

- Highlight and draw attention to a particular photograph

- Increase or decrease the visual weight of a photograph

- Add color to the page

- Emphasize colors within a photograph

- Provide a visual barrier between overlapping photographs on the page

- Fill up excess "white space" on the page

When you look at paintings or photographs in an art gallery, you will notice that with the exception of some contemporary

MATTING EXAMPLES

Matting is a great technique for enhancing photographs. You are only limited by your imagination!

(TOP) A torn paper mat adds a rustic, casual appearance to any photograph. **1.** Mark the approximate dimensions of the inner mat on light grey cardstock. This mat is approximately 4 cm larger than the photograph on all sides. **2.** Lay a ruler along an imaginary line on the mat card stock to provide a barrier against which to tear. The ruler should be laying on the part that will eventually become the mat, rather than on the part that will be torn away. While holding the ruler firmly in place, lift the excess cardstock and gently tear along the straight edge. **3.** Repeat for the remaining three sides. **4.** Cut a second mat from dark grey cardstock. This second mat should be approximately 4 cm larger than the inner mat, or 8 cm larger than the photograph.

(MIDDLE) Mat colors can accentuate details in the photograph. To accentuate the innocence of children, choose pastel colors to match their clothing. **1.** Cut the inner mat out of pastel blue paper with white polkadots approximately 3 cm larger than the photograph on all sides. **2.** Cut the outer mat about 3 cm larger than the inner mat—use a soft pink cardstock. **3.** Mount the photographs and mats from smallest to largest.

(BOTTOM) For a classic look, choose mats in the timeless colors of navy blue and white. **1.** Cut the first mat out of navy blue gingham approximately 1 cm larger than your photograph on all sides. Take special care when cutting a pattern, such as gingham, to ensure that the design appears symmetrically around your photo. You may have to adjust the size of the mat accordingly. **2.** Cut a small, solid white mat and a large, solid navy mat. Each mat should be fairly narrow, approximately 1 cm larger than the previous mat on all sides. **3.** Mount the photographs and mats from smallest to largest. When working with multiple mats, avoid the temptation to use more than one patterned paper—overuse of different patterns adds visual clutter to your page.

works, virtually all of them are matted in a variety of styles, materials, and textures. The same artistic principles that are used to create these gallery mats also apply to matting photographs on a scrapbook page.

Mat color

What color, or colors, do you want to highlight in the photograph? Do you have a photograph of a baby boy that you want to mat in blue—just to make sure everyone knows he's a boy? Is there a color you prefer to use because it accentuates elements of your page theme, even though it does not appear in the photo? Don't forget that white can also be an effective choice for a mat color.

Mat layers

Sometimes putting two or three mats of different colors and increasingly larger sizes behind a photograph can be very effective, especially if you want to emphasize the most important photo on the page. Other times using a single mat is best, especially when space is limited.

Mat width

You can create very different effects by cutting your mats in different dimensions. Mat layers usually extend between ⅛" and ½" beyond the photograph on all sides (double or triple mats may extend ¼" to 1" total or more on each side). When choosing the width of a mat consider the available space on the page. If the space is small, you will probably want to choose a narrower mat. If, on the other hand, you have a lot of space and few photos, a wider mat of two or three layers can help fill the space and add visual dimension to the page.

Mat texture

You can add texture to mats in a couple of ways. Choosing a patterned paper increases the textured feeling. Cutting one or more layers with decorative scissors also adds texture. You might tear the edges of the matting paper or embellish solid papers with rubber stamps or pen illustrations drawn by hand. Photographs with simple backgrounds lend themselves most effectively to textured mats, particularly patterned papers. Photographs with busy backgrounds can begin to feel frantic if you add busy, textured mat borders—with these photos, use simple, solid colored mats.

JOURNALING: LOVE LETTERS

Think of journaling as something that helps you capture memories with many different types of writing, whether those thoughts eventually end up as a photo caption, a paragraph on an album page, or even the basis of a mat or border.

So many thoughts in life go unsaid, while other thoughts are spoken but soon forgotten because they were never written down. This Valentine's Day, as your thoughts turn to love and relationships, take the time to write about your various loves.

FRIENDSHIP FRAME

Give a perfect gift to a very good friend. **1.** Stamp designs onto navy paper with white pigment ink. **2.** Mat a photograph with white cardstock. **3.** Mount the matted photograph on the navy blue paper.

Love letters to children

Write a letter or poem to a child who is yet to be born, or a young baby in your life. Before birth or adoption, describe your anticipation of the event. In addition to writing for your own child, you can write for a grandchild, niece, nephew, or godchild. After the arrival, write about the joy they bring to your life.

Baby notes

For a baby shower, have each person attending, and even those who were invited but could not attend, write a short note to the unborn child. These notes will be treasured in the years to come.

Once-a-year letters

Write a letter to a special child or family member each year, perhaps on their birthday or on a particular holiday, such as Valentine's Day. Over the years, the letters will tell their own unique story.

LETTERS FROM FRIENDS

Individual pockets on this page allow several letters to be mounted elegantly. **1.** For each pocket, pierce a design with a straight pin or corsage pin (see January, page 18). Remember to work from the back so the design will be raised when you are through. **2.** Mount each pierced piece on contrasting dark paper. **3.** Mount pockets at different angles, using double-sided tape.

with straight pins. Continue weaving all the horizontal strips until the design is finished.

Using a narrow (1") foam brush, brush Perfect Paper adhesive over the whole design, including the edges. Remove the pins. Let dry thoroughly, for at least two to three hours. Flip the design over and repeat the finishing process. Use scissors to trim any excess or cut it into a desired shape.

WEAVING THROUGH A BASE

Using a sheet of heavy paper or cardstock, you can create a base to weave ribbon or paper through. Using a ruler as a guide, draw lightly in pencil around the edge or in the middle of the base where you want to place each slit. Match the

OUTSIDE THE LINES: WEAVING

You can weave flat strips of paper or ribbon together to create beautiful and interesting scrapbook page design elements. A simple weave is created by working a horizontal strip (weft) over the first vertical strip (warp), under the second vertical strip, over the third, and so on, until finally over the last vertical strip. Then, the pattern is continued with more horizontal strips.

Two common weaving techniques are described below:

WEAVING A DESIGN

Cut a set of strips from paper or ribbon. If you use paper, you can vary the width and/or color of these strips or use decorative scissors to create pretty edges. Place a group of strips vertically side by side on your work surface. (It helps to tack down the strips with straight pins to the cutting mat.) Weave the first horizontal strip through the vertical strips and secure

I recently had the opportunity to read dozens of letters that my father wrote to his family while he was in the U.S. Navy in World War II, over 50 years ago. The binding is crumbling and the binder rings have rusted, but the pages are in pretty good shape. The pen that was used to write these letters must have used permanent pigment ink, because the writing is still as clear as ever. I spent hours reading every last detail.

— Anna

WOVEN HEART AND BORDER

Weaving can add exquisite detail to your layouts. To make the heart, see artwork on page 22. To make the border: **1.** Following the directions for weaving through a base on page 30, cut small slits with straight scissors into the edge of a large piece of paper to create a base for paper weaving. **2.** Weave a variety of complementary papers in a similar color palette through the base to form a border. **3.** Use Perfect Paper adhesive to secure the strips to the base at the end of each row.

length of each slit with the width of your weaving strip. You can space the slits evenly or vary the widths of the slits for a different design. As described above, if you use weaving strips of paper you can use decorative scissors to create pretty edges. Place your base on a cutting mat. Using a craft knife and a ruler as a guide, cut the slits where you've drawn in pencil. Weave a strip (of ribbon or paper) over and under the sections of the base to create a woven pattern. See above for the finishing technique using Perfect Paper adhesive and a foam brush. However, you need only add a touch of glue at the end of each strip, not the whole design, to hold it in place.

Woven design elements are excellent for pocket pages, Easter baskets, mats for photographs, borders, and corners.

PHOTO TIP: CHILDREN

One of the most important things to do when photographing a child is to get down on her level. Kneel, sit, or lie on the floor, so the camera is level with, or slightly above or below, the child's head, and your photograph will highlight more of her face.

Get close to your subject, either by moving closer or by using a zoom lens. A close-up shot shows additional detail. A good rule of thumb is to fill at least one-third of the photo with your subject.

For every rule, there is an exception. While you usually want to get in close to your subject, stepping back on occasion and showing your child as a small part of much larger surroundings can offer a nice change of pace. What you lose in detail you make up for in perspective.

CAPTURE THE EVERYDAY

Everyday activities lend themselves to wonderful pictures of children. On occasion, snap a photo of your child eating, playing, concentrating on a puzzle, or reading. These candid shots help record the multitude of "miniature moments" of your child's life. Some children who "ham it up" or smile awkwardly in photos are best caught off guard to get a more natural pose.

If you want to capture the natural spontaneity of kids, the best thing you can do is be ready at all times. Keep your camera loaded and always have lots of film on hand. Store your camera close to where the action usually takes place in your household so that you can quickly pick it up when something noteworthy occurs. Keep your camera on its auto-focus setting—kids move so fast that you may not always have time to adjust the manual settings.

Photo-worthy events don't always occur at home. Consider keeping a small point-and-shoot or

SMILES

Capture your child's beautiful smiles as she grows from infant to young adult.
1. Position photographs into the spaces of a PuzzleMates-style template to create the interlocking design. Cut photographs to fit the space. **2.** Mount each photograph onto background cardstock. **3.** Use a craft punch to punch squares around the edges of the background cardstock. **4.** Weave a pink ribbon through the squares and tie a bow at the top of the layout.

Kara Smiles

disposable camera in your diaper bag or purse to capture those photographic moments that might otherwise be missed.

PROFESSIONAL PORTRAITS

When having professional portraits taken of your children, choose a photographer who has experience photographing children. There is a definite talent to getting children to pose naturally for a portrait.

Also, consider how you dress your child. If your child is a "T-shirt and jeans" kid, consider capturing him in his natural state. You'll be happier with the results if you dress him in a new T-shirt and his nicest jeans for the portrait than if you force him to wear a collared shirt and dress pants.

Whether you are behind the camera or on the sidelines, a little attention to detail can make a big difference in the results.

PHOTO TIP

(TOP) When photographing children, remember to get close, get down to the child's level, and above all, fill the frame! **(BOTTOM)** Don't always fuss with hair and clothes. Candids capture the "real" child!

a word about

decorative scissors

You will find decorative scissors a nice addition to your collection of tools, especially when it comes to trimming mats for your photographs. Beyond the basics of straight scissors and pinking shears, you will find scissor designs with names like "seagull," "cloud," "stamp," "leaf," "jigsaw," "wave," "dragonback," and "zipper." The names of these scissors clearly give you an idea of ways you might want to use them.

- **Complement the mood of the layout.** A jagged pinking-shear edge might be appropriate for a page on river rafting or mountain climbing, but not for a page of sleeping babies.

- **Different effects.** Most scissors can give two different effects, depending on how you hold them. One effect is achieved by holding the scissors naturally. For the second, hold the scissors upside down, putting your thumb in the finger hole and your fingers in the thumbhole. Experiment with both and choose the one that best suits your layout.

- **Alignment.** Every time you have to move the blade while cutting a longer stretch, take special care to line up the design on the scissors with where the cut was already made.

- **Careful corners.** If you end up with an awkward corner, touch it up manually by cutting with straight edge scissors.

- **Don't overdo it.** Using too many different scissor designs on the same page creates visual clutter.

march

As March comes in like a lion and goes out like a lamb, our thoughts turn to the warmth of spring days—including that one day when everyone is just a little bit Irish. Whether you celebrate spring by flying a kite or searching for a lucky four-leaf clover, let the March sunshine chase away the winter blues and inspire you to start a new set of pages for your scrapbook.

MEMORIES TO CAPTURE

March is, of course, famous for that celebration of Irish heritage: St. Patrick's Day. Even if you are Irish only in spirit on March 17, you can capture the fun of the day in your scrapbook.

March also marks the first real turning point in the year as winter gives way to the first stirrings of spring. Even as we focus our thoughts on the rebirth of the earth, why not begin thinking about significant turning points to feature in your memory album, such as the birthdays of friends and family.

ST. PATRICK'S DAY

Kiss me, I'm Irish!

The spirit of friendships and good luck is at the heart of any St. Patrick's Day party. Celebrate the folklore of Ireland with a gathering of friends at a local restaurant or pub that serves Murphy's Stout and Irish fare. Have your waiter snap a group photograph for your scrapbook. Save a coaster, matchbook, or cocktail napkin from the restaurant for your scrapbook page. Ask everyone why they think they're lucky—take notes to use for journaling on your scrapbook page.

GOLD-DUSTED SHAMROCK

It's easy to make a unique shamrock decoration for a St. Patrick's Day party—or memory album layout. **1.** Trim three dried eucalyptus leaves to resemble shamrock leaves. **2.** Cut a small twig for the shamrock stem. **3.** Glue the three leaves to handmade paper, overlapping as necessary, using equal parts of paper adhesive and water. **4.** Using your fingertips, apply gold metallic powder to leaves. **5.** Mount handmade white paper atop red-orange handmade paper embedded with small twigs, and then add a thin black mat. (See June, page 86 for more about handmade paper.)

Keepsake shamrock

One of the jewels of Ireland is exquisite Irish linen. In honor of the Irish heritage, begin your collection. Host a St. Patrick's Day dinner party to show off your first pieces of Irish linen—napkins. Create a shamrock to attach to your napkin rings (see artwork above). Serve a traditional Irish menu, such as corned beef, cabbage, and Irish soda bread. Top off the meal with a frothy cup of Irish coffee or a bit of Bailey's Irish Creme. Your scrapbook page can feature your eucalyptus shamrock, photos, and a copy of the menu (perhaps penned in Celtic-style calligraphy). Use color photocopies of your new linen to make a wonderful background or border for your scrapbook pages.

ADULT BIRTHDAYS

Handmade birthday cards

Create a one-of-a-kind, handmade birthday card for a special friend or a fellow scrapbooker (see artwork on next page; also see Not Just Albums, page 166). Use archival materials, such as acid-free paper, to create a timeless keepsake. Include a picture of the two of you on the front and don't forget to express your own personal thoughts inside.

Throw a theme party!

Plan a retro cocktail birthday party with hors d'oeuvres, an open bar, and candles to set the mood. Comb antique stores or flea markets for stainless steel cocktail shakers, vintage ice buckets, cocktail glassware, and cloth cocktail napkins. Invite your friends to dress to the nines in elegant cocktail attire. Snap pictures of your guests dancing to the sounds of Frank Sinatra and Nat King Cole.

CHILDREN'S BIRTHDAYS

Birthday poses

For your child's chronological album, stage the same pose each year on your child's birthday—perhaps a close-up shot of your child blowing out the candles on the cake. Birthdays are a great time to document yearly statistics, such as shoe size, weight, height, clothing size, likes, and dislikes. Hand or feet tracings (or hand- or footprints made with paint) make wonderful additions to your pages.

FIRST BIRTHDAY

Bright colors and balloons capture the joy of a child's first birthday. **1.** Mount die-cut lettering on bright blue cardstock. **2.** Add balloon border stickers along each side of the layout. **3.** Mat photographs on brightly colored, patterned paper. **4.** Complete lettering with white ink **5.** Finish the design with additional balloon stickers.

HAPPY BIRTHDAY

A handmade birthday card with photographs is a real treasure for a special friend. **1.** Purchase an accordion book kit containing two heavy cardboard covers, middle pages, blue patterned paper, and a ribbon. Follow the kit instructions to assemble. **2.** Adhere a piece of torn blue mulberry paper to the cover; stamp with a "Happy Birthday" rubber stamp and heat emboss with gold embossing powder. **3.** On the inside pages, mount torn blue mulberry paper and then mount photographs with gold photo corners. **4.** Add journaling and "Happy Birthday" wishes.

Theme birthday parties

Host a birthday party with a theme—dinosaurs, jungle animals, tea party, pirates, or superheroes are popular with young children and create delightful photo opportunities. For a pirate theme birthday party, for example, you could use an old treasure map (perhaps traced or copied from a library book) or a treasure hunt map from the birthday party as a background on which to arrange your photographs and other mementos.

Timeless gifts

Photograph your child opening her gifts as a way to document toys and gifts that were popular during that year. Capture the giver and the gift with the birthday child. Snippets of wrapping paper and ribbon, along with birthday cards arranged in a collage, make a great background for these photos.

EXTRA SPECIAL BIRTHDAYS

First birthday

A first birthday is a very special occasion to include in a child's album. Take lots of photographs of the birthday child with guests. Make sure to document relationships for each picture with captions in the album. Have your guests "sign in" and write their birthday wishes for your one year old to include in your scrapbook pages.

Take a close-up photograph of your child at the exact time of his or her birth one year prior. Surround the child with balloons for a festive shot (even if she's sound asleep!) Use the time-stamp option on your camera instead of the date-stamp one.

Sweet Sixteen

Sixteen is a special milestone for teens. Make your child's sweet sixteen a gala affair, and record all the festivities in your scrapbook—better yet, start a new scrapbook for your son or daughter, beginning with a "sweet sixteen" layout. Include reminiscences, a personal letter to your child, and juxtapose a baby picture with shots of everyone celebrating the sweet sixteen milestone together.

- Throw a party for your daughter with her closest friends. They might enjoy a teen-only dinner at a favorite restaurant. Provide several disposable cameras to capture the fun. All young ladies love to receive flowers—send the birthday girl sixteen beautiful, pink roses to celebrate this special birthday. Embellish the sweet-sixteen scrapbook page with petals pressed from those roses (see May, page 72).

- Don't forget your son. Moms, for a wonderful picture to include in your son's album, have a photograph taken with your son to show who is taller. Perhaps treat your son and his friends to a concert of his choosing. Photograph the whole group heading out on the town, and have him save ticket stubs.

- If sixteen means "driver's license" for your teen, take the camera along to record all the details. These photographs will make a great scrapbook layout—include a color copy of your teen's new driver's license and the first insurance bill!

Milestone birthdays

Adults celebrating a milestone birthday, such as their 75th or 80th, deserve something special. Consider hosting a party and booking a big band in the spirit of his or her youth, and be sure to take photos of the guest of honor surrounded by loved ones. Perhaps have a party that conjures something special from his or her past—for instance, if your loved one was a great dancer, have copies made of a photo that shows him or her in action, and have programs made with a photo on the cover. The inside of the program can feature the menu (his or her favorite meal) and should be printed in his or her favorite colors.

- Put together a tribute album that highlights the life of the birthday star. Include old photos and memorabilia, as well as recent ones, and ask friends and family to write a special letter to the "birthday boy or girl."

- Create a scrapbook page for well wishers to sign at the party and write their best wishes to the celebrant (see artwork on next page). Remember to have archival quality pens available for writing.

OTHER NOTABLE EVENTS

National Women's History Month

Celebrate the unique gifts of the women in your family by researching and documenting their contributions in your family scrapbook. Include photographs and other memorabilia, such as newspaper clippings, or do some journaling to describe their accomplishments. Alternatively, write about the one woman who's had the most influence on your personal or professional life.

Lent

This Christian period of reflection and fasting begins on Ash Wednesday and ends with the joyous Easter

Best Wishes to a Wonderful Birthday

SARAH—
HAPPY BIRTHDAY!
HOPE THIS DAY HAS BEEN
A HAPPY AND MEMORABLE
ONE. BEST WISHES THROUGHOUT
THE UPCOMING YEAR!
—JOHN

BIRTHDAY BEST WISHES

A handmade scrapbook for guests to offer their birthday wishes adds an elegant touch to a milestone birthday. **1.** Start with a birthday message stamp, then heat emboss the stamped message using gold embossing powder (see May, page 70). **2.** Mount a single pressed pansy on each page atop gold stamped and embossed vines. **3.** Use a sheet of vellum paper as a scrapbook cover. **4.** Bind the book together with a strip of corrugated paper and a pretty ribbon.

celebration. Take time to think about your own spiritual journey. Find opportunities to volunteer in your community through programs such as Habitat for Humanity, adult literacy training, homeless shelters, or soup kitchens. Photographs and journaling from these acts of service will serve as a reminder of personal giving and commitment to helping others.

My mother is our family's genealogist. She gave me a wondrous treasure chest that I'll explore someday soon: a large box of negatives from the 1940s. I can't wait to have them printed to find out what is on them.

— Anna

ALBUM IDEA: HERITAGE ALBUM

Unlike a family chronology (see January, page 10), which records the memories of today's relationships and activities, a heritage album focuses on the memories of past generations.

Your first step in creating a heritage album is to gather photographs and other memorabilia, such as wedding invitations, birth announcements, marriage certificates, and so on. Your relatives may be able to help provide photos, anecdotes, and historical information.

SPECIAL PRECAUTIONS

There are precious few photographs from earlier eras. Take these special precautions with your heritage album:

- You may not have the negatives for many old photographs, but you can have a negative made from a print (even an old one). Especially if the original belongs to a relative, you may need to get color copies or instant enlargements made at the one-hour photo lab. If you have custody of the originals, you may still want to use copies and save the originals in a dark, safe storage setting.

- Consider mounting techniques that don't use adhesives. You can use photo corners or slotted mats to mount your photographs.

CZECH WEDDING PLAY

Honor your roots with heritage layouts. **1.** Mount a sticker border along both edges of cream paper. **2.** Mat photographs with burgundy and navy paper. **3.** Embellish photographs with sticker designs. **4.** Use calligraphy-style lettering to add journaling. **5.** Mount a small arrow on the appropriate photograph to point out a specific person in the group photograph.

ORGANIZATION

Even many experienced scrapbookers are challenged by the best way to organize a heritage album. You can start by imagining a family tree. Find ways to track family lineage as well as generations. You might choose a different page background or mat color for different family lines. Or you could increase the number of mats to indicate the generation.

Include basic genealogical information in your journaling to help readers understand the relationships between family members. Helpful information includes the person's name

~ Obšínky ~
Czech Wedding Play
1957
◆ John Janasak
(director)
‹Keith's grandfather›

Rudolph Janasak
(Keith's father)
with cousin

HERITAGE ALBUM

This two-page spread celebrates the military years of a beloved grandfather. **1.** For heritage pages, choose colors to complement the sepia tones of photographs from a bygone era. **2.** Create a personal monogram by using ornate or illuminated letters; either purchase them, as we did here, or make your own by using a rubber stamp and heat embossing using a metallic embossing powder (see May, page 70). **3.** For lengthy journaling, use a computer to allow you to include more words on the page.

(maiden and married), date of birth, date of death, who their children were, and where he or she lived, as well as special traits or remembrances of others about the person.

Make sure the colors and styles you choose for heritage layouts complement the era of the generation depicted. Try to choose colors and styles that the people in the photographs might have chosen had they created the scrapbook page.

DESIGN CONCEPT: COLOR

Of all the design techniques, the element of color probably has the most impact on the final results of your scrapbook layouts.

THE COLOR WHEEL

The color wheel provides a systematic approach to exploring and developing color schemes. By showing how colors relate to each other, a color wheel can familiarize you with the many possible color combinations. There are three basic approaches to determining color schemes.

Tints and shades

Use different tints and shades (lighter and darker tones) of a single color, such as sky blue and slate blue, to convey harmony and unity.

Complementary colors

Complementary colors are the two colors directly opposite one another on the color wheel, such as red and green. The result is a combination of both warm and cool hues. Placing complementary colors next to each other enhances each color.

A split complementary color scheme combines a single color with the two colors on either side of its complement. For example, violet, yellow-orange, and yellow-green can be combined to create a lively, charming contrast.

Triadic colors

Combining any three colors at equal distance around the color wheel is known as a triadic harmony. Using the triadic harmony of yellow, red, and blue on a single scrapbook page will create a cheerful and bright layout.

COLORS AROUND YOU

Color inspirations can come from all around you. Keep your eyes open and your "idea notebook" with you at all times.

a word about
color terms

- **Hue** identifies the name of a specific color, such as navy blue, fuschia, or apple green.

- **Tone** defines how dark or light a color is.

- **Tint** refers to a light tone created by mixing a color with white; pink is a tint of red.

- **Shade** refers to a dark tone created by mixing a color with black; burgundy is a shade of red.

- **Primary colors** are pure hues—red, blue, and yellow are pure hues, which are not mixed from other colors.

- **Secondary colors** are orange, green, and violet—created by mixing equal parts of two primary colors; red and blue make violet.

- **Tertiary colors** are produced by mixing a primary color with its adjacent secondary; red and violet make red-violet.

ADDING COLOR

Vivid colors enhance this photograph of a young girl.
1. Mat the photograph with bright pink and yellow mats.
2. Create a bouquet of punch art flowers in one corner to play off the details of the girl's hat by combining jumbo punched leaves and flowers with smaller circles and spirals in coordinating colors.

Some of the most subtle color combinations are based upon nature and the seasons; other color combinations can grow out of the mood you are trying to capture.

- Spring colors are soft and delicate: daffodil yellow, lettuce green, lime, peach, apricot, blush pink, and baby blue.

- Summer brings to mind the colors of the sky, sand, and shells, as well as the bright greens of new grass and fresh herbs, and the ripe colors of tomatoes and watermelon.

- Autumn hues are rich and warm. Autumn is pumpkin orange, burnt sienna, Macintosh red, hunter green, cocoa brown.

- Winter colors are vivid, sharp, and cool. Think emerald green and sapphire blue, or the icy shades of crystalline white or iridescent pearl.

- Colors also portray different moods. Red, orange, and yellow are cheerful, vibrant, and playful. Pastel colors portray innocence and purity—perfect for baby scrapbook pages. The rich tones of burgundy, ivory, plum, and gold lend elegance to heritage albums.

YOUR CANVAS

Consider the background of your scrapbook page to be your beginning canvas, your clean slate. Avoid working exclusively on a white background page, which is not the most flattering for your photos and other memorabilia. Keep in mind that a light colored background, by contrast, deepens the tones of scrapbook elements, whereas a dark colored background brightens light elements. A black background tends to make colors richer and more vibrant.

Experiment with neutrals and "visually textured" backgrounds, too. Add just a touch of color with a watercolor wash in earth tones of taupe, tan, and sand. Picture a beautiful layout for seashore photographs: a background of soft tan and photographs matted in muted shades of sea green and sky blue. Then add some accents of pink or purple. To create a more textured look, try a background of a pale, patterned paper in subtle shades of beige and cream, or a cheerful, dotted paper. A background color and pattern can come from your own sketch, sponge paints, vegetable stamps, elegant gift wrap, or even wallpaper samples. Numerous paper manufacturers make acid-free paper in all colors imaginable.

TECHNIQUE TO TRY: CORNERING

Cornering refers to adding decorative corners to your photographs and mats. It opens up additional possibilities for embellishing and emphasizing your photographs without necessarily cutting them.

In scrapbooks of past decades, "photo corners" were used almost exclusively to mount photographs in albums. Photo corners, still available today, are triangular-shaped pockets that you can place on each of the four corners of your photograph before mounting it on the page. Rather than attaching the photograph directly to the page, you attach the corners, which hold your photograph.

You can make your own photo corners—just disassemble a purchased corner and use it as a pattern to cut your own out of any paper that you want, using the same proportional dimensions. Triangular rubber art stamps are also available now for decorating your homemade photo corners.

For photographs that you plan to crop, one of the simplest versions of cornering involves using a "corner rounder." A corner rounder is simply a craft punch with right-angle guides inside that cuts off a curved piece from the corner of a photograph.

There are numerous punches available in craft stores that will cut a decorative design from the corner of your photographs. They range from teddy bears to starbursts and fleur-de-lis.

One particular corner punch, called a slot punch, is not intended for use on your photographs. Instead, it is to be used on your mounting paper to create a slot into which you can place your photograph. It yields a decorative look while allowing you to mount photographs without using adhesives directly on them.

Cornering scissors are another option. The scissors are constructed with plastic guides that can help you line up the paper or photograph at the correct angle for perfect corners. They have two sets of guides and can be held in two ways, which give you four possibilities for creating corner designs from one pair of scissors.

CORNERING

(TOP) A scissors-style cornering tool can cut out different designs, depending on how you hold the tool and how you align the photograph or cardstock. This photograph was matted using an art deco corner edger. Three of the four effects were used for this photograph. **1.** Take four squares of different colored cardstock and cut each with one of the designs. **2.** Experiment with combinations of the designs to find the perfect look for your mats. **3.** Consider a finishing touch; the corners here seemed to beg for bright yellow dot stickers to complete the deco look.

(MIDDLE) A tri-layered mat with a combination of corner punches adds an elegant touch to this wedding photograph. **1.** Punch out the corners of your photo with a notched punch. **2.** Cut a mat 1 cm wider and longer than your photograph, and punch the corners with a teardrop-style corner punch. **3.** Cut a second mat 1 cm wider and longer than the first. Use a corner rounder to round its corners. **4.** Mount the layers from smallest to largest.

(BOTTOM) Intricate, laser-cut photo corners (available at craft and scrapbooking stores) are the perfect embellishment for this classic heritage photograph. **1.** Cut a mat 2 cm wider than your original photograph on all four sides. **2.** Assemble laser-cut photo corners by folding on scored lines. Add adhesive as necessary to hold their shape. **3.** Place the laser-cut photo corners on the four corners of the photograph and add adhesive to the back of each corner. **4.** Mount the photograph on the mat, using only the adhesive that you applied to the back of the photo corners. **5.** Mat the photo again on a second mat (1 cm wider and longer than the inner mat) cut from a color that complements the photo corners.

JOURNALING: STORIES

Short captions along with pictures do a great job of telling a story from the recent or distant past. After all, a picture paints a thousand words. However, there are times that many words are needed to tell a story completely. For these occasions, consider devoting a half-page or more in your album to narrative.

Many of us find it difficult to write more than a sentence or two of journaling on an album page. Some people simply dislike their own handwriting. Some think they don't have anything to say. Others think that no one would read long passages. You'd be surprised who might read and appreciate what you have written—often long narratives provide a greater level of detail that will intrigue generations to come.

- If you don't like your handwriting, consider typing your stories on the computer in a sophisticated font, such as Garamond, printing them on acid-free paper, and attaching them to your album page. Even if you do like your handwriting, you may want to use the computer to print longer stories so they fit on a single page. If you use 8½" x 11" or smaller pages, you can print directly on your background cardstock.

- If you don't think you have anything to say, try again. Sit down with a spiral notebook and jot down your ideas. Ask friends or family for feedback. Add plenty of specific details. Once you have your thoughts on paper, organize them into a short story or essay. You'll be surprised at how much you have to say. Your children and grandchildren are bound to be enormously curious about whatever you divulge. Journaling is a good way to get your spouse or children involved. Ask them for ideas and remembrances of any event.

If you aren't yet convinced that there is a place for medium-to-long passages of prose in your album, consider a couple of other reasons.

- Have you ever had an experience that you wanted to include in your album but had no photographs? Perhaps you left your camera at home or no photography was allowed. Words work extremely well to paint the picture. Think of descriptive passages from your favorite novels that transport you to a different time and place with "brushstrokes" of language.

- Have you ever goofed in the organization of your album? You've carefully planned the left-side and right-side pages but suddenly discovered that it didn't come out right or there was too much white space. Write a story to fill the page recapping the experiences

One Wednesday evening when Jared was almost 3, we noticed that he was babying his right hand. There was a Band-aid on it and he mentioned that he had cut it at school. At nearly 8 o'clock, we removed the Band-aid and realized that the cut was very deep. Just to be safe, Dad took him to Primacare to get it checked out.

Sure enough, he needed a stitch to close the wound. He was such a trooper! He didn't even cry, although it was late and he was in a strange place. Dad and Jared didn't get home until 10 o'clock!

The folks at Primacare were quite smitten with this well-behaved 2-year-old who didn't even shed a tear. They showered him with gifts: bubbles, a coloring book and crayons, a squeezable key-chain flashlight, and (his favorite) a stuffed dog that he named simply "Dog".

He still talks nicely about Primacare being the place where he got his stitch.

IN STITCHES

Lengthy journaling tells the story of this little boy's first stitches. **1.** Compose journaling on the computer and print directly onto cardstock. Cut to size. **2.** Mat journaling and photographs in complementary colors. **3.** With a rubber stamp in the shape of an adhesive bandage, rubber stamp bandages on light brown cardstock using brown ink. Heat emboss with clear embossing powder. Cut out each bandage. **4.** Using a large stencil, trace title letters backwards onto the back of colored cardstock. (Tracing on the back allows any stray pencil marks to be hidden.) Cut out the letters. **5.** Using a 1/16" punch, punch two or four holes in each letter, in pairs. **6.** Tie knots through the holes using black embroidery floss. **7.** Mount matted photographs, journaling, stamped bandages, and title letters on the page with your favorite adhesive.

from the prior pages or introducing the experiences on the upcoming spread. Either way, you will have made good use of the "extra" page in your album.

OUTSIDE THE LINES: TEXTURES

Without texture a scrapbook layout would be dull. You can choose from a wide variety of textures to make your scrapbook pages unique. There are two basic types of texture: tactile and visual.

Tactile textures stimulate your sense of touch and can be incorporated into a scrapbook by layering different materials, fabrics, and other elements for a three-dimensional look. (also see August, page 103).

Visual texture refers to what the eye sees. Using media such as paint, ink, and fabric, you can create textures on your scrapbook pages. Use your imagination and don't be afraid to experiment.

Plastic wrap and foil

Carefully blot crumpled up plastic wrap or foil into an ink pad or into paper paint. Apply the plastic wrap or foil to your paper in a random pattern—blotting lightly without reinking to create delightful dark-and-light patterns (artists call this chiaroscuro).

Leaf prints

The imprints of leaves can be used to add texture to your pages. Place a leaf onto an ink pad and cover it with a piece of paper. Gently press the paper to allow ink to adhere to the leaf. Carefully remove the leaf from the ink pad and apply it to your scrapbook page. Cover the leaf with clean paper and press with your hand to transfer the leaf image to the page. You can also heat emboss the leaf image to create a raised, three-dimensional surface (see May, page 70).

Wash cloths and sand

The terry cloth texture of a wash cloth is perfect for creating "sandy pages." See the layout on the next page.

Other creative textures

You can use a wide variety of household objects for textures: sponges, scrub brushes, broom bristles, interesting fabrics (such as burlap, netting, velvet, corduroy, and lace), Koosh balls, shower body scrubbers, cotton balls, tissue paper, and bubble wrap.

PHOTO TIP: INDOOR FLASH

The key to taking good indoor photographs is the proper use of a flash. Familiarize yourself with the factors that indicate the need for an electronic flash.

Not enough available light for your film speed

With insufficient light and no flash, your photographs are likely to turn out either underexposed or blurred. If you don't leave the shutter open long enough to allow ample light in to expose the film, chances are the end result will be underexposed and dark. With fast films (400 or higher), however, you can often take satisfactory indoor pictures without a flash. Fast films can record images with less available light than the slow films.

Artificial light

Incandescent lights and fluorescent lights, the two most common indoor light sources, are different from natural (ambient) light sources. You don't often think of light as having color, but it does; incandescent light, fluorescent light, and sunlight all contain different colors. Standard films are designed to work with natural daylight; as a result, photographs taken under incandescent or fluorescent light may appear off-color, sometimes with a green or orange tinge. If your camera supports filters, you can purchase lens filters that will counteract the impact of incandescent and fluorescent light. These filters allow you to take indoor pictures under artificial light, when there is enough of it, without the color distortions you would otherwise see. There are also special films available for incandescent or fluorescent light.

Assuming you want to use standard speed films without special filters, however, your best bet is to use a flash when taking photographs indoors. The colors of "flash light" resemble those of natural sunlight, making them a better match. Even if you have ample artificial light indoors, you may still want to add a flash to counterbalance the colors of the available light.

AVOIDING RED-EYE

One of the side effects of using a flash is red-eye, especially under low-light conditions when your subject's pupils are dilated. Red-eye is caused by the reflection of the flash's light off the red blood vessels of the retina at the back of the eye.

TACTILE TEXTURE

You can almost feel the sand between your toes! **1.** Using a wash cloth, dab brown pigment ink to your paper. **2.** Heat emboss the "sand" using Desert Tapestry embossing powder (see May, page 70). **3.** Affix a small starfish or another shell with a hot-glue gun or paper glue.

PHOTO TIP

A flash is almost always necessary in a party setting. These shots were taken with an external flash, attached to a "shoe" on the camera. It is important for the flash to be away from the camera lens, to prevent red-eye.

If you have had trouble with red eye in your photographs, you can take steps to minimize it.

Turn on all available lights

By increasing the available light, your subject's pupils may shrink, minimizing the chance for the un-attractive red reflection.

Take your photograph from an angle

If your subject is not looking directly at the camera, the flash's reflection is unlikely to be recorded on the camera's film.

Use the red-eye feature on your camera

Many photographers have mixed opinions about red-eye reduction features. On most cameras, this feature works by flashing twice: once before the shot to help shrink the pupils, then again when the camera actually shoots the frame. The chief complaint that people have is about the loss of spontaneity. Because the camera flashes early, it can alert your subject to the fact that his picture is being taken.

Use a separate flash

Many camera systems, even if they have a built-in flash, have a place (called a "shoe") for attaching an external flash. The farther the flash is from the camera lens, the less likely it is that the flash will reflect back into the camera lens. Angling your flash towards the ceiling or a wall so that it "bounces" before reaching your subject also helps.

FIXING RED-EYE

If you try some of these options and still come up with red-eye, or if you are working with older photographs taken before you knew how to minimize it, you still have several options to help diminish that devilish look caused by red-eye.

Use a red-eye pen

These pens, available at camera shops and scrapbook stores, help cover up red-eye in prints by neutralizing the red. These pens are typically a greenish color that allows you to transform the red into a natural brownish color.

Allow an expert to correct the print

If you take your photograph to a camera store, you may find that they have equipment to digitally correct the picture.

Digitally correct the photograph yourself on your computer

If you have a scanner and a photo-quality printer, you can scan the picture into your computer and fix the red-eye with an image processing software program, such as PhotoShop, before you print it.

april

As winter's grays and browns turn to luscious greens and soft pastels, look for ways to reflect the harmony, color, and splendor of the natural world in your scrapbook designs. The advent of spring is ripe with photo possibilities—grab your camera, your design notebook, and your imagination and head outdoors. Then, gather all your resources and plan out a rainbow of new scrapbook ideas.

MEMORIES TO CAPTURE

April brings many opportunities for taking photographs as you celebrate cherished holidays, such as Easter and Passover. Many of us, too, start thinking about our gardens, spring parties, and reasons to get outside. Colors like robin's egg blue, lettuce green, petal pink, and lemon yellow will inspire you to create gorgeous scrapbook layouts as the world reminds us once again of the precious gift of life.

SPRING

Although spring technically begins in March, April is the first full month of spring. In many parts of the United States, April arrives as flowers begin to bloom and trees burst forth in varied shades of green. Capture the first buds in your garden on film, and celebrate National Poetry Month by recording your musings, sonnets, rhymes, and even haiku on handmade paper for mounting in your scrapbook.

April showers

April is known for its gentle rains. Imagine brightly colored umbrellas and rain gear—yellow slickers and red galoshes. Pictures of kids (or grown-ups) stomping in puddles are wonderful images for bringing a sense of fun to your scrapbook. Captions such as "It's Raining, It's Pouring" or "Singing in the Rain" come to mind as wonderful titles for these rainy day layouts.

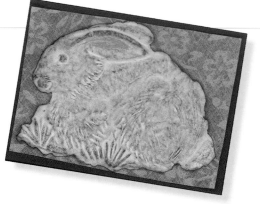

PAPER CAST RABBIT

This small bunny was made with handmade paper pulp pressed into a ceramic mold. **1.** To make paper pulp and cast the rabbit, follow the directions in the "Making Paper" sidebar in June, page 86. **2.** Pour coffee over the rabbit casting to dye it a soft brown. Allow to dry overnight. **3.** Use colored pencils to add detail to the rabbit design.

Spring has sprung

Doesn't it seem like one day all the flowers begin to bloom? Hunt out spring this year. Consider this idea: Create a scrapbook spread with 30 squares, pouches, or mini pockets—one for each day in April. Take daily nature walks with a friend or with a child. With camera in hand, snap photographs of all the first signs of the season. What are the first flowers to burst forth in color where you live? What is the first bird to return to your neighborhood after the long winter? Don't forget to record the date each photograph is taken (or use your camera's date-stamp feature). Use the squares as

Every spring my family takes an outing to find and photograph Texas bluebonnets. We've been doing this, usually on Good Friday, since my husband and I started dating. We've been known to romp in the flowers along the side of the highway, but in recent years have found a wonderful patch close to our home that blooms with multitudes of bluebonnets and Indian paintbrush year after year. Now we spend less time searching for the perfect spot and more time just enjoying the flowers and taking pictures.

— Anna

mats for your photographs (crop them to focus on the best detail of the photograph, and so they fit nicely into the square); if you make pouches or pockets instead, fill them with pressed flowers, colorful flat pebbles, and so on.

EASTER

Easter is the most joyous occasion of the Christian year—a celebration of new life and new beginnings. Along with the religious traditions, children always delight in the Easter rabbit, baskets filled with goodies, and making and hunting for colored eggs.

Take your camera to church

If you attend a church service on Easter, take pictures to capture your family in their Easter best—little girls with fancy bonnets and white lace gloves and young boys wearing suits with a tie like Dad's. Pose against the backdrop of a stained glass window or beside bright white Easter lilies with their trumpet-like blooms. For an exquisite scrapbook layout, mount your photographs on black paper and add pieces of brightly colored paper to make a collage—similar to a stained glass window.

Easter eggs

Eggs symbolize new life and have long been a part of the traditional Easter celebration. In earlier times, it was customary to roll colored eggs over fields to make

BLUEBONNETS

When working with photographs of spring flowers, choose colors from the scene to highlight the hues of the wild flowers. **1.** Using a flower stencil and a sponge dauber inked with light blue stamp pad ink, lightly tap ink from the sponge onto dark blue background paper. **2.** For a special title, embellish the letters with hand-drawn flowers and grass.

the land fertile. Today eggs are colored for Easter egg hunts and for Easter baskets. Take photographs as your family creates spectacular eggs this year with dyes, glitter, stickers, and ribbons, getting down to your child's level for some really great shots. Use pastel tints of green, blue, pink, and purple on your scrapbook layouts—enhanced with butterflies, bunnies, lambs, and chicks.

Easter traditions

Does your family have any unique traditions that you treasure each year at Easter? A special menu? Record these traditions in your family scrapbook along with photographs depicting the tradition. Family gatherings are a good opportunity to remember specifics about how your family celebrated Easter when you were a child. Did you attend church services? Where? At whose home did you have Easter dinner? Be sure to include any recipes for special foods served—such as hot cross buns, a century-old traditional Easter fare in England.

PASSOVER

The Jewish people celebrate this Festival of Freedom to relive the joy of their freedom from slavery so many years ago. In honor of Passover, a Seder meal, a religious service celebrated in the home, is served in a carefully prepared manner and order.

Preparing the Seder meal

Traditional family recipes are very much a part of the Seder meal—and the family scrapbook is the perfect place to chronicle these family recipes and traditions. If the children help with the preparation of Haroseth, a sweet apple mixture, take photographs of the steps. If they get messy, don't miss the chance to photograph your little ones with matzo meal on their noses or showing off sticky fingers.

Also, include details about any special family heirlooms used in the celebration of Passover; perhaps a special platter for serving the Seder meal, a fine linen tablecloth handwoven by a great-grandmother, or china you use only at this time of year. If you frequent a favorite Kosher bakery, get some unique photos of the baker with a piping hot tray of delicious parve rugulah.

Rituals and symbols

Since one of the purposes of the Seder is to inspire children to pass down this tradition to the next generation through the repeating of special stories, take care to document your family's traditions when serving this feast. Unless you feel photo taking detracts from the actual celebration of your family's Seder meal, include all the participants on film—the leader of the Seder, the women who light candles, the youngest child who asks "Why is this night different from all other nights?" and the child who finds the Afikomen, the hidden matzo.

OTHER NOTABLE EVENTS

Take Our Daughters to Work Day

Held the fourth Thursday in April, the Ms. Foundation instituted this event to focus on the needs and dreams of young girls. Work with your daughter to create a scrapbook layout highlighting the events of the day. Have her write a few words on what she learned and include "office treasures"—such as letterhead stationery or business cards she collected.

Display your daughter's layout on a company bulletin board or have her share it with her classmates at school. If your company has a news-

EASTER EGG HUNT

This eye-catching Easter layout features color photocopies of a popular pottery design called Dedham Rabbit. **1.** Color photocopy Dedham Rabbit pottery pieces (we used a picture frame in this layout). **2.** Cut out and mount strips of the pottery design around the outside edges of blue cardstock. **3.** Mount photographs with white photo corners embellished with a navy blue pen. **4.** Create lettering on the computer using the Scrap Swirl font and then trace with white pencil onto the cardstock. **5.** Mount color photocopies of two Dedham Rabbit Easter eggs onto the page.

PASSOVER

Food is a special part of every Jewish family's Passover celebration—many families prepare recipes that have been passed down from one generation to the next. **1.** Using a computer, print traditional recipes and a menu onto cardstock. **2.** Stamp and heat emboss leaves with malachite embossing powder (see May, page 70). **3.** Use colored pencils to add color to the leaves and grapes. **4.** Use a square stamp of grapes and heat emboss with malachite embossing powder before mounting on a thin piece of cork. **5.** Lettering with a gold metallic pen completes the look.

letter, perhaps the editor would be interested in printing the scrapbook page in the next issue.

Arbor Day

The first Arbor Day was celebrated in Nebraska on April 10, 1872. A journalist, J. Sterling Morton, organized this event to plant trees. Your family can celebrate Arbor Day by planting a tree of its own. As a family, research what trees are native to your area. Capture your planting adventure on film—including pictures of digging the hole and your children standing by the newly planted tree. Follow up by taking an annual photo of your child next to this special tree (see artwork on next page). Use the tree as a back-drop for photographs to show the changing of the seasons in your child's chronological album. Here are some other ideas for creating your Arbor Day scrapbook page:

- Save and press a leaf from your tree.

- Create a rubbing of your new tree's bark.

- Record statistics about your tree, such as height and circumference.

- Document the type of tree you planted, including its scientific name.

Earth Day

First celebrated April 22, 1970, Earth Day is a day created to focus on the importance of air, water, and the natural environment to our lives. Observe Earth Day by setting aside time to appreciate nature around you—take a nature walk in a local park or volunteer to clean up a public area in your city. Save fliers and photograph your activities to remind yourself of the responsibility of keeping your surroundings clean.

Zoo and Aquarium Month

Celebrate Zoo and Aquarium Month in April with a family trip to a zoo or aquarium. Buy postcards with pictures of your child's favorite zoo animals or fish (or if your child is old enough, ask her to draw or paint her favorite animal or fish, and use her artwork on your scrapbook page). For a zoo layout, use an earth tone background and mats in rich browns, tawny auburns, and deep greens. Cut out letters that imitate leaves, tree branches, or stone.

ALBUM IDEA: LULLABY ALBUM

If you are a parent or a grandparent, or if you dream of someday becoming one, a lullaby album can be a marvelous heirloom gift to give yourself or a parent-to-be. A lullaby album is somewhat like a songbook that combines photographs of sleeping children with the lyrics to sleepy-time songs. Any parent who has ever hummed a favorite melody to his or her child and tried to remember the words will treasure this expression of poetry and love. A lullaby album, designed with open spaces for photographs, makes a wonderful baby shower gift that can be passed down through the generations.

We planted a Silver Maple this year for Arbor Day. It was 6'4" tall; the trunk was so skinny that we used a stake to support our little tree. Kara is 5 years old and is almost 4 feet tall this Arbor Day. Together we will watch our tree grow.

April 1988

Silver Maple
Acer saccharinum

Deciduous · Height 40' to 60'

Fast growing shade tree with equal spread and height having open form, silver under side of leaves and yellow fall color. Needs any soil, full sun and plenty of water in summer months.

ARBOR DAY

Capture all the family fun as a tree is planted for Arbor Day.
1. Use an alphabet stencil to trace the letters to make the words ARBOR DAY onto leaf-print fabric. Cut out each letter.
2. Mat one photograph with the same leaf-print fabric and brown paper. **3.** Mat another photograph with leaf-print vellum paper and pine green paper. **4.** Use the computer to create journaling (we used the Scrap Swirl font), and print onto white paper. **5.** Use a brown colored pencil and a T square to draw a border around the outside of tan paper. **6.** Punch leaves from the leaf-print fabric, using a leaf craft punch. **7.** Mount photographs, journaling, lettering, and leaves on the tan paper.

Collect photographs

Search through your photographs to find pictures of children in sleep mode: getting ready for bed, hearing a bedtime story, being rocked to sleep, asleep, or fighting against sleep. Get close up for sleep shots so that you never forget the sweet, innocent expression on the faces of your loved ones (and so you can look at those photos when your kids are awake and driving you nuts!)

When I sang to my children, the lullabies all had the same lyrics — "la la la la." When I'm a grandparent, though, I'll lovingly sing all the words as we snuggle together: grandmother, grandchild, and lullbay album.

— *Anna*

List song titles

Make a list of lullabies and bedtime songs that you like. Find the words to the songs by consulting CD sleeves or songbooks— make a trip to your local library to fill in any missing lyrics.

Match the song lyrics with the photographs

Although in many cases any picture of a sleeping child will go with the lyrics to a particular lullaby, you may find some unique and special combinations. How about matching a photograph of your daughter clutching a stuffed horse with the words to "All the Pretty Little Horses"? Or pair the lyrics to "Away in a Manger" with a picture of your toddler in his Christmas pajamas.

Create pages combining the photographs and lyrics

In most cases you'll want to include only one photograph and one song's lyrics on a page. You may find special inspiration for thematic approaches in the lyrics to the songs. For instance, you might want to use a celestial motif for a page about "Twinkle, Twinkle Little Star." Since the lyrics to some lullabies are lengthy, you may find it appropriate to use a computer to format your journaling. Type the lyrics using an appropriate font, and print the lyrics directly onto acid-free paper or cardstock.

A lullaby album can be extremely easy to organize. Unlike many albums, the pages do not need to be chronological. New pages can be added anywhere that seems appropriate. In fact, new lullabies can be added a generation later. A lullaby album is also a good candidate for a smaller album. A small, soft covered album is perfect when singing to your child or grandchild cuddled up in your favorite rocking chair.

LULLABY ALBUM

A jungle theme is the perfect backdrop for "The Lion Sleeps Tonight". **1.** Choose earthy colors for your background cardstock and mats. **2.** Stamp jungle leaves onto cardstock that complements your background. For dark leaves, stamp with embossing ink from an inkpad and heat emboss with evergreen embossing powder (see May, page 70). For lighter leaves, stamp in evergreen ink and emboss with clear embossing powder. **3.** Silhouette the leaves by cutting them out very close to the edge of the stamped image. **4.** Type your lyrics and the title on your computer (choose a "jungle" font), then print directly onto cardstock. **5.** Layer your matted photograph, the lyrics, and the title on the page amid the varied leaves.

a word about

light boxes

A light box is a necessity for successful dry embossing (see next page), but it is also a valuable tool for other scrapbooking techniques, such as tracing clip art or marking photographs for creative cropping. A light box can also be helpful for sorting negatives.

A good light box has light strong enough to shine through medium-weight, light-colored cardstock. Look for a light box with a surface large enough to comfortably accommodate an entire page. Your needs may vary based on the page size you normally use in your albums.

If you don't use a light box very often and don't want to make an investment in one, there are several alternatives that you can use.

Windows

On a sunny day, you can use a window as a substitute light box. Tape the page to the window with a temporary adhesive such as Post-it dots, so that both your hands are free for tracing.

Shower doors

Even if it's dark outside, this option will work. Instead of using a window to the outdoors, use the glass door to your bathroom shower. Just turn on the light in the shower and let it shine through your pages.

Glass-topped coffee tables

Many coffee tables have glass tops. This sort of table makes an easy substitute light box. Simply put a small lamp under the glass while you work.

Clear plastic boxes

Some storage boxes are made out of clear plastic. You can put a flashlight in a clear plastic storage box (turned upside down) and use the bottom as your lighted work surface.

Note: Whenever using an electrical light source, be sure to take appropriate safety precautions.

DESIGN CONCEPT: HARMONY

One of the primary goals of scrapbooking artistry is to arrange a visually pleasing mélange of all the components you select for your layout: photographs, lettering, journaling, colors, patterns, die cuts, paper textures, and other artwork. Your goal is to achieve a balanced and harmonious design. Harmony involves two distinct, yet related, elements: unity and variety.

Unity

Balance, you will remember, is the careful arrangement of both similar and dissimilar objects. Harmony is the selection of objects that share a common characteristic, such as shape, color, texture, material, or size. By repeating these common traits within your design, you create what artists call unity. However, keep in mind that unity carried too far—with too many similar elements—can result in a very static, plain album page that lacks energy.

Variety

The key to creating harmony is to choose items that share a common characteristic but also have their own unique traits. At the same time, be aware that too much variety of color, texture, pattern, and size can be chaotic. Strive to find the ideal tension between unity and variety—this will enliven harmony and guarantee interesting scrapbook pages.

ACHIEVING HARMONY

It is important to vary the shapes of the elements that you select for each scrapbook page. Along with the oval elements on your Easter egg hunt, adding square-shaped photographs creates a pleasant visual contrast. Another way to add variety is to use differently textured handmade papers in a palette that matches your subject's clothing.

Here are some other ideas for creating unity and variety:

- Mix the simple and the detailed. Try intricate, detailed photo corners around your photographs—with a single, handmade rose along the side of your layout.

- Change the orientation of your elements. Place some of your photographs at an angle to counterpoint the placement of some straight photographs.

- Use different sized elements. Envision a large picnic basket with a trail of small, black ants marching around the edge.

■ Combine textures. Experiment with smooth, glossy papers in conjunction with thick, handmade paper with embedded dried flower petals.

When it comes to music, listening to a single note repeatedly is boring, while listening to the clash of dissonant chords is difficult on your ears. Finding the right "symphony" of similar elements and contrasts will result in a magnum opus that will be enjoyed by all. Strive for harmony with all of your scrapbook designs.

TECHNIQUE TO TRY: DRY EMBOSSING

Consider dry embossing as an elegant way to frame or mat special photographs or to add an exquisite border to a distinctive page. Not to be confused with heat embossing using rubber stamps and embossing powders, dry embossing involves creating a raised design in mounting paper using a stencil and a stylus. The resulting impression is similar to the raised monogram you've seen on fancy notepaper or envelopes. Embossed paper frames are readily available from scrapbook suppliers, but you can easily create your own.

To begin dry embossing you only need three special tools: a stencil, a light box (see sidebar on previous page), and a stylus. Start by choosing a stencil with a design that you want to transfer to your paper. Special brass stencils are made especially for this type of embossing. Their advantage is that they are completely opaque and render an excellent mask when used in conjunction with a light source. Although you can be successful with translucent, paper-thin stencils, your best bets will be brass or opaque plastic ones with a thickness about that of thin cardboard.

Once you have chosen your stencil, the steps are quite simple:

■ Position your stencil on the front side of your cardstock and affix it using a temporary adhesive, such as Post-It notes or Post-It dots.

■ Turn your work over and place it on the light box. At this point, the stencil will be sandwiched between the light box and your cardstock.

■ Using a round-tipped stylus, trace around the edges of the stencil images that you wish to transfer, working carefully to avoid stray strokes.

■ Once you have traced the entire image, you can remove the stencil and turn over the cardstock, which is now embossed. The result will be a raised image on your cardstock.

DRY EMBOSSING

You can highlight a special portion of a picture with a detailed frame. **1.** Cut an appropriately-sized circle in a piece of cardstock. **2.** Center your stencil design over the round opening on the front side of the cardstock. **3.** Dry emboss from the back side using a stylus. Add finishing color by lightly sponging ink to the raised areas through the stencil. **4.** Carefully measure and trim the cardstock to its finished size, taking care to center the opening and the design. **5.** Mount your photograph behind the opening, then mat the entire piece with a complementary color.

Dry embossing works best on medium-weight cardstock. Lighter weight papers do not hold the shape as well, and heavier cardstocks are harder to emboss.

Dry embossing, when used alone, yields a monochromatic design that looks and feels textured. The feeling of texture is accentuated by the reflection of light off the raised surfaces of the embossing. As an alternative to a monochromatic raised image, your embossing can be colored for a distinctive look. Colored pencils, chalks, a sponge dauber and ink pad, and even watercolors are good options for adding color to a dry embossed design. You can either color your image after the stencil has been applied, and before you actually emboss, or after the stencil has been removed. Your choice of media will determine the best time and method for adding color. Most techniques are best used before embossing, but some, such as chalks or sponging, can be used gently afterwards.

Do not be concerned about the raised embossed image flattening over time—the designs are usually quite sturdy. As long as you store your albums upright most of the time, your embossed images should last for many years to come.

JOURNALING: CREATIVE LETTERING

One of the features of a creative scrapbook that lends a particularly polished look is creative lettering. Perhaps you have looked in awe at the lettering of others and thought that doing such work was beyond your reach. Although creative lettering takes considerable practice, most scrapbookers can develop enough personal flair and expertise to draw their own titles and captions.

DESIGNING LETTERING STYLES

One of the most popular lettering styles in scrapbooking is called "dot lettering." It involves beginning with straight, fat letters, much like a stylized version of the elementary school script of years gone by. The ends of each letter are then embellished with an enlarged dot. Once you have mastered this style, you can innovate your own variations. Use serifs instead of dots. Or substitute hearts, flowers, stars, squiggles, or any other small, personalized detail.

When you are ready to try something new, begin experimenting. Instead of fat letters, try tall, skinny ones. Work in italics. Draw letters without any curves—pretend you only have straight sticks of varying lengths available to build your let-

ters. Try embellishing the insides of your letters instead of the ends of the lines. Look around for other sources of inspiration for your creative lettering; magazines, computer fonts, and even advertisements can give you ideas on ways to enhance your lettering. Many bookstores sell whole books of alphabets in hundreds of styles. When you experiment with a style and come up with something you like, draw the entire alphabet in that style on a piece of notebook paper. Save it for a time in the future when you may want to refer to that style again.

Remember that your titles, captions, and journaling do not always need to run horizontally across the page. Sometimes you may want to write up one edge or down the other. At times you may want to write around the edge of a photograph. Now and then you may even want to write on a curve or in a spiral.

KEYS TO SUCCESS

Draw, don't write

Remember that creative lettering is not handwriting. You need to draw your letters, rather than write them.

Plan your work

Before you draw a title or caption on your scrapbook page, draw it on a piece of scrap paper. Count your letters, figure out your required spacing, determine how many lines you will need to use, and decide how you will center your lettering.

Draw lines

Don't trust yourself to write straight without a line to guide you. Using a gentle touch, sketch in pencil the lines on which you will write your caption. For extra help, you may want to draw a faint line to guide the tops of your letters as well. When you have completed your lettering and let it dry, you can erase the lines with an art eraser. If you are working on light-colored paper or cardstock, instead of drawing the lines in pencil, you can place a lined piece of paper beneath your page and use a light box. As the light shines through both layers, you can use the lines for guidance.

Start in pencil

Lightly draw your lettering first with a pencil, so that way you can easily erase any mistakes before you make them permanent with ink.

Work towards yourself

It is much easier to draw lines and curves towards yourself rather than away from yourself. Turn your paper as needed so that you can draw most of your straight lines and arcs in the preferred direction.

Sleep, my child, and peace attend thee,
All through the night;
Guardian angels God will send thee,
All through the night;
Soft the drowsy hours are creeping,
Hill and vale in slumber sleeping,
Mother dear her watch is keeping,
All through the night.

CREATIVE LETTERING

Your creative lettering can make or break a layout. **1.** Type the text of the song. **2.** Print the lyrics onto cardstock. Cut out and mat. **3.** Choose a "word art" option from your computer program to create the title. Spread the title over two lines, selecting the same font that you used for the text, and distort it into a stop sign shape.

4. Print the title on cardstock. Cut it with a circle cutter and mat it. **5.** For the background, gently tear a piece of mulberry paper to a size slightly smaller than your background cardstock. **6.** Layer your matted photographs, lyrics, and title along with angel wings from a craft store.

Embellish last

Draw your entire phrase before embellishing any of the letters. You can adjust your embellishments to counteract any inconsistencies in your base lettering.

PROBLEMS TO AVOID

Inconsistent heights

If you have trouble keeping your letters the same height, lightly mark your page in pencil showing the top and middle of each line, in addition to the bottom. As you practice, the extra lines will become unnecessary.

Inconsistent widths

Before starting, take into consideration the desired widths of your letters. If you are drawing a title with a tall, skinny style, make sure your letters are consistently tall and skinny. Likewise, if the style calls for broad, fat letters, make them all proportionately wide.

Conflicting slants

When choosing your lettering style, determine whether you will use an upright look or an italic slant. Once you decide, make sure all your letters have a consistent slant.

Residual pencil marks

Light-colored inks, such as pink and yellow, will not completely cover up your pencil marks; however, they will cover the marks enough to make them difficult to erase. When working with light-colored inks, be sure to erase each letter almost completely before you begin to trace it in ink.

Smudges

Although pigment inks usually dry quickly, it is still possible to smudge them while you work. Take care to avoid placing your hand on your finished letters and hold off on erasing until they have had a chance to dry completely.

OUTSIDE THE LINES: EMBROIDERY

Why not combine the art of creating lovely scrapbook pages with the Victorian-style craft of ribbon embroidery or the very popular craft of counted cross-stitch? By using these stitchery techniques, you add a personalized, one-of-a-kind look that will make each scrapbook layout a charming keepsake of heirloom quality.

For my daughter's first Easter, her grandmother cross-stitched a wonderful bonnet in pastel colors. Rows of pink and purple flowers and a pretty yellow ribbon adorned the small bonnet. Today, the Easter bonnet is wrapped in tissue and stored in my daughter's Treasure Box along with the beautiful, hand-smocked dress that she wore. However, a color photocopy of the Easter bonnet made a wonderful addition to my scrapbook pages titled "My First Easter."

— Debbie

EMBROIDERY

Ribbon embroidery uses the same traditional stitches, such as straight stitch, lazy daisy stitch, and French knot, that are used when embroidering with thread or floss. Embroidery with satin and silk ribbon brings a unique elegance to your album pages that can be further set off with lace, pearls, and other beads. You can embroider directly onto thick cardstock by first punching small holes with a micro-size hole punch or by using a sharp needle that will pierce the paper (see artwork on next page). Or stitch your design in fabric for mounting on a scrapbook page. Be careful of the fabric you choose to use in your scrapbook—some fabrics are not safe for archival-quality albums.

There is a huge selection of ribbon styles—wonderful rich colors and luxurious textures. Satin ribbon and 100 percent silk ribbon are the best choices for using in your scrapbook. While silk is a strong, natural fiber that won't flatten on your scrapbook layouts, satin ribbon's best feature is softness and ease of handling. Ribbon widths are expressed in millimeters—for scrapbook pages choose 1.5 mm for stems and lines, 7 mm for leaves, and 9 mm for roses and other larger flowers. A chenille needle size 18 to 22 is large enough to accommodate the larger width of the ribbon. While stitching with ribbon, it is important to keep the ribbon flat and loose to create the designs.

COUNTED CROSS-STITCH

Counted cross-stitch is worked on an even-weave fabric, such as Aida cloth (available wherever embroidery floss is sold), or a perforated paper designed especially for cross-stitch. A

VICTORIAN RIBBON EMBROIDERY

Traditional embroidery, such as French knot, straight stitch, and lazy daisy stitch, can easily be woven onto cardstock. **1.** Lightly trace in pencil a design from a pattern book onto a piece of cardstock using a light box. Using a micro-size hole punch ($\frac{1}{16}$"), punch small holes along the design where your needle should pass through. **2.** Stitch all background elements first, such as stems and leaves; work forward to design elements, such as the flowers and roses. Follow an instruction book for the various embroidery stitches.

Keeping the ribbon length to 12" to 18" will guard against fraying and make stitching easier. To minimize bulkiness, weave ribbon ends behind existing stitches, leave a long tail to be caught into the next stitch, or knot at the back (see inset above). **3.** Erase any pencil marks showing around your stitches.

series of small x's creates a pattern by using different colored embroidery floss. There are so many wonderful counted cross-stitch patterns that can be used to embellish your scrapbook pages.

Cross-stitch designs can be stiffened with gloss adhesive and used directly on your scrapbook pages. Stitch the design on fabric or paper, then apply a thin layer of archival gloss adhesive over the design and let it dry. Carefully cut out your design leaving a ⅛" border all around, then apply another layer of gloss adhesive covering the raw edges of the design. Once your design is dry, you can mount it as a design element on your scrapbook page.

Other designs can be stitched onto cloth to be used in your home, such as bread basket liners, wall hangings, furniture doilies, and table runners. Once the design is complete, make a color copy of the finished piece for your scrapbook pages. Or, if you already have other cross-stitch pieces in your home—gifts from relatives, a sampler stitched by your grandmother, or a wedding announcement stitched by your mother-in-law—copy them as well.

Dust off your old cross-stitch books and practice or learn the traditional embroidery stitches, as these crafts will add a wonderful new dimension to your scrapbook layouts.

PHOTO TIP: PHOTO COMPOSITION

In many ways the principles of good photo composition are quite similar to the design principles that we present throughout the chapters of this book. The principles of balance, color, and harmony apply to well-composed photographs as well as to scrapbook pages. Most of us can recognize a well-composed photograph when we see it, but we don't necessarily know the best way to compose one.

There are two basic ways to alter the composition of a photograph. The first is to move the subject; the second is to move

COMPOSITION

The composition of these two photos results in a simple, clean portrait. Each child is "framed" at the bottom by clasped hands or folded arms in front of the body and at the top by positioning the viewfinder to just "skim" the top of the child's head. The background (grass on the left, a sandy beach on the right) adds subtle color—which contrasts well with the bright solid-colored clothing—but is deliberately kept out of focus.

the photographer. You will often do a combination of the two. Let's take a look at the attributes that influence the composition of your photographs.

Point of interest

A photograph should have a single focal point of interest, even if that point of interest is a group of people or things. Determine what is the most important subject to capture in the picture, then arrange your composition to highlight and emphasize it.

Simplicity

The reason for a photograph should be obvious. Try to avoid cluttered backgrounds, which can draw attention away from the focal point that you want your viewer to see. If the background is cluttered, try to change your angle or perspective to minimize it. For example, shooting from a low angle may allow you to use a simple blue sky as a backdrop for your photograph.

Contrast

A light subject will usually be more effective against a dark background. Likewise, a dark subject should usually be photographed against a light background. Often you can change the contrast between your subject and the background by changing your angle.

Point of view

The easiest perspective for shooting your subject is your own natural point of view, but you can also take on the point of view of a child or a pet who sees things differently than you do. Experiment with different angles to find the one that most pleases you.

Balance

In general, asymmetric balance is preferable to symmetric balance. To accomplish asymmetric balance, place your subject off-center and allow less important and smaller objects to balance your focal point.

Movement

Diagonal elements are usually perceived as more dynamic than horizontal elements. Photographing roads and fences at a diagonal adds an energetic perspective. For animals and people, your subject should look into, not out of, the picture. Similarly, a moving subject should be photographed entering the photograph rather than leaving it; this works better visually since it suggests that there is room to "complete" the action.

Perspective

You can add dimension to a photograph by framing the subject with a foreground object that adds perspective. Placing a tree branch or window frame in the foreground can actually draw your attention to the subject while also providing a sense of size and space. The foreground frame, however, should link thematically with the subject of the photograph such as a rose trellis in the foreground of a garden photograph of a bride.

Proximity

Always ask yourself if the photograph you are taking would be better if you were closer to your subject. A good rule of thumb is that your subject should take up at least one-third of the photograph. If in doubt, take several photographs, moving closer to your subject (or zooming in) with each one.

Mergers

A merger is any situation in which one subject seems to merge with another element in the scene. Mergers detract from good photo composition. The most commonly seen merger is a tree or pole appearing to grow out of a person's head. Train yourself to look for mergers and adjust your angle to eliminate them.

Borders

The borders of your photographs can be as important as the focus. Pay attention to what appears in the edges of the photograph. If you crop out arms or legs,

THE RULE OF THIRDS

This landscape, taken on the Pacific coast in Mendocino, California, illustrates the Rule of Thirds, a principle of composition used by photographers and designers. Look at the photograph and visualize three horizontal sections: the sky, the water, and the foreground. Then visualize three vertical sections on top of that; the focal point of the picture, the woman, falls at an "intersection" of a vertical and horizontal line, just to the left of center.

do it on purpose, not by accident. There may be times when it is better to move closer and crop out more rather than moving back to keep the whole person in the photograph.

The Rule of Thirds

The Rule of Thirds is a principle of photography and graphic design alike that divides your frame into three equal sections horizontally and three sections vertically. Imagine a grid of nine rectangles overlaid on your photograph—in effect a window with nine panes. The most pleasing photographs will usually have the subject at one of the four intersections of the imaginary lines.

Make sure that the horizon of your photograph does not cut your picture exactly in half. Using the Rule of Thirds, place your horizon one-third from the top or one-third from the bottom of your photograph. A high horizon suggests closeness, while a low horizon emphasizes spaciousness. Choose your composition according to the feeling you want to portray.

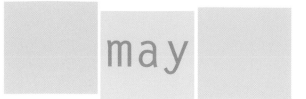

may

May is the month to enjoy the beauty of nature and the great outdoors. As the school year winds down and the weather warms up, take some time to view the world through the eyes of a scrapbooker. Fix yourself some lemonade, or better yet, pack a spring picnic along with a notebook and camera, and plan a bouquet of new layouts to capture the essence of May in your memory albums. On your outing, you might also pick some spring flowers to try your hand at pressing them.

MEMORIES TO CAPTURE

May offers many opportunities to honor the people who have made an impact on our lives—from the mothers who nurtured us to the men and women who gave their lives in defense of our country. It is probably no accident that May is also thought of as the month for flowers—beautiful blooms to celebrate May's many festivities, or to grace the gravesites of loved ones. This May, pause and reflect on the important people in your life, and then let those reflections inspire your scrapbooking.

MOTHER'S DAY

Ever since 1914, the second Sunday in May has been set aside to commemorate mothers. Whether you celebrate this day with a kid-made breakfast in bed, an exquisite, hand-crafted card, or a gift picked to please, make sure to capture your Mother's Day experience in your album. If you're a mom, encourage your husband and children to take some photos of you enjoying your special day. And whether or not you are able to be with your own mom, you will also want to remember her in a way that is meaningful to both of you.

Family heirlooms

This Mother's Day is the perfect time to begin a tradition of taking a family photograph that is repeated

PRESSED BOTANICALS

Pressed flowers and leaves look lovely framed with pretty blue cardstock. **1.** Trim a piece of blue cardstock and a piece of pale lilac cardstock to 4" x 4". **2.** Using a circle cutter, cut a 3¼" circle from the blue cardstock and a 4" circle from the lilac cardstock. **3.** Trim a second piece of lilac cardstock to 4" x 4"; arrange pressed flowers and foliage on this cardstock. **4.** Using a small brush, apply a clear-matte paper adhesive thinned with water onto the back of each pressed element and mount on the 4" x 4" lilac cardstock (use a pair of tweezers to move pressed elements around, if needed, before adhesive dries). **5.** Mat the design on a 4¼" square piece of blue cardstock. Let dry completely. **6.** Mount onto a second piece of blue cardstock cut to 4¼" x 4¼". For more about pressed botanicals, see page 72.

each year. As props for these annual portraits, choose a special heirloom for each child to pose with, such as Mom's pearl necklace or an antique teacup. It will be

MOTHER'S PEARLS

A black-and-white photograph of a mother with her daughter is a classic when embellished with black velvet paper and a pretty pink ribbon. (This is Debbie and her daughter Kara.) **1.** Mat the photograph with pink and cream plaid paper, then mount it on a piece of black velvet paper. **2.** Place a small white button in one corner of the pink and cream plaid paper. **3.** Thread a needle with a strand of pink embroidery ribbon. Starting from the front and inserting the needle through to the back, sew the button onto the frame, leaving a tail of 2". Have your last stitch come from the back into the front, leaving a tail of 2". **4.** Tie a pretty bow with the tails of the pink ribbon. **5.** Repeat steps 2 through 4 for the three remaining corners.

a treat to watch the progress of your children's growth as these photographs accumulate over the years. You can take this idea a step further by creating a special "keepsake album" for each child in which you mount the annual photographs.

Plan to continue this tradition until the year when the heirloom is actually passed down to the child—perhaps on your daughter's wedding day, or the day your son graduates from college. Capture that special occasion in a final photograph, and create a special layout to "close" the album. Of course, the keepsake album will be included as part of the gift along with the heirloom itself.

A gift for mother

Your mother will cherish a handmade journal containing memories of times that you have enjoyed together. The recollections may be written in your own handwriting; if penmanship is not your forte, experiment with different fonts on your computer. Perhaps each page could begin with "I remember when . . . " If you

have favorite photographs of yourself with Mom, mount them in the journal, too. Pressed flowers (see page 72) and favorite quotations are wonderful ways to complement these pages. Use archival quality paper and ink when creating this unique journal to be sure it will last a very long time.

The mother-to-be

Don't overlook a pregnant friend or relative this Mother's Day. How about sending her ready-made scrapbook pages for her baby album (see February, page 24)? There could be a pocket page for cards she receives this Mother's Day (see September, page 120), several mats for photographs, and a place to journal her thoughts about impending motherhood.

HIGH SCHOOL PROM

The high school prom is a milestone for so many teenagers. Although the prom is often thought of as a premier "photo opportunity" for young ladies, don't leave out the guys. Consider sharing reprints with the parents of your teenager's date or even making a finished scrapbook page to share with them.

Getting ready

Preparation for the prom presents almost as many photo opportunities as the event itself. Take your camera along as your daughter searches for the perfect gown or as your son is measured for his tux. Before the big day bring the dress to a copy shop and make color photocopies of the fabric. These make a great background setting for your layout, especially if the fabric is a pretty floral or damask pattern.

PROM NIGHT

Elegant pages are ideal when teens are dressed up for the prom. **1.** Mat photographs with marble-design paper and handmade paper in pretty party colors. **2.** Mount a piece of harlequin-style ivory paper atop a sheet of raspberry cardstock. **3.** Mount your matted photographs atop the ivory paper. **4.** Punch flowers and leaves using paper punches and handmade papers. Affix punched designs with your favorite adhesive. **5.** Use the computer to create a title for your page with a fancy font. (Our title was printed onto ivory striped paper with navy ink and embellished with a plum metallic pen.) Cut a rectangle around the title and mat with marble-design paper.

Maybe your daughter will allow you to tag along to the hair salon to snap a few pictures of her hair-do in progress; a shot with the manicurist works well, too.

The main event

Whether or not you really have a grand staircase, you will want to include shots of your daughter's "grand entrance" and of her receiving her corsage. Have your son bring his date by the house for some additional photographs of the couple. You'll have photographs of the actual prom from a professional hired for the event, but the fun and spirit of the night is often best captured in the candid shots. Send a few disposable cameras along to be shared at your teenager's table and offer to share reprints with everyone.

Memorabilia and memories

When you lay out the scrapbook pages for the prom, leave room for journaling and special memories. Consider mounting a pocket or envelope to store these writings. Also leave room in the scrapbook for keeping memorabilia from the prom—such as the dinner program, pressed flowers from the corsage and boutonniere, ticket stubs, and other items.

GARDENS

In May our senses are captivated by the natural beauty of the outdoors. For novices or avid gardeners, it's a time to start gardens or to enjoy those planted earlier in the year. Bring a bit of May inside your home with a spray of fresh cut forsythia or pussy willow fronds. This springtime bouquet will serve as the perfect accent for your everyday photographs.

Planting a garden

Whether your family simply plants flowers along the front of the house or gets involved in an intricate backyard garden, all will enjoy sharing this special time of working on the garden together. Capture a child's delight at digging in the dirt and putting in seeds for marigolds, zinnias, and morning glories. Take a few shots of your husband planting your family's favorite vegetables—such as tomatoes, peppers, cucumbers, and sugar-snap peas—in neat rows. Empty seed packets are a colorful addition to your scrapbook pages. Or you may want to create a background from color photocopies of seed packets. The children's song, "Inch by inch, row by row—gonna watch our garden grow" would make a wonderful title for your gardening pages.

Arranging flowers

Photographs help you remember favorite floral arrangements long after the blooms themselves have wilted. Create a special scrapbook to commemorate your flower arrangements—a small spiral album would do nicely. Be sure to note the names of all the flowers and foliage in the arrangement and any special techniques used. You may even want to embellish your pages with actual pressed petals or greenery from the arrangement. Also include any awards you may have won (see artwork in this chapter, page 72). Adding favorite verses or quotations pertaining to flowers gives the album an old-fashioned touch.

Finding a natural garden

If you're not a gardener, visit a local wildflower preserve or botanical garden. You will not be able to pick the flowers, but pack a picnic lunch and take some photographs of your family or friends surrounded by colorful blooms and flowering trees.

OTHER NOTABLE EVENTS

Memorial Day

On Memorial Day our thoughts turn to loved ones who have passed away, especially those who died in defense of our country. This is an occasion for placing flowers and other decorations on their graves. Spend time this Memorial Day writing in your family scrapbook about the lives of departed friends and family members. Remembering their special stories in words and pictures ensures that memories will be passed on to future generations.

Derby Day

The Kentucky Derby is held on the first Saturday in May. For those fortunate enough to attend, this event is a gala affair—both men and women dress in their finest for the day's festivities. Host your own Derby Day party, complete with friendly wagering on the outcome of the race. Offer mint juleps, and serve Derby Pie for dessert. Save a pressed mint sprig to include on your scrapbook page.

National Bike Month

Now that the weather is warming up, it is a great time to get some exercise outdoors. Celebrate National Bike Month by cycling with friends and family. Take your camera along for the ride. If you have a child who is receiving a new bike, take photographs of him "test driving" at the bicycle store. Learning to ride a bike is one of those special accomplishments that you will want to document in your child's album (see artwork in June, page 86). Wheel-shaped photographs made with a circle cutter are a wonderful way to accentuate the bicycle theme.

ALBUM IDEA: WEDDING ALBUM

Your wedding photographs are probably the most elegant in your collection and, as such, deserve a special showcase. Wedding photographers often sell their clients 5" x 7" and 8" x 10" enlargements bound in a fancy album—but this type of album doesn't leave room for journaling. And while bridal shops sell wedding albums preprinted with questions to answer about your family background, your engagement, and your wedding, these albums lack the truly personal touch.

By creating your own scrapbook-style wedding album, you have the opportunity to combine the best of both worlds: a fine showcase for the professional photographs, plus a home for the candid shots from your shower and honeymoon. And when you make your own album, you can include the stories and memorabilia that enhance the photos.

Choosing a motif

If you look at preprinted albums in a bridal shop, you will note that each has a recurring motif, such as doves or interlocking wedding bands, printed on each page. When you create your own wedding album, you may want to choose a motif as well.

Color

Use the colors from your wedding for your album's color scheme. By including at least a dash of these colors on each page, you will create a look that is unified from cover to cover.

Design

Choose a stencil or a set of wedding-related rubber stamps, such as ivy, roses, champagne flutes, or bows. Use them to create borders or corner designs that will be the same on each page.

Flowers

Visit your local florist and purchase flowers to represent those in your bridal bouquet. Press the flowers and use them on your pages (see "Outside the Lines: Botanicals," page 72).

BRIDAL SHOWER

For a contemporary adornment of pages devoted to a bridal shower, make your own packages. **1.** To make the gifts, begin by cutting a piece of white cardstock the shape of each package. **2.** "Wrap" each cardstock "package" with wrapping paper, just like you would a gift, affixing the gift wrap on the back with acid-free tape. **3.** Add any sort of ribbon or flat bow to further adorn each package. **4.** Mount photographs, journaling, and flat packages to your page with your favorite adhesive.

Bridal Shower Luncheon
August 17
The Crystal Garden Restaurant
Hyatt Regency Princeton

Guests
Ellen Saxon
Natalee Fogel
Sheila Berkelhammer
Andrea Kane
Celeste LePrevost
Kathy Leopold
Virginia Lippincott
Felicia Lowenstein
Kerry Paone

WEDDING PORTRAIT

A delicate floral papercutting enhances this beautiful wedding portrait. Use an adhesiveless mounting technique and a decorative slot punch to punch the corners of the mat for your photograph. Any time you need to remove the photograph, just slip it out of the mat. **1.** Create a design for your papercutting. The papercutting shown here was designed on lightweight paper using a straight edge and a rose stencil. **2.** Tape your design to the front of a piece of cream-colored cardstock. (The taped edges will later be discarded.) **3.** Using a craft knife, cut along the lines you have drawn on your pattern, cutting through both the pattern and the cardstock. Remove the pieces as you finish cutting them out. **4.** When the cutting is complete, trim the edges of the cream-colored cardstock with a paper cutter. Smooth any rough edges with your fingernail. You now have a papercut, cream-colored frame. **5.** Trim a piece of pale green cardstock to ⅛" wider in each direction than the papercut frame. Cut out the center of the pale green cardstock to create a frame (your photo should be ¼" wider on all sides than the pale green frame). **6.** Mount the papercut frame onto the pale green frame. **7.** Glue the matted papercut frame onto your page, placing glue or double-side tape on outer edges of papercut frame. Be sure to leave an opening at the top into which you can slip your photo.

PHOTO OPPORTUNITIES

If you are planning a wedding—your own or your child's—take plenty of pictures along the way. Many special aspects of the wedding preparations are overlooked as photo opportunities.

China, crystal, and silver

Take pictures of your wedding and shower gifts, especially your collection of china, crystal, and silver. Not only are these photographs useful for insurance purposes, they also can be used for a collage-style page for your album.

Shopping for gowns

Take along a camera on gown-shopping trips. Have a friend photograph the bride-to-be in each gown that she considers. Not only can the bride refer to the photographs to help her make a final decision, but the shots can also be used to create a page for the wedding album.

My wedding photographer sold me the proofs and negatives but no enlargements. My husband and I were responsible for getting all of the reprints in various sizes for ourselves and our families. It was a lot of work at the time, and I know we saved some money. But I didn't realize until several years later what a good deal that was — I own the negatives to all my wedding photographs and can get additional copies any time I choose.

— Anna

DESIGN CONCEPT: RHYTHM

The principle of rhythm is based upon the repetition of design elements to encourage the natural movement of a viewer's eyes across the page. By creating a repetition with your photographs and design elements, you set the stage for telling a story in a visually-pleasing context.

Begin by paying attention to the placement of photographs on a scrapbook page. It is better to draw the viewer's eye into the layout instead of outside the page's boundaries. One way to accomplish this is to avoid placing photos of people who are looking to the side on the very edges of your layout. Another idea is to place a focal point, such as the most important or "final" photograph, in the center of your layout.

You can also create rhythm by placing elements that share a common trait near each other. For instance, cut photographs from the swirling teacup ride in Disneyland into circles, then mount near each other in a curved pattern. Or, try overlapping photographs with design elements. To further encourage the sense of whimsy and movement, slightly tilt some of the photographs on your page.

When developing a sense of rhythm, remember to use design elements that complement your chosen theme. Simple green ivy borders project a graceful and flowing rhythm for a wedding layout; a border of small geometric shapes has a crisp and sharp rhythm that might be perfect for those dancing shots taken at the prom.

TECHNIQUE TO TRY: STAMPING

Rubber stamping is one of the fastest ways to add visual appeal to your scrapbook pages. Stamps are available in many designs, from country charm and Victorian elegance to art deco and children's themes.

One of the key attractions of stamping is that it allows you to repeat designs in order to unify your scrapbook pages. You can also create new looks using a single rubber stamp by employing mixed media to color or embellish the stamped image. Another appeal of rubber stamping is the ease with which you can add artistic designs to your pages. When you purchase a stamp, you are buying the right to use professional designs for your personal projects.

Kara at Disneyland
(age 10)

KARA AT DISNEYLAND

This layout illustrates the design concept of rhythm. The teacup photographs are mounted on circular mats and placed in an arc to mimic the spinning cups and saucers on the Mad Hatter's Tea Party ride. **1.** Begin with a layout of striped blue paper. **2.** Mat photographs in coordinating colors of purple and yellow. **3.** Stamp Mickey Mouse balloons with black onto yellow and purple paper. Heat emboss with clear embossing powder. **4.** Tie white embroidery floss around balloons. **5.** Mount photographs on the blue striped paper. **6.** Mount the balloons onto the layout.

GARDEN GLORY

Rubber-stamped flowers seem like the perfect way to highlight this photograph of a young girl who just picked a hibiscus to put in her hair. **1.** Stamp and heat emboss plenty of flowers and one basket on colored papers. Stamp half of the flowers on green (these will become the leaves) and the other half on petal colors, such as pink and red. **2.** Silhouette the basket and each flower by trimming close to the edge of the design. **3.** Trim away the leaves from the petal-colored flowers; trim away the petals from the green flowers. **4.** Layer the petals, leaves, and basket into a realistic design and affix to your page with your favorite adhesive. Add some more flowers around the page for continuity.

a word about

heat embossing

One of the most dramatic ways to enhance a stamped image is to use heat embossing. Heat embossing involves covering the still-wet stamped image with a special embossing powder, then heating the image with an embossing gun. The embossing powder melts and then hardens, causing the image to become raised and shiny.

Embossing powders are available in many different colors, including metallic gold, silver, and bronze. One of the most practical colors, however, is clear, because clear embossing powder will take on the color of the ink you used beneath it.

Stamp

To begin heat embossing, first stamp an image with ink as you normally would—but do not allow the ink to dry.

Sprinkle

Sprinkle the image with embossing powder, making sure that all the ink is covered. Gently dust the excess powder off the page and onto another piece of paper. (Tap, blow, or brush until all of the excess powder is removed from your stamped page.) The excess that you have removed can be returned to the bottle for later use.

Heat

Apply heat to the underside of the image by using an embossing gun (hold the gun approximately 3" to 5" from the underside of the image, or follow the manufacturer's instructions for usage). An embossing gun works like a hair dryer except that it applies more heat with less force.

SUPPLIES

Although it is possible to spend a large amount on stamping supplies, there are only two necessary items for getting started: rubber stamps and inks.

Stamps

Literally thousands of rubber stamps are available—they come in designs to suit every project. Good quality stamps have a hard rubber design surface backed by a layer of foam and are mounted on a wood block. Consider your stamp purchases carefully—it's easy to get carried away. Choose stamps for which you already have a scrapbook page in mind. Versatile stamps, such as geometric designs, are always good buys.

Inks and ink pads

The same criteria that you use for purchasing good ink pens apply to the selection of an ink pad: ink pads for stamping in scrapbooks should be made with lightfast, pigment-based permanent inks. There are dozens of ink colors available from several manufacturers.

Ink pads come in a variety of shapes. A large rectangle is appropriate for the colors you use most, but a small square is more practical for colors you'll use only a few times. As an alternative to an ink pad, permanent pigment markers with brush tips also can be used to ink your stamps. Ink pads are preferable for monochromatic stamping, but the brush markers allow you to use multiple colors on different parts of your stamp at the same time (for example, see artwork in September, page 114).

Pencils, markers, and chalks

A stamped image may be pretty, but in some cases you may want to further enhance the image by coloring it in with another medium. Chalks, colored pencils, and brush-tip markers work well for this.

TECHNIQUE

Ink it

Tap the rubber portion of the stamp against the inked surface of the ink pad. If you prefer, you may turn the stamp face up and tap the ink pad against the stamp. The effect is the same, but some people find the second approach easier, especially with oversized stamps.

Inspect it

Before stamping on the page, always inspect the stamp to ensure that you have adequately covered it with ink.

Position it

Position the stamp on the page or paper. If you need extreme precision in the placement of your stamp, you may want to use a stamp positioner. A stamp positioner is a device that has a temporary surface (usually plastic or thin paper) on which you can make a test image. After making the test image, place it exactly where you want the final image to be, remove the temporary surface, and then stamp your final image onto the page.

Press it

Apply even pressure to the stamp. You can gently tap on the back of large stamps to ensure that the design is completely transferred to the page. Avoid rocking the stamp back and forth, this can cause the image to appear fuzzy; it can also leave stray marks from the edges of the rubber.

Lift it

Carefully lift the stamp from the page, taking care to lift straight up to avoid marring the stamped image.

Reink it

In most cases, you will want to reink before stamping another image.

BEYOND THE BASICS

While simple stamping can yield nice results on your scrapbook pages, you can add even more pizzazz by using advanced stamping techniques.

Layering

Add texture and depth to your pages by stamping on a separate piece of cardstock, cutting out the image, and mounting it on the page. Especially pleasing results can be achieved by stamping several related prints, perhaps on different colored paper, cutting each out, and combining them for a three-dimensional effect. For example, imagine a basket stamped on brown paper, filled with flowers stamped on white paper and colored in various shades with colored pencils or watercolors. For a realistic touch, combine a stamped basket with actual pressed flowers.

Echo prints

You can create echo prints by stamping more than once before reinking your stamp. For designs of objects that remain stationary (such as plants), overlapping the repeated images at an angle gives a sense of depth and

BUTTERFLY IN MOTION

This photo mat illustrates the techniques of masking and echo printing. **1.** Stamp a butterfly on a scrap of paper and cut it out. This will be your "mask." **2.** Reink your stamp, and stamp the first butterfly. **3.** Cover the first butterfly with the mask and stamp the next butterfly slightly to one side or above the first butterfly without reinking your stamp. **4.** Repeat until you have the desired number of butterflies. We used a yellow opaque marker to color the first butterfly. **5.** Cut around the butterflies with a craft knife so that you can place your photograph underneath.

distance. For objects that can be mobile (such as birds), the same technique of overlapping repeated images at an angle gives the impression that the object is moving towards you.

Masking

Try combining stamped images in such a way that they overlap to make a complete picture. In order to do this effectively, use a technique called "masking." Consider using two stamps—one of a pot, one of flowers—to create a flowerpot with a hydrangea in it. First, stamp the flowerpot on the page. Then stamp it again on a scrap of paper (a Post-It note works nicely). Cut out the image on the scrap and place it precisely over the image on the page. Then stamp the flower, allowing part of its image to fall on the scrap. When you remove the scrap, you'll see the flower planted in the pot.

Pink roses

Rosemary

Blue Salvia

Evelyn's arrangement of spray roses, waxflower, limonium, blue salvia and rosemary won a Blue Ribbon at the Sunbonnet Lou Garden Club competition.

FLOWER SHOW

We created this layout for a friend of ours who won first place for this beautiful flower arrangement. **1.** Choose lovely handmade paper embedded with flower petals to use as a background. **2.** Mount some of the pressed flowers and greenery used in the award-winning arrangement and label across the top. **3.** To complete the page, include information about the flower show as journaling.

Record the hidden facts

Some of the most interesting facts about an event may not be obvious from photographs. For instance, when journaling your wedding, include information such as your happiest moment or excerpts from the best man's toast. Make a list of the menu that was served at the reception. What was the weather like that day? Who traveled the farthest to attend—and how far did they travel? Use your imagination. You can ask yourself similar questions about almost any event you have captured on film.

Transcribe from video

The videotapes you have are a wonderful asset, whether they are home videos, commissioned videos of a high-profile event such as a wedding or bar mitzvah, or mass-produced videos of a dance recital. The next time you're trying to fill in details for the journaling in your scrapbook, take time to view your video. You'll be amazed at what you start to remember. Keep a notebook and pen—and the remote control for the VCR—handy. Write down details as they occur to you as well as direct quotations from the video. Later, you can use the information for journaling on your scrapbook pages.

JOURNALING: CAPTURING THE DETAILS

The details in your journaling will bring your story to life for your readers. But too often, we forget details before they are captured. Take steps now to ensure that your scrapbook pages are filled with detailed journaling.

Write it down immediately

One of the best ways to capture the details of the moment is to write them down as soon as possible. In your camera bag or purse, carry a pen and small notebook in which to record the names, dates, and places that correspond to your photographs. Whenever appropriate, include the frame numbers in your notes to help you easily match the information with the photographs. Jot down the facts as soon as possible, then fill in the remainder as soon as you can. Don't worry about the format of your notes. Later when you are working on the scrapbook pages and using your notes to add to the journaling, you'll have the opportunity to decide on the best presentation format.

OUTSIDE THE LINES: BOTANICALS

Have you ever pressed the delicate petals of a flower between the pages of a thick book so that you could preserve the flower and the memories associated with it? The old-fashioned handicraft of pressing flowers can be used in your scrapbooks to create beautiful decorative elements and focal points. Include flowers from special occasions such as weddings and birthdays or favorite flowers, leaves, or even herbs from your garden.

WEDDING INVITATION

Preserve a wedding invitation in style.
1. Arrange pressed flowers and greenery in the corners of your page first (don't use adhesive until you are happy with your arrangement). **2.** Using a small brush, apply a clear-matte paper adhesive thinned with water onto the back of each pressed element and mount on the page. Use a pair of tweezers to move pressed elements around, if needed, before adhesive dries. **3.** Let dry completely. **4.** Mat your wedding invitation, using cardstock in the color scheme of your album. **5.** Mount your matted invitation in the center of the page.

PRESSING FLORAS

Many types of flowers and leaves can be pressed and dried quite easily to preserve their color and form. Using the traditional method of pressing in a thick book or a flower press produces beautiful specimens, but it can take several days to dry the flowers. On the other hand, investing in a microwave flower press allows you to produce pressed flowers with great color in just minutes.

You can also purchase pressed flowers and leaves. This option allows you to choose magnificent wildflowers and tinted leaves that are not native to your area.

AFFIXING PRESSED FLOWERS

Pressed flowers can be mounted directly onto a scrapbook page or to a separate piece of acid-free paper that is later added to your layout. Use a small paintbrush to apply a mixture of equal parts of water and glue to the back of the flower (use an archival-quality glue such as Perfect Paper Adhesive). Position the flower on the page and press it into place. Then, add a protective covering by coating the flower with Perfect Paper Adhesive (diluted as above). Try the gloss version of your adhesive for a really unique look.

Overlay especially delicate flowers with a Sanwa tissue (an ultra-sheer Japanese paper), then coat the paper with a diluted adhesive (as above) until the tissue disappears.

USING PRESSED BOTANICALS

Use your imagination to find different ways to use pressed botanicals in your scrapbook layouts beyond the obvious wedding and gardening pages. Here are a few ideas to get you started:

- Frame portraits with an arrangement of flowers and greener (see October, page 134).

- Mount pressed ferns to create a background for matted photographs (see December, page 155).

- Add pressed pansies to a scrapbook page of you and your daughter wearing a pansy-print hat.

- Use pressed greenery for a Christmas wreath layout.

PHOTO TIP: NATURE

Among your most beautiful photographs will be those of flowers, gardens, and landscapes. If you keep these tips for outstanding nature photography in mind, you will be rewarded with many magnificent shots.

GET THE BIG PICTURE

When face-to-face with the grandeur of a landscape such as the Grand Canyon, few can resist snapping picture after picture. Unfortunately, those landscape shots often turn out to be disappointing. This is because the camera captures only two dimensions, rather than the three dimensions we actually see. Nevertheless, there are techniques you can learn to help you take more satisfying photographs.

Stop and look

Take a few moments before snapping the shutter to assess what it is that impresses you about this scene. Is it the striking color of the flowers or the unusual shape of the trees? Perhaps it is the mist rising from a pond or the shaft of sunlight slanting through the clouds. Remember that each photograph needs a focal point—make sure that your focal point emphasizes whichever aspect of the scene you find most inspiring.

Capture your vision

Look carefully through the viewfinder as you compose your shot. Stepping forward, backward, or to the side can drastically alter a landscape photograph. Remember the Rule of Thirds: Place your focal point at one of the intersections of two horizontal and two vertical

LANDSCAPES

To add depth to landscape photography, include an attractive element from the setting in the foreground, such as the tree on the right-hand side of this photo.

imaginary lines. Make sure that the horizon of your photograph does not cut the picture in half.

Landscape photographs are considered to have four parts: the foreground, middleground, background, and sky. If you want to convey distance, catch your viewer's attention with something in the foreground, then draw his eye towards the background via a road or winding river. Another way to emphasize distance is by placing an item in the foreground but focusing on the distant focal point. The foreground item will serve to convey perspective.

The lens on your camera also affects the photograph. A telephoto, or zoom, lens allows you to get a close look at the subject. In addition, it can allow you to crop the photograph before you even take it. A wide-angle lens, on the other hand, allows you to fit more in a single photograph, adding a sense of spaciousness. Some cameras can take panoramic photographs, allowing you to capture a very wide expanse on a single shot (see artwork above).

CAPTURE THE DETAILS

There are times you will want to catch the essence of a scene through close-up photography. Whether you are shooting the rare mushroom that you found beneath a tree in Muir Woods or the roses blooming by your back door, by getting in close you can reveal details and convey a powerful sense of drama.

GRAND CANYON

Wide panoramic photographs call for large scrapbook pages. **1.** For this spread, we chose three panoramic shots of the Grand Canyon to show its grandeur and complemented them with two smaller photographs. **2.** To create the title and "icon" images, stamp rubber-stamped letters and petroglyph designs onto individual squares of earth-tone cardstock. **3.** Heat emboss each one with terra cotta embossing powder, and then double mat each. **4.** Mount letters and icons onto your layout.

While professional-quality close-up photography requires special equipment, most 35-mm cameras do a fine job at close range. Consult your camera's manual to determine the minimum distance between the lens and subject that your camera supports. You may be able to compromise by working from a greater distance and using a zoom lens.

"Depth of field" is the distance from the nearest item in the photograph that appears in focus to the farthest in-focus item. The closer the lens is to the subject, the shallower the depth of field will be. A shallow depth of field can work to your advantage in close-up photography. By tightly focusing on a single rose, for instance, the remainder of the rose bush will blur and recede into the background, returning attention to the main subject and creating a soft frame for the rose.

june

Summertime, like no other time except New Year's Day, is a time of resolutions. Who doesn't have one or more projects that they plan to complete during the summer months? This summer let your resolutions turn towards scrapbooking. Resolve to catch up on organizing all of the photographs that you have taken since the beginning of the year, and capture this summer's sun-warmed memories in creative ways. Consider starting a new theme album.

MEMORIES TO CAPTURE

SUMMER SOLSTICE

Feel the heat from this golden sun mounted on a sky of deep blue. **1.** Ink a sun pattern rubber stamp with black pigment ink, and press onto gold-colored metal. **2.** Heat emboss with clear embossing powder. **3.** Tap the gold-colored metal with a stylus to create small, decorative depressions. **4.** Mount design on a piece of deep blue paper.

As the days become longer and warmer, take time to slow the pace of life. With the children out of school for the summer, you will find many opportunities to enjoy family outings, such as a trip to the zoo or a baseball game, or a special celebration for Father's Day. And don't forget to take some much-deserved time for yourself: Treat yourself to a day in the city with a friend, an outdoor concert or festival, or a walk along the river or beach. Remember to bring along your notebook and camera.

FATHER'S DAY

Even though some dads may shrug off the importance of Father's Day, they do appreciate a heartfelt gift or card or breakfast in bed.

Memory box for Dad

Your father probably cherished the gifts you made for him while you were growing up—from the macaroni artwork to the elaborate wooden box for storing cuff links and coins. Bring back this tradition by creating your own memory box for Dad this Father's Day. You can find patterns and kits for making decorative paper boxes at many craft stores. Using a permanent ink pen, write out special memories of your father or express what he means to you on a long strip of cardstock, to be attached to the inside of your box. You may want to include favorite photographs of you and your dad together. If you have children, you can help them make memory boxes for their father.

Memories of Father

Take time this Father's Day to preserve precious memories of your father in your family album. Interview him by asking questions about his childhood, favorite

FATHER'S DAY BOX

Dad will love this fancy paper box full of memories of his children. **1.** Follow a pattern to create a paper box (pattern books for boxes are available at craft stores or you can purchase a decorative box from a paper goods store). **2.** Cut a strip of cardstock to fit inside the box. The length of the strip should be based upon the number of photos and amount of journaling you want to do.) **3.** Fold the strip of cardstock accor-dion-style. Trim the last fold as necessary if the strip was a little too long. **4.** Mount photographs and stamp designs to the strip of cardstock. **5.** Add journaling, if you wish. **6.** Apply a clear, acid-free lustre-finish l aminate over each photograph. **7.** Using adhesive, attach one end of the strip to the bottom of the inside of the box. **8.** Add a loop of ribbon to the other end of the strip to allow Dad to pull it from the box.

I can remember a handmade gift that I gave to my dad on Father's Day when I was younger. It was a wooden stagecoach that I made in wood shop class at school. I remember meticulously cutting dowels to form little spokes for the wagon wheels. That stagecoach is still in its treasured spot on top of my dad's dresser. Father's Day is always a very special day for me and my dad.

— Debbie

foods, pets, hobbies, childhood activities, and first job. If your father has passed away, interview other relatives and his friends. Be sure to include in the album any special memories that you have of your father. If you have a sample of your father's handwriting, mount it along with your journaling.

Through the years

Father's Day presents another great opportunity to stage an annual photograph of your children. Place copies of these yearly photographs in a special album for each child. Choose a different setting each year—here are some suggestions:

- Your toddler getting a piggyback ride from Dad
- Your daughter helping her dad with his tie
- Father and son all dressed up for a dinner out or special family occasion
- Dad reading the comics or a favorite book to his child
- Dad and child playing in the yard, a treehouse, or favorite park
- Dad and the kids blowing bubbles against a sunny sky

TAKE ME OUT TO THE BALLGAME

Who doesn't love attending a baseball game? The screaming fans, the great outdoors, the traditional seventh inning stretch, the organ music, the wave, and of course, peanuts, Cracker Jacks, hot dogs, and cotton candy. This summer, capture all the fun and excitement when you attend a baseball game with your family or friends. Decorate your scrapbook pages

with baseballs created with a circle punch, white paper, and a red pen. Or mount your Cracker Jacks label and the prize found inside along with the words to the song "Take Me Out to the Ballgame" around the edges of your page. Remember to record the names of the teams and the final score.

GRADUATION

Without a doubt, the highlight of every student's school days is graduation. Whether you are creating scrapbook pages about a high school or college graduation, save memorabilia from this momentous event.

Graduation collage

Create a collage of graduation memorabilia: On a color photocopier, arrange a composition of mementos, such as a graduation ceremony invitation, a name card, a graduation cap tassel, a class ring, a photograph of the school, a yearbook portrait, a student ID card, and a final report card. (Instead of a color photocopier, you can also use a digital imaging station—such as the Fuji "Aladdin," the Kodak "Picture Perfect," the Polaroid "Make-A-Print," or the Agfa "Innovatouch"—available at many one-hour photo labs.) Add scraps of decorative paper in the school's colors to pull the layout together. If you wish, cover the collage elements on the copier with graduation gown (to create a background color for the final collage) before you make the copy. Your collage copy can be used as a page all by itself or as a background for mounting a special graduation photograph.

OTHER NOTABLE EVENTS

Flag Day

Celebrated on June 14, Flag Day offers Americans the opportunity to honor their country by displaying the American flag. Take photographs of your children saying the "Pledge of Allegiance" and write down the actual words that they use. Sometimes children hear words a little differently than adults. This will garner a chuckle years down the road.

Summer solstice

When the sun reaches the northernmost point of its circuit, around June 21, daylight hours get longer and summer officially begins. Plan an outdoor meal in a scenic place near home to celebrate the summer solstice by watching the rising or setting of the sun with family and friends. Your photographs will look especially striking mounted in your scrapbook with a background of blues, oranges, and pinks (also, see artwork on page 76).

ALBUM IDEA: HOBBIES

Some photographs don't seem to have a place in the family chronological album. Activities that involve only one family member might be more appropriate for a personal album. And some interests or hobbies that carry through the years can get lost amid the other activities represented in the family album. If you or a family member enjoys a special pastime, devote an entire album to that activity.

CHILDREN'S ACTIVITIES

Sports

What parent hasn't taken photographs of his child playing on a soccer team or his 12-year-old playing basketball? If your child is involved in a particular sport, create a sports scrapbook in which you add a few pages each season. If your child dabbles in several you could either create an album for each sport or make one album that combines them all. For a special touch, make a color copy of your child's sports uniform and use it as a background for one of your pages.

Performing arts

If your child is a budding dancer or a musician, create a few pages in your memory album for each recital. You might want to include programs, a violin string or guitar pick, and even pieces from costumes, such as

TAKE ME OUT TO THE BALLGAME

The familiar words to this popular tune make a wonderful border for a summer layout. **1.** Type the lyrics on the computer and print them out on red cardstock (the font used here is ScrapMarker in 36 point, by Inspire Graphics). **2.** Create borders by cutting the cardstock into horizontal strips with a pair of deckle-edged scissors. **3.** Mat your photographs in complementary colors and mount them on the page. **4.** Mount an empty bag or box of Cracker Jacks. **5.** Add a few baseball stickers to play up the baseball theme.

sequins, taffeta, or netting from a tutu. If your child is a member of a theater group, create a spread for each play. Include photos from the performance, the playbill, and ads and reviews from the local paper. Decorate the pages based on the theme and title of the play.

ADULT PASTIMES

Sports

Whether you're passionate about volleyball, basketball, golf, skiing, sailing, cycling, running, or hiking, take pictures and collect memorabilia for a theme scrapbook. Include team photos, tournament photos, pictures of any trophies, and award ribbons.

Performing or fine arts

If you play an instrument, sing with a choir, or act in community plays, an album dedicated to your art is the perfect tribute to your talents. Include sheet music,

ALL MY SPORTS

If your child participates in more than one sport, you can create a single spread to portray the highlights of a given year. **1.** Choose colorful photographs and mat with patterned paper appropriate for each sport. Use solid-colored narrow mats as needed to separate the patterned paper from the photograph or background. **2.** Trace letters onto the patterned paper using a letter stencil. (We used a font called Helvetica.) Cut out the letters and mount on black paper. **3.** Silhouette the letters by trimming the black paper close to the original patterned letters. **4.** Journal the team names and records on colored cardstock and mat in black. **5.** Draw a border around the edges of the spread using a black pigment pen. (We drew one solid line and one dashed line to play up the sports theme.) **6.** Layer all the elements (letters, photographs, journaling) on the pages and affix with your favorite adhesive.

song lyrics, playbills, ads, and reviews along with your photographs. If you paint, sculpt, or draw, a "scrapbook portfolio" can be the perfect setting for keeping sketches, final art, photographs, or works in progress.

Hobbies

Document your hobby in a theme album.

- If you're wild about quilting, sewing, or weaving, include fabric swatches and yarns with photographs of your finished pieces.

- If your hobby is flying remote controlled airplanes, take pictures at the competitions and use an aviation motif to create your album.

- If you're learning how to decorate cakes or arrange flowers, take pictures showing the different steps of your art—then plan scrapbook pages to help you remember your creations.

Clubs

If you are a member of a garden club, a mom's club, a sorority, or a church group, volunteer to be the club's historian. That way you'll have access to lots of photographs of club events besides the photos you have already taken. Make a scrapbook for the club, but also create a few pages for your own special album devoted to your activities and memories.

DESIGN CONCEPT: ANCHORING

Anchoring elements adds visual weight to an element so it doesn't appear to be floating in the white space on your layout.

Small design elements should be grouped together rather than scattered individually across your scrapbook page. For instance, a single element, such as a small rubber-stamped flower, loses its impact when placed by itself on a layout. However, a grouping of three small flowers stamped near or even overlapping each other creates a new element with additional visual weight. By repeating a few more groupings of similar elements around the scrapbook page, you will keep the unity of your layout intact. Include an odd number of elements in each group to promote variety and keep your layout interesting.

"Silhouetting" is another great way to focus attention on a single element in the photograph and to remove distracting backgrounds or elements. A photograph can be silhouetted by cutting around the outside of a predominant element in the photograph. However, you will want to avoid mounting a silhouetted photograph by itself on a scrapbook page; instead anchor the silhouette to your design (see artwork on next page).

CAPTURE YOUR HOBBY

What better way to remember your gifts of handiwork than to create a scrapbook page?
1. Take before and after pictures to highlight the process of making the hat. Crop photographs with a circle cutter and mat on slightly larger solid circles. **2.** Type the title and journaling using your favorite word processing program, and then print out and mat. **3.** Mat a piece of the yarn packaging on coordinated cardstock. **4.** Punch holes around the edge of two of the matted elements, using a ⅛" handheld hole punch. Lace leftover yarn from the knitting project through the holes. **5.** Combine the matted photographs, label, title, and other journaling on the page to tell the story.

Here are some ideas for anchoring silhouetted photographs:

- Mat the silhouette with contrasting color paper to create a small border.

- Mount the silhouette against a background in a color different from that of your entire scrapbook page.

- Add a strip of colored paper to the bottom of the silhouette to create a "base."

- Mount the silhouette at the very bottom of your scrapbook page.

- Create a grouping of silhouetted photographs and layer them upon your scrapbook page.

- Mount the silhouette behind another element, such as a die-cut flowerpot, in a fashion that allows the viewer to feel as though he is peaking over the edge.

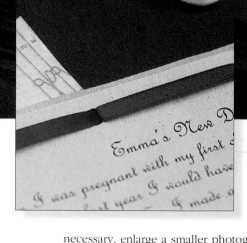

ANCHORING

Fabric, dress patterns, ribbons, and buttons are used to anchor a silhouetted photograph. **1.** If necessary, enlarge a smaller photograph to 4" x 6", using a digital imaging station or ordering an enlargement from a photo lab. **2.** Use a pair of sharp, precision scissors to silhouette the figure in the photo. **3.** On tan background paper, mount strips of fancy ribbon at the top and bottom of the page with a hot-glue gun. **4.** Cut a square of burgundy velvet and mount it on the tan paper. **5.** Create journaling with your computer (here we used a font called French Script) and print it directly onto a sheet of tan cardstock. **6.** Punch two holes at the top of the tan paper (with journaling on it) with a hole punch and weave a small burgundy ribbon to create a flat bow. **7.** Mat journaling on a sheet of gold wrapping paper. **8.** Make a color copy of a piece of a dress pattern and reduce it to 64 percent to create a smaller pattern. **9.** Mount the dress pattern, journaling, and silhouetted photograph onto layout, layering so that fabric is showing behind the silhouetted photograph. **10.** Weave gold thread in an x pattern into the holes of each button, then tie a knot at the back of each button to secure the thread. **11.** Hot glue the buttons onto the design.

TECHNIQUE TO TRY: TINTING

After many years of favoring color photography, many scrapbookers begin to experiment with black-and-white film—especially for portraits. Consider embellishing that extra-special portrait with hand coloring. Such tinted treasures are not new—in the years before the invention of color film, artists once hand-colored black-and-white photographs to give them a more realistic look.

TOOLS

There are several tools available for hand-coloring photographs. No matter which coloring tools you choose, read and follow the manufacturer's directions and recommendations carefully. In general, photographs printed on matte paper work better for this technique than those printed on glossy paper.

Oil paints

Oil paints for tinting photographs are lighter in color and more transparent than traditional oil paints. The transparency is necessary to allow the detail of the original photograph to show through. Following the manufacturer's instructions for diluting the paints can further lighten the colors. You can blend the paints to create your own unique colors. For a smooth finish, apply and blend the paints with cotton swabs. Because oil paint takes a long time to dry, you can easily correct mistakes before the paint has dried. Paints are a good choice when you want to apply overall color.

Markers

You may find it easier to work with markers designed for tinting photographs. These markers have a brush tip that allows you to color in medium-sized areas with ease. Ink from markers should be applied with a circular motion. You can blot off any excess color and blend your remaining colors with a sponge. We like to use regular pigment-ink brush-tip markers to highlight our black-and-white photographs. Using the markers you already own could be a great way to experiment with tinting techniques before investing in special supplies.

Colored pencils

Colored pencils are excellent tools for highlighting small areas of a black-and-white photograph (see artwork on next page). You can use them alone if you only want to tint small areas, such as flower petals, or you can use them in conjunction with markers or oil paints to provide detail in larger areas. Any colored pencils can be used, although special pencils for tinting photos are available.

TIPS FOR SUCCESS

- Color the larger areas first. Leave the fine details for last.

- In general, work from the top towards the bottom of the photograph to avoid smudging your work.

- For landscapes, begin with the farthest items and work toward the foreground.

Look to the photographs themselves to find inspiration for your photo coloring: blue denim, red lips, rosy cheeks, green foliage, blue sky. Your goal should not be to turn a black-and-white photograph into a color one; your goal should be to turn a black-and-white photograph into your own personal work of art. If you have a color photograph that you think would look outstanding as a hand-tinted black-and-white, you can still create one. A custom photo lab can print your color negatives as black-and-whites.

Take some time before coloring your first photograph to get a feel for the technique. You can practice on a photocopy of a black-and-white photograph. In fact, some people like using color copies (of black-and-white photos) as a basis for their finished product because the texture of a color copy makes it easy to apply the color.

JOURNALING: WHO'S WHO

Accurate journaling about the people in your photographs provides a legacy for future generations. Such documentation is easy when there are only one or two people in the picture but can sometimes be tricky when it comes to groups.

TAKING THE PHOTOGRAPH

You'll have an easier time documenting who is in a group photograph if you take your scrapbook needs into consideration when you actually take the picture.

- For a small group of five to six people, pose them in a single line. If you have a panoramic option on your camera, you might be able to get even more people in one line. You might also consider a circular arrangement so you can create a caption that begins "Sitting clockwise from the top are: . . ."

TINTING

We chose soft grays, yellows, and greens to accentuate the colors of the hand-tinted photographs in this layout. **1.** Have your black-and-white photographs printed on matte-finish paper. **2.** Color small details, such as the flowers, with colored pencils designed for tinting photographs. **3.** Rubber stamp a vase using taupe ink on a piece of light blue cardstock. Rubber stamp a second vase using taupe ink onto cream cardstock. **4.** Stamp an extra vase on a Post-it note to use as a mask (see May, page 71, to learn about masking). Use the mask to cover the original vases precisely. **5.** Using brush-tip markers or small inkpads, cover the petal portion of a flower stamp in yellow ink and the stem and leaf portions in green ink. Stamp three flowers in each vase, reinking the stamp between impressions. **6.** Compose journaling and a page title using the computer, and print onto cardstock. **7.** Mat all items in coordinating tones of cardstock and mount on the page. We chose a striped handmade paper for the background to complement the striped fabric in the photo.

- For larger groups, ask the people to stand or sit in discreet rows, the way school classroom photographs are posed.

- If rows seem too formal, arrange your subjects in "casual" small groups rather than one large jumble.

IDENTIFYING EVERYONE

The easiest way to identify all of the people in a group photograph is by listing the names from left to right, row by row.

Draw a "map": Make a copy of the photograph and trace the silhouettes onto a piece of cardstock. Write each person's name on her silhouette on the cardstock. If the images are too small for the names, number them and cross reference to the names below. Mount the cardstock map next to or under the original photograph.

IDENTIFYING JUST ONE PERSON

You may find occasions in which you want to identify only one person in a group shot—for example, a photograph of a graduation class of 100 that includes your child. Any of the following techniques will draw focus to the important person in the photograph.

- Add an arrow sticker, triangular punch, or other design element to the photograph pointing to the person you want highlighted.

IDENTIFYING GROUPS

When there are many people in a photograph, a photo map is the perfect way to document who's who. **1.** Make a photocopy of the photograph using the reduction feature on the copier to get the size you want for your photo map. Note that the photocopy does not have to be a color copy. **2.** Place your photocopy over a piece of graphite paper (available in art supply stores) that you have placed on top of a piece of cardstock. **3.** Trace the edges of the people on the photocopy with a pencil, using enough pressure to transfer the graphite to the cardstock. **4.** After removing the copy and the graphite paper, use a pigment pen to redraw the graphite marks that were transferred to the cardstock. This is your photo map. **5.** Add names to the map. **6.** Mount the map on the same page as the original photograph. **7.** We chose to embellish this heritage layout with a punch art bouquet made with various punches, including a jumbo daisy, circle, snowflake, birch leaf, medium sun, small spiral, and small circle.

- Use a thin strip of paper or a long thin sticker to fashion a line from a person in the photograph to an area on the background page where you identify him and journal about him.

- Make your own "magnifying glass" by punching and mounting one or two layered rings of paper and adding a traditional or decorative handle.

OUTSIDE THE LINES: PATTERNING

Although there is an abundance of patterned, acid-free paper available to scrapbookers these days, sometimes you won't be able to find just what you are looking for. Why not make your own patterned paper?

a word about

making your own paper

If you are new to paper making, we recommend you begin with a paper making kit. Following are the supplies included in most kits and sample directions:

■ **Paper mold. A rectangular frame covered with a mesh screen. (You can use an embroidery hoop and nylon window screening to create circles or ovals.)**

■ **Deckle. An empty frame the same size and shape as the paper mold. The deckle fits onto the mold to hold the paper's edges.**

■ **Cotton linter sheets. Cardboard-like material made of compressed cotton fibers.**

■ **Paper clay. A powder that increases the hardness of the paper's surface.**

1. **Wet a cotton linter sheet with cold water and tear into 2" pieces. Place in a kitchen blender filled with 1 quart of cold water. Soak for 10 minutes.**

2. **Blend for one minute on slow. Add 1 teaspoon of paper clay; blend for 20 seconds. Let the mixture sit for 20 seconds; blend again for 20 more seconds.**

3. **Optional: add flowers and blend gently.**

4. **Prepare paper mold and deckle so that screening is sandwiched in the middle; use rubber bands to hold together. Float mold and deckle in a tub of water, deckle-side up.**

5. **Pour pulp from blender into deckle, patting lightly to spread evenly.**

6. **Lift the frame and deckle out of the tub; drain. Turn over onto a towel; press firmly with another towel to remove excess water. Lift frame off paper.**

7. **Place paper in a flower press; allow to dry a few days.**

Stencils

Stencils can be used to create patterns on cardstock or heavy paper. Position a stencil over your paper and apply pigment ink with a small hand roller (called a brayer) or a sponge.

Color copies

Patterned paper can be made from color copies of pretty fabrics, lace trimmings, or baby's favorite blanket. Don't overlook the not-so-obvious designs found in china patterns or wrapping paper.

PATTERNED PAPER

It's easy to make your own patterned paper to create just the look you want. **1.** Using a ruler, draw in very light pencil lines to aid in keeping the pattern along a diagonal line. **2.** Stamp a small bicycle rubber stamp diagonally across a piece of blue paper. **3.** Allow to dry overnight before erasing the pencil lines, so the ink won't smear. **4.** Use a computer to type and print letters with black ink onto pink cardstock. Cut out each letter. **5.** Print a larger bicycle design from computer clip art. **6.** Color the larger design with embossing pens, and then heat emboss.

PHOTO TIP

Creative portraits are easy to achieve if you look through the camera with a "photographer's eye." **(TOP)** This portrait illustrates what we call "point and shoot" or "just do it"—in other words, you "see" the picture, grab your camera, point it at the subject, and shoot. Don't fuss about camera settings or lighting. This picture benefits from ambient light—daylight under a tent at an outdoor party—and a little bit of movement by the girl. The shutter speed was 1/30th of a second. Keeping standard 200 or 400 ASA film in your camera lets you take "grab" shots like this. **(MIDDLE)** This relaxed portrait of a boy at his bar mitzvah, shot with 100 ASA film, takes advantage of a natural outdoor background. Taking your picture under a tent or awning eliminates overhead sunlight and forces the main light to come from the side. **(BOTTOM)** Take advantage of a great natural setting for portraits. This little boy was photographed on a South Carolina beach at twilight with 100 ASA film. The photographer, eying the seagull through his lens, encouraged the boy to pretend he was a seagull.

PHOTO TIP: CREATIVE PORTRAITS

You can take fantastic portrait photographs on your own—here are some hints.

Setting

In the spring or summer, a portrait in a real flower garden or on the beach is much more captivating than an indoor or studio setting. For a winter portrait, have your subject pose in front of a roaring fireplace or wear her favorite dress coat in front of a stunning, tall evergreen tree.

Clothing

Except for the most formal portraits, keep clothing simple. The subject of the photograph is the person, not the clothing. Capture the essence of your subject by allowing him to dress in whichever way he feels most comfortable.

Props

Props can really help set the mood in a portrait. For example, have an adult sit in an antique wingback or rocking chair by a window, or have a child sit in a Radio Flyer wagon. Give your subject a pet rabbit to hold in her lap or a few wildflowers for an Easter portrait.

Lighting

Take a photograph by a window and allow the natural sunlight to illuminate your subject. Or take the portrait in a slightly darkened room with candles or firelight illuminating your subject.

Filters

If your camera supports the use of filters, try using a multiple-image filter for a surreal look. The effect will be striking—the filter causes your subject to be repeated several times on the negative. Depending on your choice of filter, the repeated images may be in a circular layout, resembling a gemstone's facets, or a linear layout, giving the impression of motion. For a romantic look, use a diffusion filter. It will give a soft-focus appearance to the photograph, resulting in a dreamy impression. Diffusion filters are also flattering to people with uneven skin tone or wrinkles. Diffusion filters come in several types, but the weakest one (#1) is usually used for portraiture.

july

By July, summer is in full swing. Just as you commemorate patriotism and national history with the special holidays of the month, take some time to celebrate your own personal history. Gather with family and friends to reflect on the memories of years gone by and make new memories for the future. Take a break from the heat and plan a scrapbooking party or informal get-together with a few of your closest friends or relatives to work on your family scrapbooks.

MEMORIES TO CAPTURE

July finds us half way through the year—already! Summer is well underway, and we find many opportunities for creating memories. Be deliberate in your planning of summer activities—seek out new and exciting ways to fill your days. Prepare to fill your scrapbook pages with wonderful photographs of summertime fun.

INDEPENDENCE DAY

Flags and fireworks

Salute the birth of the United States with a spectacular celebration on the Fourth of July. Capture this fun-filled day of picnics, parades, and flags for your scrapbook. And what better way to end the day than with the brilliant explosions of color and light called fireworks? Add a little Americana to your scrapbook by decorating your Fourth of July layouts with patriotic themes, such as red, white, and blue bunting or stars and stripes.

Parades

This year, organize your own neighborhood Fourth of July parade. Encourage your neighbors to decorate bikes and wagons in the patriotic colors of red, white, and blue. Snap photographs of all the parade partici-

SUMMER WATERMELON

Paper paint creates a watermelon with colors so brilliant you will be tempted to try a bite. **1.** Using your finger, cover a watermelon stamp with red and green paper paint. **2.** Stamp the watermelon image onto white paper. Allow it to dry for one hour. **3.** Mat your watermelon design with red-checked patterned paper.

pants and collect decorative remnants for a neighborhood scrapbook page.

SUMMER

Nature's gifts

We all love the fresh fruits of summer—blueberries, strawberries, and peaches. Plan an outing to a local orchard or farm to pick your own fruit. Of course, you will want to take your camera along to capture evidence of who eats more fruit than they pick. Plan a scrapbook

Since 1982, my father's family has had a reunion every three years in Waco, Texas, where he grew up. No one in the family lives in Waco anymore, but we still return there for the reunions.

A special aspect of these reunions is the location — we always return to the same clubhouse in the same park. We take the same family group photographs on the same porch every time. It is inspiring to watch the families grow over the years.

—Anna

page with rubber-stamped baskets depicting the first gifts of summer (see artwork on next page).

Backyard barbeques

Plan your favorite summer menu for the grill and invite your friends over for a casual get-together. Festive yard torches and decorative outdoor candles create an intimate setting for a summer evening under the stars. Remember to choose a fast film speed to capture the nighttime shots.

Summer excursions

Summer days are a great time for day trips to the art museum, beach, or theme park. Schedule these outings on your calendar and take time out to enjoy the sights in your own neighborhood. You may be surprised at how much fun you can have so close to home. Gather memorabilia from your outings to add to the photographs on the pages you create.

Watermelonfest

If summer had a taste, it would taste like watermelon. Watermelon is sweet, cool, and wonderfully messy. Capture the fun of eating watermelon for your summer scrapbook pages. The bright colors will look fabulous. We like to create a two-page layout in our family chronological album highlighting all of summer's fun. Photographs of our families eating watermelon always show up on these pages.

FAMILY REUNIONS

Photo opportunity

A family reunion is the perfect occasion for taking photographs. In addition to the classic "big" photo of everyone together, be creative with your photo groupings. Here are a few ideas:

JULY 4TH BIKE PARADE

July 4th is a wonderful day for a bike parade! **1.** Cut letters from navy paper patterned with white stars and stripes. **2.** Punch stars from white paper with navy stars, using a star craft punch. **3.** Create two border strips for mounting above and below the photograph, using a border craft punch. **4.** Punch scalloped border in navy paper and mount on a piece of white paper to show through the design. Punch small red stars using a craft punch and mount on scalloped design. **5.** On a piece of red cardstock, mount a row of stars and a raffia ribbon at both the top and bottom. **6.** Mount lettering and photograph to finish the layout.

PICKING BLUEBERRIES

A favorite summer pastime is picking blueberries for pies and muffins.
1. Use a computer to print letters onto white paper. Mat the white paper with a strip of blue paper. **2.** Rubber stamp baskets with brown ink, and then heat emboss with clear embossing powder. **3.** Cut out each basket and mount individually on the page. **4.** Mount lettering and photographs on blue-checked background paper.

- Photograph the oldest family member with the youngest family member.

- Group all the family members with a January birthday together and take a photograph; do the same with the remaining 11 months.

- Take a photograph of each generation separately.

Photo scavenger hunt

Organize a photo scavenger hunt to keep people busy before dinner (and to provide you with photographs for your scrapbook). Split into teams; each team should be given a loaded camera and a list of items to photograph. Make sure they keep track of who and what they are shooting. Fun items to photograph could include five people whose names have "ie" at the end (Katie, Annie, and so on), two people with the same birthday, the person who brought the chocolate cake, or the family member with the biggest shoe size.

Story exchange

Find time while everyone is together to exchange stories and memories. Provide cardstock cut into 3" x 5" squares along with archival-quality pens to encourage relatives to write about their favorite stories or memories. Compile all these stories and "publish" them in your scrapbook.

Family reunion scrapbook

Create a family reunion scrapbook featuring the events of the reunion. Use photographs of the entire family together, pictures of their favorite foods (Aunt Carolyn's homemade pickles and Cousin Mary's famous lemon cake), and snapshots taken of the Family Olympics (sack race, water balloon throwing, and egg toss). Using an 8½" x 11" page format allows for color copies to be made for family members. Be sure to take your scrapbook to display at the next family reunion as well.

Scrapbook layout for each family

Ask each family group to create a scrapbook page (8½" x 11" format) about their family—hobbies, occupations, favorite sports, recent trips—to bring to the reunion. (Encourage participation by mailing "starter supplies," such as a blank scrapbook page, some patterned papers, and archival-quality pens.) Add these pages to your family reunion scrapbook and offer to mail copies to family members. Families that cannot attend the actual reunion can still participate by mailing their layouts.

National Picnic Month

Picnics are a natural part of summer. Pack a wicker basket full of your summer favorites—fried chicken, home-grown tomatoes, potato salad, fresh peaches, pound cake, and of course, lemonade. To capture your summer outing, toss a camera into your basket also. Decorate picnic scrapbook pages with brightly-colored gingham ribbon, and mat photos with gingham paper.

We all scream for ice cream

July, quite appropriately, is National Ice Cream Month. Visit a favorite ice cream parlor or make banana splits at home (experiment with toppings and see how creative you can be). Decorate your pages in Neapolitan colors of cream, strawberry pink, and chocolate brown. Have each family member write about his or her favorite ice cream.

ALBUM IDEA: VACATION ALBUM

Next time you take a vacation, dazzle your friends by showing off a completed album or set of scrapbook pages soon after you return. Instead of narrating through a large stack of loose photographs that quickly become out of sequence, let your friends experience your trip vicariously through the pages you have created.

Why not dedicate an entire album to that once-in-a-lifetime trip to the Far East or to your 25th anniversary tour of Europe? You probably took enough photographs and gathered enough memorabilia for a whole album anyway. If you usually take shorter trips, devote a single album to all your trips collectively. If you like to visit the same vacation spot year after year, what could be more special than a scrapbook that chronicles your annual visits?

Let your trip be the inspiration for your pages. Draw motifs from the natural surroundings of the places you visited. For a visit to the beach, use tropical colors with sand, surf, and shell motifs. For a vacation in Washington D.C., find inspiration in the architecture—use crisp clean lines with pillars and columns. For that trip to Asia, choose oriental papers and folded origami as a backdrop for your photos (see artwork in December, page 160).

VACATION ALBUM I

A wine label and a postcard complement these photographs taken on a trip to Napa Valley, California. **1.** Draw grapevines around the border of the page using an embossing pen (available at rubber stamping stores). **2.** Heat emboss the grapevines with gold metallic embossing powder (see May, page 70). Work in small sections, first drawing a few grapevines and then heat embossing them—the process will not work well if the embossing ink is allowed to dry before applying the embossing powder. **3.** Draw the page title and journaling with embossing ink, and then heat emboss. **4.** Stamp grape clusters at key points on the page, then heat emboss. If needed, add additional grapevines to connect the grapes to the vine border.

PHOTO OPPORTUNITIES

Keep your camera busy while on your trip. Have a travel partner (or innocent bystander!) take plenty of photographs of yourself and your traveling companions in famous (and even not-so-famous, but picturesque) places. Did you travel by train? Take photographs at all the train stations. Capture the lesser-known details on film as well. Take close-up shots of the inscriptions inside the Jefferson Memorial or the gilded gate at Versailles. Capture the flavor of your destination by photographing the local residents going about their everyday business, such as at a Provençal market or Turkish bazaar. Photograph a family in the park or workers gathered in the town plaza at lunchtime.

Let your photographs inspire your journaling. Take pictures of street, building, and monument signs where you visit—the front of your hotel and the restaurants you eat in. If you're taking a cross-country road trip, stop at the state borders and photograph the family with the "now entering" sign for each new state.

FOOD, GLORIOUS FOOD

What's a vacation without great food? Whether you're using chopsticks in San Francisco's Chinatown or having your first sushi in Kyoto, capture the experience with photographs and memorabilia. Save napkins, menus, and matchbooks to accompany your photographs.

VACATION ALBUM II

Two pages would never do justice to a once-in-a-lifetime trip to Italy—but they serve as a great introduction. **1.** Choose one or two photographs from each city visited. **2.** Add a small map of the country, some rubber-stamped suitcases, and the cover of an expired passport (you could also color photocopy the cover of a current passport). **3.** Add some currency that you have saved from the trip. Matting the paper currency on marble green paper really makes it stand out on the page. **4.** Mount the coins by making a square from two clear giant photo corners.

FILL YOUR POCKETS

While on vacation, collect items of interest that you can use to embellish your scrapbook pages while capturing additional memories from your trip. In addition to the obligatory photographs, postcards, and brochures from places visited, keep maps, receipts, and ticket stubs. If you travel to a destination with unique vegetation, gather leaves and flowers to press (see May, page 72) and use on your album pages. If you travel abroad, when you make a trip to the post office to buy stamps for your postcards, buy a few extras to include in your scrapbook. Likewise, for international travel, save a few coins and small-denomination bills. Pack a stack of zippered plastic bags. They're great for collecting and organizing all the memorabilia you collect on the trip.

TAKE NOTE

Reserve a little time each day to document your activities and experiences. Pack a simple spiral notebook or bound journal in which to record where you went, what you did, who you met, what your children said, how the sand felt between your toes. What unique dishes did you try? What was your tour guide's name? (Take his picture, too.) By recording information consistently, you will remember each day as a special adventure that you can include in the journaling you do when you return.

BE PREPARED

A once-in-a-lifetime trip is no time to find yourself out of film or with a dead battery in your camera. Always take an extra battery and a few more rolls of film than you expect to use. While you will probably be able to buy film at your destination, you may pay an exorbitant price. Depending on your destination, you may not even be able to find a fresh battery.

Even if you are traveling light, you can pack a miniature tripod. While not as versatile as a full-sized tripod, the mini version can be set up on a ledge or other flat surface and used with the timer option on your camera so that your entire traveling party can get into the pictures.

DESIGN CONCEPT: MOTION

A sense of movement, both in your photographs and your decorating elements, will engage the viewer's eye and make for more energetic, lively layouts.

MOVEMENT IN PHOTOGRAPHS

Begin by capturing movement within your photographs—good friends sailing across a blue lake on a beautiful summer day or children racing at dusk to catch fireflies in an old mason jar. Don't limit your scrapbook pages to only stationary photographs of people.

Get as close as you can to take these action shots. Try to capture hair blowing in the breeze and sea spray leaping against the sailboat. Choose a fast shutter speed (or the "action" option on your camera) to freeze the motion and minimize blur. Take the photograph as the person enters the frame rather

CAPTURING MOTION

You can use portions of unused photographs to create playful lettering and crop chosen photographs to accentuate the motion theme of the layout. **1.** Cut swimming photographs into circles, saving the extra part of the photograph. **2.** Crop other photographs to focus on the action in the picture. **3.** Using a plastic alphabet template, trace each letter on the backside of photographs where there is a picture of water. Cut out each letter. **4.** On a dark blue background, mount a strip of water design stickers and the lettering at the top. **5.** Mount your photographs, matting some if you choose. **6.** Repeat lettering on the bottom of the layout.

than when she is leaving it. Some cameras have a continuous-drive mode (that sports and fashion photographers use) that allow you to take a great series of action shots.

MOVEMENT BY DESIGN

Design elements and techniques can also be used to portray movement in your albums.

- Stamp an image on your page, then drag a portion of the rubber stamp across the paper to make a trail.

- Make echo prints with a rubber stamp by stamping the page several times before reinking (see artwork in May, page 71).

- Add two small curved parenthesis (( )) around an element to make it appear to be moving back and forth, like cartoonists do in comic strips.

- Draw short dotted lines in patterns across your page to show movement, such as the path a bee might take, a basketball swooshing through a net, or a frog leaping across the bottom of a page.

- Place footprint stickers (or use a footprint paper punch) across your scrapbook page to show movement from one photograph to the next.

- Silhouette similar photographs and include all of them on one page. For example, use a series of photographs taken at a diving competition to show the different stages of a dive—standing on the board, bouncing, piking in the air, reaching for the water, entering the water. Mount them in sequence on your page to show the continuum from start to finish.

TECHNIQUE TO TRY: DIE CUTS PLUS

Die-cut shapes are one of the first embellishments that many scrapbookers use in their albums. They are readily available in stores and come in hundreds of shapes. Die cuts can be used to quickly add color to a page. Here are some more advanced techniques.

MATTING

Although die cuts are made from a single sheet of solid or patterned paper, you may want to add more than one color to your layout. Mount your chosen cut on a coordinating piece of cardstock and cut close to the original shape, leaving ⅛" or so around the die cut. The cardstock cut out becomes a

mat for the die cut. For an striking look, mat a patterned die cut with a solid cardstock to enhance the shape on the page. Using decorative scissors to cut the mat can give a lacy look.

Similarly, you can mount two identical die-cut shapes in coordinating colors, slightly askew from each other, in a technique called shadowing. The bottom die cut becomes a "shadow" of the top one, adding depth to the page.

PIECING

Many die cuts would look more realistic if they were not a solid color. For instance, a blue crayon die cut would look better if part of it were black. Similarly, a yellow beach umbrella would be more interesting if each section were a different color. To achieve this look, purchase matching die cuts in each color that you need for your finished design. Place the color that you will use the most on the bottom, then cut out portions of the remaining colors of die cuts and layer them on top of the bottom one.

DIE CUTS

The creative possibilities for embellishing die cuts are nearly endless. This assortment includes a matted heart with stamp-edge scissors border, a heart whipstitched with silver lamé thread, a "pieced" umbrella, a paper pierced shamrock, a three-layered star, a yellow oak leaf embellished with an embossing pen and embossing powder, an orange corrugated oak leaf, and a flower rubber-stamped within a die-cut flower.

a word about

corrugating

A corrugator, also known as a crimper, is a fun tool for adding dimension to your pages. A corrugator works by running a piece of cardstock between two spindles that interlock like gears. The pressure from the two spindles folds the paper uniformly, giving a crimped appearance.

Corrugated page embellishments retain their shape quite well as long as your albums are stored upright most of the time.

Corrugated die cuts

Simple die cut shapes jump off the page when you corrugate them. In some cases you can even create new shapes with a corrugator—a tan oval quickly becomes a Ruffles-style potato chip when you corrugate it.

Mats

Corrugating a mat is a very effective way to add visual texture to a photograph. Remember that cardstock changes shape slightly when you crimp it, so you'll need to cut your mat longer than usual to allow for the "shrinkage." You can trim it again after you have corrugated it.

Borders

For a fun border, cut a strip of contrasting cardstock using a straight edge along one side and a wavy ruler edge on the other. Make the border slightly wider than your page to allow for shrinkage. When you corrugate and mount it (and trim off any excess), it will look like the borders teachers use on their classroom bulletin boards.

PIERCING

The paper piercing technique discussed in January (page 18) can easily be used to embellish die-cut shapes. For simple shapes, pierce an all-over decorative design. For more intricate shapes, draw in the missing details on the back side of the die cut and pierce along the lines. Then turn it over, and you will find your shape enhanced by the pierced holes.

RUBBER STAMPING AND STENCILING

You can turn a simple solid die cut into a unique page embellishment by adding texture with rubber stamps or stencils. Any design that fits your theme can be used—stamp fireworks on a star, or stencil flowers on a heart. Depending on the look you want to achieve, either place your design carefully so that it falls entirely within the bounds of the die cut, or allow your stamp or stencil to overlap the edge of the die cut.

PENSTITCHING

Using your pigment pens, you can add a face to a teddy bear or clothing details to a die cut of a child. You can also use pigment pens to add faux stitching—a running stitch around the inside or outside of a die-cut jacket or a whipstich or blanket stitch over its edge. For a gilded appearance, trace the edges of your die cut with an embossing marker, then heat emboss with a metallic embossing powder.

EMBROIDERY

Embroidery can be used on die-cut shapes to add an elegant or sophisticated touch. Try using lamé thread for a whipstitch or blanket stitch. Add a running stitch (using standard embroidery floss) to mark the joints of a teddy bear, then add French knots for the eyes. Create a floral design on a heart shape using ribbon embroidery.

CORRUGATING

Corrugated die cuts can easily add a three-dimensional effect to your page. Pre-corrugated die cuts are available in stores, but the selection is limited. With a corrugator (also known as a crimper, available in craft stores), you can make your own (see sidebar at left).

JOURNALING: SEQUENCING

f a picture is worth a thousand words, a group of pictures must be worth many, many more. Nevertheless, a few well-chosen words can turn a group of pictures into a complete story. Imagine a series of photographs of a mother and

Labels visible in the layout:

FEBRUARY 6
ALMOST READY TO MOVE IN. ALL WE NEED IS A LITTLE LANDSCAPING AND FINAL INSPECTION

DOWNSTAIRS BATH

DINING ROOM

KITCHEN

OCTOBER 4
THE WINDOWS ARE IN AND THE ROOF IS READY FOR SHINGLES

CHILDREN'S BATH

NOVEMBER 29
THE ROOF IS ON AND THE BRICK IS GOING UP

BUILDING OUR HOUSE

SEQUENCING

Chronicle the tremendous accomplishment of building your dream house in your memory album. Take lots of notes and photos as your house is being built. **1.** Include a color copy of the actual blueprints used to build the house for the background of the layout. **2.** Add swatches of wallpaper to record your interior decorating decisions (you could also use paint chips and upholstery or drapery fabric). **3.** Include the dates on each of the photo labels—they add to the sense of progression. **4.** Arrange photos chronologically from the upper left corner down to the bottom center of the spread and up to the upper right corner.

child making a gingerbread house. The arrangement of the photos on the page is important, but the words will tie it all together.

When you place your photographs on the page, lay them out in sequence—left to right, top to bottom, or clockwise. To make clear the order in which the photographs should be viewed, add arrows that you have cut from appropriately colored cardstock, pointing the way from photograph to photograph. If you make the arrows large enough, you can do some of your journaling on them. Simple words such as "next" or "then" or "10 minutes later" may be sufficient for some sequences, but in other situations you may want to write more about what happened between the photographs. For fun with the gingerbread house photographs, you could document how many candies your little helper ate at each step.

Add captions to each photograph. What is happening in the photograph? How does it relate to the photographs before and after it? Why is it a significant step in the series? Many occasions lend themselves well to a sequence page:

- Building a house (see artwork on previous page)
- Preparing for a wedding ceremony
- Building a snowman
- Getting ready for a first date
- Making a favorite recipe, such as a cake
- Celebrating with a birthday party
- Re-decorating a room in your house
- Your child climbing a tree
- A favorite tree changing with each of the four seasons
- Building a sand castle
- A kitten or puppy growing during the first year of life
- Carving a pumpkin (see artwork in October, page 127)
- Decorating a Christmas tree

You can expand the sequence concept from a single page or spread to an entire mini-album. Spread the photographs out over multiple pages and add more extensive journaling about the events pictured. This can be an especially rewarding chronicle for a child's album. Follow a theme similar to one in a children's book, such as *The Carrot Seed* by Ruth Krauss. Take pictures of your child planting seeds, watering and caring for his plant, and recording its growth. Use a small 5" x 7" album and include one photograph per page. Follow the subject from beginning to end through pictures and journaling.

OUTSIDE THE LINES: SPLICING

Have you ever thought to splice photographs together? Splicing—merging one or more photographs together to create a new image—is a great technique for creating wonderful group shots for your scrapbooks. We discovered this technique by accident when working on scrapbook pages from a family trip to an Arkansas state park. We had the park to ourselves, so there was nobody to ask to take a photograph of the whole family (and our camera did not have a timer option). When we got home, we cut photographs and silhouetted them to create a single photo of our family.

It is easiest to splice together silhouetted photographs, since you have already cut the background from around the group. Simply layer the various silhouetted photographs to create a single image. Another method is to combine two group shots to create a panoramic-type photograph. This technique is great for a group shot at a school dance or for photographs of your tour group posing on the steps of Notre Dame in Paris.

If you are in a setting where you can't take a single photograph of the entire group, think beforehand about taking photographs to splice together. Pose all the people to be included into the photograph, placing the two photographers at each end. The first photographer should take the picture, then rejoin the group. The second photographer should stand exactly where the first photographer did and snap a second photograph. Try this technique at your next family reunion so that everyone can be included in a group photograph.

PHOTO TIP: FIREWORKS

Summertime celebrations offer great opportunities to watch fireworks. Most people who have been dazzled by the bursts of color have dreamed of catching the glory with their camera.

LONG EXPOSURE

The ability to take a long exposure is a key requirement for taking good photographs of fireworks. Fireworks are really not as bright as they seem; therefore, a long exposure is required to capture them on film. Using a 100 ASA film, you'll need at least a one-second exposure, and sometimes two seconds

or longer. Even if you have an automatic camera that does not allow you to set the exposure directly, try it anyway. You may find that your camera recognizes the situation and keeps the shutter open long enough for a good shot.

DON'T MOVE

Another requirement for good fireworks photographs is a steady camera. You'll need a tripod for your camera, because any minuscule movement of the camera will result in a blurred photograph. If you don't have a tripod, place your camera on any solid platform—the roof of your car or a fence post will do. Use a remote shutter release (a cord that attaches to the camera), also called a cable release, to further minimize jarring and motion.

FOCUS

Since you'll be far away from the fireworks, be sure to set your camera on "infinity." An auto-focus camera will probably choose the correct focus point, as long as you ensure that other items are not in its focusing window. Since all of the fireworks will probably be shown in the same portion of the sky, you should be able to get your camera aimed and focused during the first few bursts.

NO FLASH

What about using a flash? A flash will not travel far enough to illuminate the fireworks. In fact, it may draw attention to something in the foreground of your photograph that you don't want to be accentuated. So, turn your flash off. If you can't turn it off, try covering it with your hand or a piece of electrical tape.

Try composing some of your photographs so that a statue, boat, or skyline is in the foreground and the fireworks are bursting behind it. This will give your photographs an extra element of interest and also show where they were taken. Take lots of photographs. Since you're shooting a moving target, not every shot will be a masterpiece. Take plenty to increase your chances of having a few really good ones.

PHOTO TIP

These photographs of fireworks on a beach in Martha's Vineyard were taken with 100 ASA film, an F-stop of F-8, and a tripod. Hold the shutter open with your hand or a cable release while the fireworks are going off—use your personal judgment as to when to let go, for example, just after the peak of the fireworks explosion.

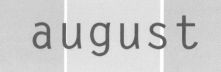

august

Hot. Hot. Hot. That's August. When you're outside in the sun, you'll have many opportunities to take lively photographs of the fun. And when the heat drives you indoors, you'll have plenty of time to work on your scrapbooks. So stretch out on your favorite lawn chair, review your summer photographs, and then head for your scrapbooking table to create some fantastic layouts. If possible, plan a trip to the seashore to gather shells, sand, and starfish and to take family photos.

MEMORIES TO CAPTURE

The motto for August should be "Just Add Water." Whether you take a trip to the beach or go only as far as the public swimming pool, water is an indispensable part of summer. Your scrapbook layouts depicting splashing and swimming will be bright and fun.

LAZY BEACH DAYS

Colors of sea and sand

The colors of the sand, the ocean, the sky, and the brightly-colored beach umbrellas pointed towards the sun are just waiting to be photographed. Zoom in for tight shots of your friends and family at the beach. Catch children running in and out of the surf as the waves break.

Sandy kingdom

Get down to the business of building the perfect sand-castle. Snap photographs of your kingdom—before and after the tide comes in. Embellish your sandcastle pages with pails and shovels cut from paper, and add texture with faux sand (see March, page 46).

She sells seashells

It is so relaxing to stroll barefooted along the ocean's edge hunting for beautiful seashells. If your camera

SEASHELLS

This design is created with a single rubber stamp. Layering a colored shell upon a black and cream background creates a three-dimensional look. **1.** Ink the rubber stamp with black pigment ink and stamp it onto a piece of cream-colored cardstock. **2.** Ink the portion of the rubber stamp with the large scallop seashell again with black pigment ink and stamp the shell onto a piece of peach patterned paper. **3.** Cut out the seashell stamped onto the peach paper around the edge of the shell. **4.** Trim the edges of the cream-colored paper to the edge of the seashell design. **5.** Mount the peach seashell over the corresponding seashell on the cream paper. **6.** Mat the entire design on peach paper.

has a macro setting, photograph some of your favorite shells close-up to include in your scrapbook. Smaller, flat seashells can be mounted directly onto your scrapbook pages.

NEAR THE SEA

A lovely layout with watercolor pencils captures a wonderful day spent near the sea. **1.** Stamp scallop seashells onto metallic cork paper with black pigment ink. Heat emboss with clear embossing powder. **2.** Stamp the "Near the Sea We Forget to Count the Days" lettering onto tan paper with black pigment ink. Heat emboss with Turquoise Tapestry embossing powder. **3.** Mat photographs as desired. **4.** On cold-pressed watercolor paper, draw a horizon line across the top of each page with a navy watercolor pencil. Draw a shoreline across the bottom of each page with a tan watercolor pencil. **5.** Lightly scribble various shades of tan, brown, gray, and blue together in the shore area. With a wet paintbrush, lightly blend the colors together. **6.** Scribble a black watercolor pencil and tan watercolor pencil onto a piece of scrap paper. Wet an old toothbrush and scrub into the black watercolor. Pull your thumb across the toothbrush bristles to spray black dots onto the shoreline. Repeat the same with the tan color. **7.** Sprinkle table salt into the wet colors of the shoreline. **8.** Lightly scribble various shades of blue and purple into the middle section of the page to create the ocean. Layer the colors and overlap colors. With a wet paintbrush, lightly mix the watercolors together, blending the colors until you get the look you want. **9.** With a clean, wet paintbrush, pull blue color from the ocean and lightly paint a blue sky. **10.** Mount watercolor paper onto tan paper. **11.** Mount shells and starfish onto shore. **12.** Add blue mulberry paper to the page and to your photographs. **13.** Mount lettering with a piece of blue mulberry paper showing from behind.

WATER FUN

Pool party

If you're lucky enough to own a pool, host a poolside party for your friends (or host a party at a community pool). Think tropical. Decorate with a luau theme and invite your guests to wear Hawaiian shirts. Greet your guests with leis and piña coladas, and serve a Hawaiian menu. Take plenty of group shots of your guests.

Swimming lessons

Disposable underwater cameras are a must if your child participates in swimming lessons. Inexpensive and easy to use, these cameras take great photographs. Capture several lessons on film to show how your child's swimming has improved. Mount his swimming certificate or patch on the same layout.

Water sports

Water skiing, sailing, snorkeling, and scuba diving are all activities that capture the essence of summer. Take a waterproof camera along. Look for the vivid colors of the catamaran's sails against the crystal blue water and clear sky. If you're a snorkeler, take plenty of photographs of the fish—and your snorkeling buddy.

SUMMER CAMP

Pack right

Along with the bathing suits, T-shirts, and insect repellent, send a labeled camera (disposable ones are great for this) and a journal along to camp with your child. Include some fun camp stickers in a letter for your child to use in a camp journal. Teach him how to use the camera before camp starts. Explain all the steps—especially when to use the flash and when a flash is not required. It is a good idea to develop

SUMMER CAMP

Preserve your child's camp memories in a special small-sized album, and add to it each year. **1.** Mount sticker borders across the top and bottom of golden yellow cardstock. **2.** Use a computer to print journaling directly onto cream-colored cardstock (we used the ScrapWood font and the Kidsprint font). **3.** Mat journaling with rust-colored cardstock. **4..** Mat the photograph with a leaf-print paper and rust-colored cardstock.

EXPLORING CAMPING HIKING

Camp Gilmont

I had fun at Camp Gilmont this summer. My friend, Kerry, was in my cabin. I swam in the swimming pool. I learned to paddle in a canoe. I got stuck in the middle of the lake in my canoe. But a counselor came and got me. I stayed at camp a whole week.

practice photographs before the trip and to review them with your child. Encourage your child to write daily about his experiences and emotions and to take photographs of all the activities and his new friends. These photos and journaling will become a memorable layout.

Operation: Photographs

Perhaps your child needs a little encouragement to remember to take photographs while away at camp. Along with the camera, send a list of fun "assignments." Suggest items to photograph: the bunk where he sleeps, all his cabin mates gathered in front of his cabin, some pretty scenery, a new friend, his counselors. Also include ideas for collecting items that you can use later in scrapbook layouts, such as acorns, leaves, feathers, and tree bark.

Letters home

Before your child goes to camp, help him or her address postcards to family and friends. Go ahead and add the necessary postage. Provide a list of items that your child might want to write home about—a blank postcard is intimidating for a young child. Of course, letters that you receive from your child should be mounted in your child's scrapbook.

OTHER NOTABLE EVENTS

Friendship Day

National Friendship Day is observed on August 2. Celebrate—and commemorate—your friends in photographs. Gather a group of close friends and neighbors and schedule a sitting with a professional photographer. Or plan a special afternoon (or evening) out and bring along your camera.

National Night Out

Held the first Tuesday in August, this event was designed to heighten crime prevention awareness in neighborhoods, but it is a great excuse to organize a block party. Create a scrapbook layout depicting the streets and houses in your immediate neighborhood. Include photographs of your neighbors (mounted near their house on the layout); note family member names and their street address.

National Smile Week

Celebrate this hint from Heloise by taking photographs of family and friends sporting big smiles. Organized annually (the first Monday in August through the following Sunday), Heloise invites you to "Share a smile and it will come back to you, bringing happiness to you and the giver."

ALBUM IDEA: COLLECTOR'S ALBUM

At some point in your life, you've probably enjoyed collecting something. In fact, you probably have at least one collection now. Perhaps it is Lladro figurines or antique linens or family quilts. A collector's album is a great way to show off your collection.

TWO-DIMENSIONAL COLLECTIONS

Items that are two-dimensional, or flat, such as stamps, foreign currency, and wine labels, fit nicely in a scrapbook. Depending on the type of items in the collection, you can decide whether to mount them permanently on your scrapbook page or mount them in a fashion that will allow them to be removed. For instance, baseball cards and stamps may have intrinsic value that would be destroyed if you mounted them permanently. Valuable objects should be included in your scrapbook using adhesiveless, or temporary, mounting techniques, such as photo corners or Mylar sleeves. Others, such as a collection of wine labels, may have no dollar value above the memories that they represent. Such items can be mounted using either permanent or temporary mounting techniques.

3-D AND LARGE-ITEM COLLECTIONS

Some collections are much too large or bulky to be included directly in your scrapbook. Collections of items such as fine art, Christmas ornaments, linens, quilts, Navaho rugs, hand-painted china, or antique jewelry can still be included in a special collector's album.

The most obvious solution for large or bulky items is to take a photograph, and then mount the photograph in your album. For some items, such as linens or needlework, a color photocopy better captures the detail. Consider combining both—make a color copy of your collectible linens to use as a background on the page, then add a photograph of the linens in use on your table. Be conscious of the setting you choose for photographing your collection. Photograph your antique jewelry collection against a solid, simple background, such as forest green velvet. Take a look at magazines devoted to interior decorating or food for ideas for styling your photographs.

ORGANIZE YOUR ALBUM

If your collection is complete—you have all of your grandmother's quilts—pick an album and plan its design from beginning to end. If you are still adding to your collection, choose a flexible album style that will allow you to add pages as you acquire additional items.

When I was a teenager, I collected decorative napkins — pretty floral ones, whimsical ones, custom imprinted ones, and everything in between. Those napkins are long gone now. Too bad I didn't know about scrapbooking at the time! They would have made a charming album, and captions would have told the story behind them.

— Anna

TELL A STORY

Everything you can document in journaling about your collection is a bit of history, both personal and public. What is unique about the piece? Does it have special engraving or markings? When and where was it made? Where did you acquire it? How much did it cost? If you think you may eventually sell the piece, leave room for the selling price.

DESIGN CONCEPT: DEPTH

The design concept of depth is what differentiates creative-style scrapbooks from their photo album-style counterparts. By layering design elements with different textures and patterns, you can create a perspective of depth within a scrapbook layout.

Shadowing is a technique for creating depth within a scrapbook design. One easy way to shadow an element is to add a contrasting color mat offset to one side. For example, cut a dark green mat and mount it behind a patterned-paper tree. Allow the dark green mat to show only on the right side and bottom of the tree (see artwork on page 106). Or try drawing a line with pigment ink on two joining sides of a photograph to create your shadow. A cluster of small black dots around the edges of a design element creates a shadow—and depth.

You create a pattern by repeating a motif in your design. Imagine rubber stamping a beach umbrella repeatedly across a page. Mounting brightly-matted beach photographs atop the umbrella designs gives depth to your layout. Additionally, if you stamp a combination of light and dark umbrellas in different colored inks, you create a contrast that enhances the perception of depth.

Let your shadowing techniques extend to your journaling, titles, and creative lettering. Hand-drawn or stencilled

This locket was worn originally by Lucretia Eleanor Tubbs. Note the "LT" engraved on the back.

It was probably made in the 1910s or 1920s, prior to Lucretia's marriage to Carlos Collins in 1930.

The locket has since been handed down from Lucretia to her stepdaughter Emmilou Edmonds (nee Collins), who in turn passed it down to her daughter, Anna Swinney (nee Edmonds).

COLLECTOR'S ALBUM I

The back of this antique locket is as beautiful as the front, so we decided to include both in the layout. **1.** Use deckle-edged scissors to cut the mats to enhance the old-fashioned look. **2.** Add fancy appliqué letters (available in fabric stores) for a personal monogram. **3.** To attach flat buttons to the page, mark locations by penciling a small mark through each hole after arranging the buttons on the page. **4.** Prepare the holes by punching them with a large chenille needle. **5.** Stitch the buttons onto the page through the holes you prepared using metallic thread.

block letters can easily become three-dimensional by adding color on one or two edges (see School Portrait in September, page 116). Choose a corner (such as the upper left) for the "sun" to shine from, and add a shadow on the opposite (lower right) edges. There are also many fonts with a three-dimensional appearance available for computer journaling and titles (see "High School" lettering in artwork in September, page 117). You can increase the three-dimensional effect by using colored pencils after you print them.

Texture is another way to add depth to a layout. A simple mat around a photograph adds texture to a layout. Using different weights and styles of cardstock creates even more depth within your design. See artwork on previous page and in March, page 46, to find other ways to add texture.

A word of caution—don't confuse depth with busyness or clutter. The design elements that you use to project a feeling of depth should not overpower your overall page but rather enhance the entire design.

TECHNIQUE TO TRY: POP-UP PAGE

When a friend leafs through your scrapbook and happens upon a pop-up page, she is bound to be delighted. There is nothing like a pop-up page to add dimension to your album.

The most common style of pop-up page consists of two adjacent pages joined at the album's binding. The objective is to decorate a "base" that will lie flat when the album is closed and spring open when you turn to the page.

BEFORE YOU BEGIN

Before creating the page, decide which element would be most effective as a pop-up. Just as you design any layout, you need to compose your pop-up and its surrounding pages. Choose the elements you want to remain on the page and the ones you want to stand up on the pop-up. Die cuts, silhouetted

COLLECTOR'S ALBUM II

Who hasn't collected matchbooks from restaurants they've visited? You can show off many matchbook covers on a single page with this technique. **1.** Remove all matches from covers to reduce the risk of fire. **2.** Cut four strips of cardstock approximately 1½" wide and 12" long. **3.** Cut four strips of cardstock in a contrasting color, approximately 1" wide. Glue the 1" strips to the 1½" strips. **4.** Arrange your matchbooks on the four strips. **5.** Punch a pair of holes at the beginning and the end of the 1" strip using a ¹⁄₁₆" hole punch. Punch additional pairs of holes at intervals on the 1" strips. **6.** Attach the strips to the page with permanent or temporary adhesive. Trim strips to the width of the page, if necessary. **7.** Strengthen the bond between the strips and the page by making a stitch with embroidery floss through each set of holes and tying the stitches off on the back side. (Without the added stitching, the horizontal strips of cardstock could sag under the weight of the matchbook covers.)

photographs, and heavy cardstock shapes work well on pop-ups. On the other hand, stickers and lightweight papers work best on the base page because they are more delicate. Of course, there are always exceptions—stickers mounted on heavy cardstock can certainly work as part of your pop-up scene.

THE BASE

Before you can create a decorative pop-up, you'll need to build an extension of your page to serve as a base. Using a pattern (see Resources appendix for books containing patterns) cut a base out of a folded piece of heavyweight cardstock large enough to match your page size and the size of your pop-up scene. The fold will become the center of your base. Remember to leave a flap which will later be glued to your page. As you add embellishments to the base, you can adjust its height by either cutting it or adding other decorative pieces of cardstock to make it stand taller. You will eventually mount the base across the center of your album, spanning two adjacent pages. Fold the base into a slight V, with one side on the left page and the other on the right page. Later, after decorating your pop-up, use a strong adhesive to attach the base to the page.

EXPERIMENT

Just as you would experiment with the placement of your pictures on the page, you will want to experiment with the placement of your pop-up and with the decorations mounted on your pop-up. We like to start by attaching the pop-up to the page with removable Post-it dots. This facilitates moving it later, if desired. You can also use the removable dots to temporarily attach your embellishments to the pop-up. At each step of the way, you will want to make sure that your album still closes correctly.

You can also experiment with the actual placement of the pop-up base on the page. One placed near the top of the page adds dramatic height; one placed lower is inviting and integrates better with the rest of the layout. (Make sure that your pop-up doesn't extend past the bottom of the page when the album is closed.)

Try putting more than one pop-up on a page to create a stadium effect. Make each base slightly smaller than the previous so that each can be seen when the page is open. Mount the smaller pop-up an inch or more closer to the bottom of the page than the larger one.

ASSEMBLE

Once you are happy with the composition of your pop-up and the surrounding spread, permanently attach the elements. Use faint pencil marks to note the exact location and orientation of the base and embellishments on the page. Use permanent adhesive to reattach the pieces.

CREATING DEPTH

This layout illustrates how to create depth by using shadowing. **1.** Using a plastic template and a pencil, trace a tall, skinny pine tree onto the back side of a piece of patterned paper. **2.** Use the same template to trace another tree onto a piece of solid green cardstock. Cut both trees out. **3.** Create a rustic border with a brown colored pencil for your layout base. **4.** To create a shadow for one of your photographs, mat the photo with yellow cardstock showing on the right side and bottom only. **5.** Mat the other photographs in complementary colors. **6.** Mount all photographs on a tan layout base. **7.** Layer the patterned tree and the solid green tree to create a shadow effect, and mount on your layout. **8.** Add small trees, using colored pencils and a plastic template.

POP-UP PAGE

The die-cut dolphins leap out of the water with a pop-up page. **1.** Begin by cutting two bases using a pattern. Trim one base to have a smaller radius (this will be the front base). Fold both along the center line of symmetry and along the intersection of the base with the tabs that will hold it to the finished page. **2.** Temporarily affix the bases to your scrapbook pages with Post-It dots, making sure the pages can still close easily. Mark the location of the bases, then remove them from the page. **3.** Add embellishments to your pop-ups. First place dolphins with Post-It dots to make sure they are correctly placed. Then apply permanent adhesive to glue the dolphins to the base. **4.** Return the base to the page with Post-It dots, again checking the positioning. **5.** Add permanent adhesive to bond bases to the page.

a word about
alternative pop-ups

For spiral-bound or three-ring albums that don't support traditional pop-ups well, try these other options.

Strip pop-up

Cut a strip of cardstock approximately 6" long and your desired width. Fold it down the middle vertically, and fold vertical flaps on each end. Attach one lap vertically to the left page. Attach the other flap parallel to the first on the right page. This will provide you with a pop-up base that spans the center like a tent but which leaves room for the spiral or the gap of a three-ring binder.

Slider

Hide a photo behind another photo and let your readers pull out the hidden picture with a tab. Cut your hidden picture so it's at least 1" shorter in length than the top and the bottom edges of the top photo. To the back of the hidden picture, attach a strip of cardstock about ¾" wide and several inches longer than the photo is wide. Leave about 1" sticking out from one edge of the hidden photo for a tab, and leave the remaining length of the strip on the other edge of the photo. Cut a ¾" slit in your page underneath where you will mount the top photo. Slip the long end of the tab strip into the slit, from front to back, and attach a 1" square of heavy cardstock firmly to the end of the strip that's on the back side of the page. This creates a "brake" that prevents the strip from being pulled out of the page entirely. The strip and the attached photo should move freely in the slip. Attach the top photo or design element along the three edges covering the slit, the strip, and the hidden photo, leaving the fourth edge free so the tab can be pulled out. The hidden photo will sit behind the top photo with a tab available for pulling it out to view.

KEYS TO SUCCESS

We strongly recommend experimenting with every pop-up to achieve the angles and dimensions that work for each particular layout. Here are additional tips for creating pop-up pages.

Choose the right album style

Pop-up pages work best with post-bound or flex-hinge albums because their pages meet closely in the center. Spiral-bound and three-ring binders pose a problem because of the distance between the left- and right-hand pages when open.

Work in your album

For many page layouts, the easiest way to work is by removing the page from the album. Not so for pop-ups. The placement of the pop-up base on the page is directly impacted by the way the pages lay within the album itself. For this reason we recommend working directly in your album when making a pop-up.

JOURNALING: LAYERING

Since capturing memories in words is such an important part of preserving our experiences, it is useful to know different ways to journal on scrapbook pages.

PENS, PENS, PENS

When you first began scrapbooking, you probably used a black pigment pen to journal on your pages. There are dozens and dozens of colors and pen styles available, however. Branch out from navy, red, brown, purple, and green. Try silver, gold, or opaque markers for writing directly on dark cardstock. Experiment with pen tips, such as fine point, broad tip, calligraphy, and brush tip. Between the colors and tips available, there are limitless combinations for unique journaling on your pages.

Write directly on the page

In many cases, you will want to write directly onto your scrapbook page. Use creative lettering to draw titles (see April, page 56). Write captions under photographs. Journal entire paragraphs. Capture the highlights of an event in a bulleted list. Journal around the perimeter of a photograph or a page. Write to fill in a circle, a triangle, oval, or spiral.

Write on a separate piece of cardstock

Write your journaling on a contrasting piece of cardstock, cut it out, and mount it on the page. Such layered journaling adds dimension to your page. Even if

BUDDIES
Chase
Jared
Chase and Jared were born just one day apart
in the same hospital.
When they were 10 months old,
they "met" again at daycare.
From that time forward, they were inseparable.
They were graduated from the infant class
to the toddler class
and eventually to pre-school on the same day.
When they were turning three,
it only seemed natural to have
a joint birthday party.
S I N C
B U

BUDDIES

Double matting highlights the story of these two young friends. **1.** To make the title, cut 1¼" squares of yellow cardstock. **2.** Place a sticker letter in the center of each yellow square. As an alternative to stickers, substitute stenciled letters or your own creative letters (see April, page 56). We like stencils or sticker letters for this technique because they are easiest to center in the cut squares. **3.** Mat the yellow squares in white. **4.** Complete lengthy journaling using your favorite font on your computer, and print on yellow cardstock. Mat the journaling in white, and then again in red. **5.** Mat photographs in solid and patterned primary colored cardstock. **6.** Layer all items on the page and attach, giving prominence to the journaling block. **7.** Embellish the page by adding clusters of punched geometric shapes in primary colors.

your cardstock is the same color as its background, you can mat it in a contrasting color to increase its visibility. Short and long captions alike can be overlapped with the pertinent photographs, adding to the rhythm of the page. This method is especially helpful if you have fears about making mistakes. If you make a mistake in your journaling, you can re-create it without redoing the entire page.

Write on a die cut

Similar to writing on a piece of cardstock, you can journal directly onto a die-cut shape, such as a bell or a house. For added interest, have your journaling conform to the shape of the die cut.

OTHER IDEAS

Computer journaling

For longer passages of journaling, we like to use a computer. Just type the text into your favorite word processing program, format it however you like, choose an appropriate font, and print it directly onto a piece of cardstock. Cut it out, mat it if you like, and mount it on the page. For scrapbook styles that use removable 8½" x 11" cardstock as the background pages, you can print with your computer printer directly on the page—no cutting required.

Sticker letters

Sticker letters, available in a wide variety of colors and patterns, are especially great for quick and easy titles. Try using two of each letter in different colors and overlapping them for a shadowed effect. For lengthier journaling, use a sticker letter as the first letter of each paragraph and complete the paragraph with a pen. This creates a simple "illuminated letter" or "dropped cap" for your paragraph of journaling.

Die-cut letters and words

Most die-cut letters and words are about 2" in height, which make them good options for page titles or illuminated letters. You can further embellish these larger letters with stickers or penstitching, or with any method for dressing up die cuts (see July, page 95).

Stencils

Alphabet stencils, or templates, are available in many sizes. Those from 1" or smaller up to 2" can be useful in scrapbook journaling. You can find stencils in traditional styles, such as Helvetica or Script, and in more decorative ones, such as Log Cabin and Funky. You can use stencils to trace directly on your page with ink or trace with a pencil and then add detail in ink.

Hand-cut letters

A fun way to use alphabet stencils, or templates, especially those that are not overly detailed, is to trace them onto paper or cardstock to be cut out individually for mounting on the page. Lightly trace the letters in reverse on the back of the paper (instead of on the front) so that any stray pencil marks will be hidden. After cutting out the letters, mount them on contrasting solid cardstock and silhouette them. This allows you to overlap the letters slightly when you mount them on the page while allowing the individual letters to stand out from each other (see All My Sports in June, page 80).

OUTSIDE THE LINES: WATERCOLOR

You can add a light wash of color to create a sandy beach or bold colors to make a brilliant sunset. The only drawback to using watercolors within a scrapbook is that watercolors are not permanent. If your album should ever get wet, your colors will run. Be sure to store your albums in a safe place if you decide to use watercolors for decorative purposes.

SUPPLIES

Watercolor pencils

Unless you already have watercolor paints on hand, we recommend using watercolor pencils. Watercolor pencils can be applied dry like colored pencils—then use a wet brush to gently blend the color(s). Another method is to scribble watercolor pencils on a scrap piece of paper, then draw a wet brush into the color and apply the color from the brush to your paper.

Brushes

Although there are a wide variety of watercolor brushes available at any art supply store, you can easily begin with brushes that you already have on hand.

Paper

One of the drawbacks of watercolors is that your paper gets wet. Scrapbooking cardstock is too thin to withhold much watercolor painting (it will warp). If you are adding just a wash of watercolor to a few small designs, cardstock will be just fine. However, if you are painting scenes or an entire background, use a thicker paper, such as 140-lb cold-pressed paper.

METHODS TO TRY

Apply a light wash of color

Stamp or draw designs with permanent ink. (Avoid water-based inks, which will run when you apply the watercolor.) You can even heat emboss a design before applying watercolors. Apply color directly from your brush to color in the design. Or try coloring a portion of a design with a dry watercolor pencil and then using a wet brush to blend the color into the entire design. Don't worry about going outside the lines of your design—you might like the effect.

Paint scenes and background

For large areas, use thick paper that can be mounted on cardstock once it is dry. Again, you can apply color dry with a watercolor pencil or wet from a brush. For a textured look, pour some table salt into the wet paint. As the salt expands and crystallizes, a beautiful mottled effect is created that can be snow, a field of wildflowers, or a sandy beach. Another interesting technique is to splatter watercolor paint from an old toothbrush onto your page. Load an old toothbrush with paint and draw your thumb across the bristles to splatter paint (see artwork on page 101). You can use a mix of colors to create different effects, such as pebbles on a beach or the spray from waves in the ocean.

WATERCOLOR

Bright blue morning glories are a favorite summertime flower. **1.** Ink a morning glory rubber stamp with permanent black ink. On the left side of your page, stamp out a design and allow to dry about an hour. **2.** Scribble various shades of blue watercolor pencils onto a piece of scrap paper. Wet a small brush with water and take up some of the color by rubbing the brush into the blue scribbles. **3.** Paint the morning glories blue. Add shading by picking up different colors of blue or by adding more water for a lighter blue.
4. Scribble green watercolor pencils onto another piece of scrap paper. Proceed as in steps 2 and 3 above to paint the leaves and vines green. Don't worry about staying within the lines; the loose feeling lends a visual softness to your art. **5.** Mount a photograph to the right of the morning glory watercolor.

PHOTO TIP: BLACK-AND-WHITE FILM

Only a small percentage of family photographers use black-and-white film. Color photography is appealing because it captures what we see. On the other hand, black-and-white photography forces us to imagine the color—and we imagine it in the most vivid fashion. Black-and-white photographs are often far more memorable and dramatic than color photographs.

Black-and-white photography was once the arena of professional photographers and enthusiastic amateurs with darkrooms in their basements. Recent advances in technology have made available additional black-and-white films that can be processed in a one-hour lab using standard C-41 processing. The ready availability of these films and the

FAMILY PORTRAITS

Black-and-white photography is a wonderful way to expand your portrait repertoire. **(ABOVE)** The dark background and backlighting from the sun create a subtle glow around the family. Block the overhead sunlight from your lens with your hand, someone else's hand, or a card. **(BELOW)** This intimate portrait of mother and baby was shot 10 feet from a window on a very bright day, with a 1/60th of a second exposure. Remember, if you see a great picture starting to happen, don't hesitate for a second—grab your camera and shoot!

My first experience with black-and-white photography was through a class my senior year in college. I learned to process and develop the film myself in the school darkroom. The excitement of watching my photographs appear before my eyes was magical. Although I enjoyed developing my own pictures, it was also difficult to get a print perfect — perfect shades of black, gray, and white.

Our assignment was to shoot a particular subject all semester. First I tried shooting trees but these prints turned out to be boring. So I chose "children" instead. I photographed my daughter and her classmates at school. I photographed children playing at the park. Then there were the photo showings, posting a series of prints that "had something to say." My fellow classmates critiqued the photos and discussed my photo message. I just took pictures that I liked.

— Debbie

accessibility of processing has led to a rise in the popularity of black-and-white photography among non-professionals. Nevertheless, black-and-white photography is different from color photography and requires attention to additional details.

SIMPLICITY

By its very nature, black-and-white photography offers visual simplicity. Given this, it allows you to concentrate on form, lighting, and design, as well as the gestures and expressions of people.

Take advantage of the simplicity and focus your attention on one or two key aspects you want to capture on film. Just as in color photography, avoid cluttered backgrounds that can draw attention away from the focus of your photograph and detract from its simplicity. Remember to move in close to your subject to compose photographs that are simple in subject matter and composition.

SHADES OF GRAY

Black-and-white photographs are made up of many shades of gray. Lighting is more important than in color shots, and texture becomes more obvious. Black-and-white photography emphasizes contrast; dark shadow and rays of light will be noticed easily. However, a red dress, blue chair, and a green tree, all of which stand out brilliantly in color photography, may all be rendered in a similar shade of gray on black-and-white film. The similarity of grays can lead to boring black-and-white photographs if you are not careful in composing your photographs. You'll want to choose subjects and settings with high contrast in tone that will be captured well on black-and-white film, translating your images into a wide range of shades of gray.

Shadows can add drama to black-and-white photographs. Sidelighting adds shadow, dimension, and depth, whether you are using color or black-and-white film. With black-and-white photography, sidelighting can increase the contrast depicted in your photo. For example, if your light source comes in directly from your subject's left, the left side of her face will be brightly lit, contrasting significantly with the right side of her face, which will be bathed in dark shadow.

THINK BLACK-AND-WHITE

This lovely portrait was taken by the boy's mother on their annual summer trip to visit family in Athens, Greece. She took advantage of late morning sunlight coming in from under a canopy, using a 1/60th of a second exposure and an F-stop of 4, with no flash and a telephoto lens.

THINK BLACK-AND-WHITE

Because we see everything around us in color, it takes practice to think in black-and-white. Study the photographs of great black-and-white photographers, such as Ansel Adams, and consider how they were composed. Begin exploring black-and-white photography on your own. Instead of experimenting on your vacation photographs, however, take your family to the park for practice black-and-white portrait sessions. Record the settings you use on your camera along with the frame number and information about the lighting. Look critically at your photographs and determine which techniques work best.

Black-and-white photography is not appropriate for every photo opportunity. Black-and-white film works well for portraiture, nature, and architecture, and classic activities, such as a college graduation. On the other hand, color photography is more appropriate for a child's birthday party or a hot air balloon festival. Analyze each situation separately and evaluate whether black-and-white or color photography is appropriate. If you have two cameras, keep one loaded with color film and one with black-and-white. Then you'll have the luxury of taking both types of photographs of any occasion.

DO IT YOURSELF

Although one-hour processing is now available for some black-and-white films, part of the allure of black-and-white photography is the ability to process and print the photographs yourself. When you print your own photographs, you have total control over the results. If this idea appeals to you, take an adult education course on the subject and give it a try.

september

Whether you are a student, a former student, or the parent of a student, September brings thoughts of going back to school. And with the venture back into the classroom come visions of schedules and a new routine. Schedule time this month to work on your scrapbooks. Make a weekly appointment with yourself to sort photographs or design new layouts—just as you would schedule time for studies or classes if you were back in school.

MEMORIES TO CAPTURE

September is the month that signals the end of summer vacation and getting back to the routines of everyday life. Children are back in school, and life's hurried pace resumes. Don't neglect your scrapbooks this month. Organizing and mounting photographs from the summer helps you remember the fun times while you keep your albums up-to-date.

GRANDPARENT'S DAY

Celebrated the first Sunday in September following Labor Day, this is a day set aside to honor our grandparents.

Grandparents' album

Create a special album for your children's grandparents. Instead of periodically sending an envelope of new photographs, create a few new scrapbook pages to add to their album. Don't forget to include some photographs of your children doing everyday things, such as eating breakfast, riding their bikes, or brushing their teeth. If your grandparents are still living, make an album for them as well. What more treasured gift than to be given a window into your grandchildren's and great grandchildren's lives.

Generations

If grandparents live close by, plan a visit on Grandparent's Day. Take lots of photographs while you're there.

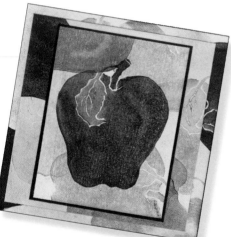

ORCHARD APPLE

1. Using markers, color directly onto an apple rubber stamp: red for the apple, green for the leaf (also rub the green on both sides of the apple to add shading), brown for the stem (also rub the brown on the edges and bottom of the apple to add contrast), yellow to color a section of the apple for a highlight. **2.** Huff (blow) onto the stamp to moisten the ink. **3.** Stamp onto a sheet of cream paper. Immediately (without reinking) stamp again on another portion of the cream paper. Continue stamping on different parts of the paper until the ink is gone. **4.** Repeat steps 1 to 3 on slightly larger sheets of cream paper. **5.** Mat the center piece of stamped cream paper with black paper. Mat with a second sheet of stamped cream paper, then mat with a third sheet of stamped cream paper.

(You can never have too many photos of older family members.) Snapshots that contain multiple generations will be especially treasured in years to come.

GRANDPARENTS' PHOTOCARD

This card can be used as a frame for display or mounted in a memory album. To display, fold the card with the collage frame facing out. Tie the gold ribbon, leaving a little slack so that the card will stand (as pictured above).

To create the collage frame: **1.** Tear small pieces of colored paper into different shapes and sizes. **2.** Cover a small portion of a precut cardstock black paper frame (purchased at a craft store) with a liquid adhesive. **3.** Position paper pieces randomly over the glue, overlapping or leaving black space as desired (work quickly in small sections, because the glue dries quickly). **4.** Apply a layer of paper adhesive, covering the entire surface of the paper and frame. (Place the frame on a scrap piece of paper before applying glue—it is a little messy.) **5.** Apply a dusting of gold pigment powder over portions of the paper pieces while the adhesive is still wet. **6.** Allow about one hour for the frame to dry, then apply a second covering of paper adhesive. **7.** Allow another two hours for the frame to dry.

To create the photocard: **1.** Fold a piece of black linen paper in half, creasing with a bone folder. **2.** Mat a photograph with the collage frame and mount onto black paper with adhesive. **3.** Ink a patterned rubber stamp with black ink, stamp on the front of the card, and heat emboss with gold embossing powder (see inset). **4.** Punch a small hole in the card for a ribbon. (You may want to reinforce the punched hole with a small circle of heavy, gold cardstock.) **5.** Thread a gold ribbon through the holes and tie it into a bow.

BACK TO SCHOOL

The first days of school are usually exciting as children don their new back-to-school outfits and become reacquainted with friends after the summer break.

First day poses

Begin a tradition of taking a special posed photograph each year on the first day of school. Stage the same pose every year—perhaps by the front door with your child wearing his backpack and holding his lunch bag. Begin a work-in-progress layout for all these first day photographs. On a work-in-progress layout, you create a basic completed design with extra spaces to mount new photographs. You will look back and smile as your child grows over the years and the lunch box changes from cartoon characters to pop idols to a plain, brown paper bag (see artwork on next page).

Signs of the times

Cut pictures from magazines or advertisements from "Back-to-School" sales showing popular trends and colors in fashion, and use them to create a scrapbook page for your child's school album. Or better yet,

The first day of school was always a highlight in my life. Ordering new clothes from the Sears catalog and shopping for pencils and paper was such fun. I could hardly wait to receive my text-books — and even homework — during those first days of school.

— Debbie

photograph your child modeling her "fashion garb." Your child will have proof that bellbottoms were really cool when she was a kid.

Sign here

On the first day of school, have your child write his name for his school days album. Remember to use an acid-free, permanent pen on acid-free paper to ensure that the signature will last. On the last day of school, you can compare how his handwriting has changed.

Away for college

College-bound children are often encouraged—or nagged—to keep in touch with their folks. As a parent, you can follow your own advice by maintaining contact with your son or daughter. Send an empty scrapbook album with your teen to college. Then, when you mail a care package of her favorite cookies, include a completed scrapbook page to keep her apprised of all the goings-on at home.

SCHOOL PORTRAIT

A classic apple motif highlights that special school portrait.
1. Use an alphabet stencil to trace two sets of lettering on cardstock in coordinating colors. Trace the letters in reverse on the back side of the cardstock so that any stray pencil marks will not show. Cut out both sets of letters with sharp scissors. (Use a craft knife to cut out the centers of letters such as O and D.) **2.** Using an apple design paper punch, punch two large apples from red cardstock. Cut tiny leaves freehand from green cardstock. Mount on a square of tan cardstock. Mat the squares with red paper. **3.** Use several mats to accentuate your focal photograph. We used a narrow tan mat, two narrow red mats, and a wide mat of apple-patterned paper. **4.** When assembling the page, layer the darker letters under the lighter ones to create a shadowing effect.

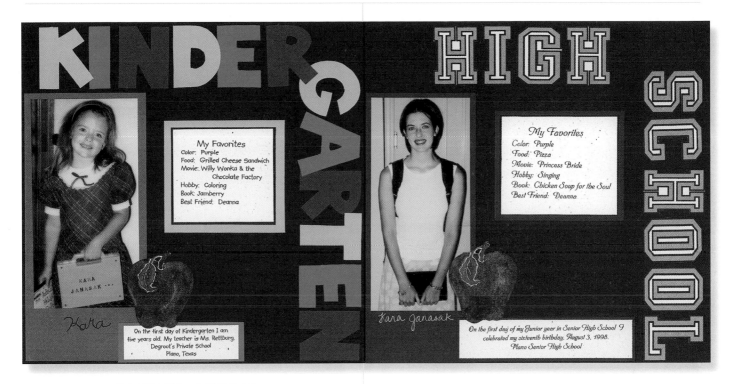

My Favorites
Color: Purple
Food: Grilled Cheese Sandwich
Movie: Willy Wonka & the Chocolate Factory
Hobby: Coloring
Book: Jamberry
Best Friend: Deanna

On the first day of Kindergarten I am five years old. My teacher is Ms. Rettburg. Degroot's Private School Plano, Texas

My Favorites
Color: Purple
Food: Pizza
Movie: Princess Bride
Hobby: Singing
Book: Chicken Soup for the Soul
Best Friend: Deanna

On the first day of my Junior year in Senior High School I celebrated my sixteenth birthday, August 3, 1998. Plano Senior High School

BACK TO SCHOOL

These title pages introduce each new grade in a school days album. The kindergarten photo is an enlargement of an old Polaroid. **1.** Lightly trace large letters onto paper using a pencil and an alphabet stencil (remember to trace letters onto the back of the paper and to turn the stencil over so that the letters are reversed). Cut out the letters. **2.** Color an apple-shaped rubber stamp with red, green, brown, and yellow markers, overlapping the colors to create a shadowed effect. Cut out the apple. **3.** Use your computer to journal information about the first day of school. Also create a small block of text containing information such as your child's favorite color, favorite snack food, favorite movie, favorite book, and favorite friend. **4.** Mat first day of school photograph on colored cardstock, leaving enough paper at the bottom for the student's signature. **5.** Mount the school grade letters around the outside of a piece of red cardstock. **6.** Mount the photograph, journaling, and apple on layout.

OTHER NOTABLE EVENTS

Rosh Hashanah and Yom Kippur

In the Jewish faith Rosh Hashanah is the beginning of a new year. It is a time of introspection and of personal awakening to the call of the shofar (an animal horn that is blown like a trumpet). Yom Kippur, the Day of Atonement, is the most serious day in the Jewish calendar. On Yom Kippur the faithful devote their thoughts to becoming closer to God and asking for forgiveness. The personal diary you keep during this journey of self-reflection may provide ideas or thoughts for journaling in your scrapbook.

Labor Day

Labor Day is the first Monday in September. Create a scrapbook page featuring photographs of your workplace and coworkers. In your journaling describe why you chose the profession or job that you have today, what you like about your work, or special projects and goals for the coming year.

ALBUM IDEA: SCHOOL DAYS ALBUM

Devote a theme album (or series of albums) to cover the activities of your child's school years. Without even trying, you are bound to collect a multitude of photographs and memorabilia related to every school term.

SCHOOL PHOTOS

Almost every child has a formal picture taken each year at school. Use a 5" x 7" or 8" x 10" photo as an introduction to a new year in your child's album. Mount wallet-sized photos from each year on a title page spread as an introduction to the entire album. You don't have to wait until your child has graduated from high school to create this introductory page—just save room for all 12 photographs and mount the ones you already have. This page can be a work in progress.

If you're lucky enough to have a class photo as well, especially for the elementary years, be sure to document the names of all the children in the class—or at least the names of his closest friends (see June, page 85).

Devote a page each year to your child's teacher (or teachers). If you don't have an official portrait, take your own photographs at an open house or school event. Have your child comment on what he liked most about his teacher and include that as journaling on the page.

SCHOOL ACTIVITIES

Many students are involved in extracurricular school activities. Create a layout for each significant activity so your child will have a memento of the French club, the school literary magazine, or the varsity hockey team.

Sports

If your child's involvement in school sports is significant enough for inclusion in the school's yearbook, it is certainly significant enough to be included in his school album. When you create a page for his album, he can be the star of the team—even if he sat on the bench for most of the season.

Music

Capture your child's involvement with the band, orchestra, or choir with pictures from performances, flyers from concerts, and lyrics and song titles. Take some extra photographs that focus on the instrument your child plays. Sheet music can make a great background for these pages.

Clubs

Highlight your child's involvement in school-affiliated clubs by saving the club logo and charter to use with your photos. Keep disposable cameras on hand and encourage students to take photographs to document any service projects that the club participates in.

Special days

Gather photographs and memorabilia of special days to include in your child's album. What activities did she participate in during the Student Olympics? What about that school trip to Colonial Williamsburg? Encourage your child to take photographs at high school dances and pep rallies as well.

SCHOOL HONORS

Honors big and small should have a special place in a child's school album. Big honors, such as being named prom queen or elected to the student council, are often accompanied by photographs, certificates, and other memorabilia that can be used to create a page for an album. Also, include smaller honors, such as "Star of the Week" or "Weather Person" for a preschooler, that are important to your child's self-esteem and sense of recognition. And don't overlook group awards. If the school choir won first place at a district competition, get a copy of the certificate to include in your own tenor's album.

SCHOOLWORK AND ARTWORK

Years from now you'll enjoy reviewing samples of schoolwork from a school days album. Include a representative spelling test and math worksheet, and photographs and summaries of major school projects. What was the title of your child's semester-long research project? What was her science fair experiment? Choose—and photograph or color photocopy—a few pieces of art that your elementary school student made during a given year (see artwork on next page).

DESIGN CONCEPT: DOUBLE PAGES

Due to the design of albums, you will almost always have two pages side by side. Whether these facing pages are dedicated to the same event or different events is, of course, totally up to you. While there is no right or wrong way to handle single pages vs. double pages, we can offer some suggestions.

LIMITED PHOTOGRAPHS

When you only have two or three good photographs from an event, here are some options:

- Enlarge the photographs to 5" x 7" or 8" x 10" size to expand the layout from a single-page to a double-page.

- Add extensive journaling to tell the story of the photographs, allowing you to use two pages instead of one.

- Use a complementary color scheme for the design of facing pages, even if the events depicted are different.

- Tie two unrelated events on facing pages together with a common vertical border along the outside edges of both pages.

A CHILD'S ARTWORK

We chose a bulletin board as the background for displaying this child's school artwork. **1.** Create the bulletin board by attaching a thin sheet of cork to a piece of cardstock. Mount on red and black plaid paper, and in turn mount on black cardstock to give it a clean edge. **2.** Silhouette each photograph or color photocopy of a piece of artwork by cutting close to its edge (if you make color photocopies, you can use the reduction setting on the copier to make smaller images). **3.** Use an alphabet stencil to trace the letters for your title onto red cardstock. Trace the letters in reverse on the back side of the cardstock so that any stray pencil marks will not show. Cut out the letters with sharp scissors. **4.** Glue the red letters onto a piece of black cardstock. Cut out each letter again, leaving a narrow border of black around each letter. **5.** Arrange and mount the lettering and silhouetted photographs onto the cork background to resemble a school bulletin board display.

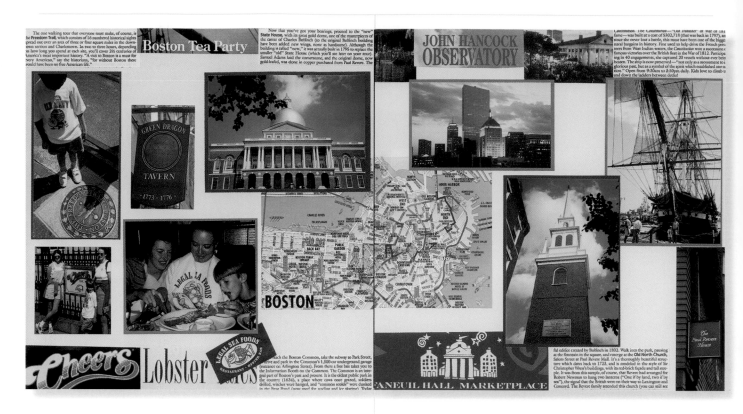

DOUBLE-PAGE LAYOUT

Portions of a tour book and pamphlets picked up during a trip to Boston were used to decorate this double-page layout while also supplying journaling of the sites visited. **1.** Mat your photographs as desired to match the color scheme. **2.** Cut words, descriptions of tourist sites, and maps from tour books or pamphlets collected on your trip. Mount these at the top and bottom of the page. **3.** Cut a map of the city into two equally-sized pieces and mount on facing pages, making sure the edges line up properly. **4.** Mount your photographs.

TIE DOUBLE-PAGE LAYOUTS TOGETHER

When creating a layout across two pages, make sure you link the two pages visually. Here are some ways to create visual continuity:

- Create an element that straddles the centerline of the album, such as lettering that spans both pages.

- Add an outside border that encompasses both pages (see Take Me Out to the Ballgame in June, page 79).

- Create a pop-up to coordinate a layout across two pages (see August, page 107).

SERIES OF THEME PAGES

Create a section of pages in an album related to a single theme, such as "Kindergarten" in a school days album or "Birthdays" in your family album.

- Make a title page on the right-hand side of a two-page layout to create a "chapter" heading. Mount a single photograph with lengthy journaling on this page to introduce the section.

- Coordinate the colors of background papers and borders to tie a section together. For instance, use a red and cream plaid background paper along with an apple-patterned paper.

- Use a common design element on every page in the section, such as a small apple in one of the top corners.

TECHNIQUE TO TRY: POCKET PAGES

In addition to photographs, scrapbookers love to collect other pieces of memorabilia. Travel brochures, playbills, birthday cards—all are candidates for inclusion in your scrapbooks. But there will be many kinds of memorabilia that you don't want to mount permanently on your scrapbook pages. A pocket page can be an outstanding way to include these items in your albums.

WHOLE-PAGE POCKETS

Whole-page pockets are perfect for items that are almost as large as your scrapbook pages, such as oversized brochures, certificates, and children's artwork.

A whole-page pocket actually requires two pages glued together. If you use cardstock pages, the two will each be a piece of cardstock that will end up in a single page protector. If your pages are designed specifically for a particular album binding, such as a post-bound or flex-hinge album, you'll be using two actual pages attached together.

Begin by cutting some portion off the top of the front page of your pair. You can cut a semi-circle out of the top, or a V, or you can cut off the top third of the page for a straight-edged pocket. You can decorate the front of the pocket. For a baby album, you might use a semi-circle cut and adorn the edge with a baby bib design. For a wedding album, turn your pocket page into a tuxedo—use a slit at the center top and fold back triangular "collars"; add a bow tie at the neck and a cummerbund at the bottom. You can also use the front of the pocket to mount photographs.

After you have decorated the front of the pocket, attach it to the back page of your pair (the uncut page). For a sturdy bond, use a strong adhesive, such as double-sided tape or acid-free liquid glue, and apply it to the bottom, left, and right edges. Leave the top edge open so that you can slip in your memorabilia.

SMALL POCKETS

For smaller items, such as a love letter, a postcard, foreign paper currency, ticket stubs, or even the receipt from a special dinner out, a small pocket on the page can highlight the item and still allow room for several flat items or photographs on the page.

To make a small pocket, simply cut a piece of cardstock or decorative paper in the shape of your desired pocket—square, pentagonal, circular, or oval. While designing your layout, place the pocket on your page and tuck its contents beneath, making sure the layout appears as balanced with the pocket filled as with it empty. When you are pleased with your layout, add strong adhesive (we recommend double-sided tape) to the left, right, and bottom edges of the back side of the pocket and attach it to the page.

POCKET PAGE

When making a pocket page to store playbills and ticket stubs from a weekend of attending Broadway plays, a "big city" motif is perfect. **1.** Mount a piece of skyline-patterned paper (8¼" x 10¾") on a piece of solid black cardstock. This will serve as the back of your pocket. **2.** Cut a piece of gray cardstock (8½" x 8½") in half diagonally, making two right triangles. **3.** Lay the two triangles over the rectangular back, each with one of its shorter edges along the bottom. These two pieces together will become the front of your pocket. **4.** Attach the front of the pocket to the back of the pocket by applying double-sided tape along the left, right, and bottom edges of the two triangles. **5.** On a strip of black cardstock 2" to 3" wide, draw a skyline scene. Using a ruler and a craft knife, cut out the silhouette of the skyline. **6.** Attach the silhouette skyline to the front of the pocket with double-sided tape around the edges, creating a second pocket. **7.** Using a font that mimics the style on the playbills, create a title using black ink on yellow cardstock. Attach it to the front of the skyline. **8.** Slip playbills into the larger pocket and ticket stubs into the smaller one.

a word about

mounting memorabilia

Although pocket pages work well for many souvenirs, some mementos can be mounted directly onto your scrapbook page. Include a swatch of wallpaper from your child's nursery in her baby book. Incorporate a swatch of fabric on a layout about a hand-sewn outfit (see Anchoring in June, page 82). Similarly, postcards, canceled stamps, and wine labels can be placed directly on your page. (Remember to use caution about allowing such items to come in direct contact with your photographs, as most are probably not photo-safe.)

While paper money can be adhered directly to the page (or placed in a pocket if you might want to spend it later, or see the reverse side), coins provide a unique challenge because of their weight. You can place them in a small pouch made by placing two clear photo corners in the shape of a square (see Vacation Album II in July, page 93).

Three-dimensional items, such as a baby bonnet or ballet slipper, may seem too bulky to have a place in your scrapbook. (See Feburary, page 26, for an example of how to include a baby bonnet.) However, several manufacturers now offer specialty pages that contain raised areas in which you can display such items. While you would probably limit yourself to one such page in any given album due to its bulk, these pages do offer a new opportunity to display three-dimensional items along with your photographs and flat embellishments. (See December, page 164, for more about mounting three-dimensional items.)

Your small pocket can be simple or ornate. For a simple pocket, use a piece of plain cardstock or patterned paper and add penstitching around the edges to add definition. For a western layout, rubber stamp the image of a blue jeans pocket, cut it out, and add it to your page (see October, page 128). Try paper piercing to create elegant pockets. (For an example of love letter pockets with paper piercing, see February, page 30.)

JOURNALING: HANDWRITING

Handwriting is an important part of your scrapbooking legacy. While you may not want your everyday scrawl on your title page or most elegant layouts, including your handwriting on some pages is a special gift you leave for future generations. Whether or not you are fond of your penmanship, choose places in your scrapbooks where you can journal your thoughts and emotions in your own unique style. If your writing is truly illegible, include a typed "translation."

Through the years, your child's handwriting will change many times. Capture it on a regular basis in his school days album. Once he is old enough to write, have him fill out an annual "survey." Ask questions such as his favorite color, favorite TV show, and best friend. Leave ample room for the answers. Give your child a permanent pen to use and be sure to have him sign his name, as his signature will change frequently through the years. The first day of school is a good time for the annual survey.

I think back with amusement on how my handwriting has changed over the years. I remember struggling with capital cursive J's in the fifth grade. They were so hard to make correctly. Eventually, I developed a legible cursive style — about the time we stopped receiving grades in penmanship. Like most of us do, I now use a mixture of printing and script, but for my scrapbooks I try to choose one or the other on any given page.

— Anna

I LOVE TO DANCE

Find opportunities to include your child's handwriting along with pictures of her. **1.** Offer your child a pigment pen and cardstock to write a special story or letter. Draw horizontal lines lightly in pencil to help her keep her writing straight. (Erase the lines when the ink has dried.) If your child has trouble thinking up something to write, offer her a photograph or ask questions to inspire her. **2.** Create a title for your page on a separate piece of cardstock. We drew this dance step title freehand—but it was modeled after a computer font called DanceStep. **3.** Mat the journaling, title, and photograph in various combinations of black, green, and metallic paper. **4.** Silhouette a second photograph of tap shoes and mount on a circle of gold cardstock cut with a circle cutter. Mat the circle on a slightly larger circle of silver cardstock. **5.** Mount all items on your page using your favorite adhesive.

I LOVE TO DANCE!

I like to dance and tumble. It's really fun! The two places I go to are Plano Academy of Dance, and Dallas Power House of Dance. My favorite kind of dance is tap. At Plano Academy of Dance I take tap, ballet, and jazz and at Dallas Power House of Dance I take tumbling, and Power Squad.
Jenna

There are other ways to capture your child's handwriting. Save stories written at school (or for younger children, transcribed by the teacher) and postcards from camp. Save his letters to Santa—but don't put them in the album until all your children are old enough to have outgrown the mystery. Have your children write a short note at Thanksgiving telling what they are thankful for. Include these cherished samplings in your memory books.

OUTSIDE THE LINES: ADDING COLOR

Decorating chalks, colored pencils, and spritzing with an airbrush tool are great ways to add color to scrapbook pages. You can color a clip art design printed from your computer, add detail to a rubber stamped image, or embellish a page directly with different hues. You'll find it most effective when adding color to apply the colors in layers from the lightest to the darkest. Add a shadow in a darker shade to make your design more realistic.

CHALKS

Chalks create a soft pastel finish. They can be blended and shaded easily and quickly. Apply chalks in a circular motion with a stiff brush or a cotton or sponge applicator. When finished, spray your design with a fixative spray so the chalks don't smear. (Be sure to spray your page before adding your photographs.)

We like to use chalks to add color to the crevices of small heat-embossed images. Use chalks to adorn scrapbook pages that include photos of your "Sidewalk Picassos"—children using chalk on sidewalks.

COLORED PENCILS

Colored pencils, which come in a wide variety of colors, are an excellent choice to add exquisite detail and look beautiful when shaded and blended into designs. Choose a permanent pigment with a soft lead for easy blending. When using colored pencils, make all your strokes in the same direction for a neater appearance.

For a lovely look, use light-colored pencils on darker papers. Applying white pencil on black paper is an especially creative way to decorate school pages, making them resemble an old-fashioned chalkboard.

SPRITZING COLORS

An airbrush tool can be used to add a splash of color to your designs. A simple device with a plastic or rubber bulb to blow air through the nib of a wet marker, airbrush tools are

SPRITZING AND COLORED PENCILS

Church friends took these photographs of lighthouses during an autumn trip to New England. **1.** Ink a lighthouse rubber stamp in black pigment ink and stamp it on tan paper. Heat emboss with clear embossing powder (see May, page 70). **2.** Color in the lighthouse design with colored pencils, shading colors where desired. **3.** Spritz rust, gray, and yellow splatters of ink on the lighthouse design with an airbrush tool. **4.** Draw a black ink border around the outside of two pieces of 12" x 12" tan cardstock. Then spritz the pieces of cardstock with rust, gray, and yellow splatters of ink with an airbrush tool. **5.** Mat the photos with complementary colors. **6.** Mount the lighthouse design and photographs on the prepared tan cardstock.

available at most art and craft stores. Depending on the blast of air, you can control the pattern of ink splatters from the marker to your paper. We recommend that you choose a marker with a larger nib, such as brush-style markers.

PHOTO TIP: CANDID VS. POSED

As nice as it is to have a posed group shot of your son's kindergarten class on the field trip to the zoo, most of the best photographs are candids.

Somewhere around the age of four or five, we lose our ability to act naturally in front of a camera. For this reason, most people photograph best when they are less aware, or unaware, of the presence of the camera.

In family photography, the goal is to record real life, not fiction. In addition to posed photographs, take pictures of ordinary activities, such as the family cooking a meal together, your daughter reading *The Little Mermaid* (for the twelfth time), or your son building a tower from Legos. When on vacation, pose your family in front of the sign at Sea World for an "identity shot," but also take a picture of your son feeding the dolphins, or your daughter's face when she sees the shark tank.

Make the most of poses

Aim for spontaneity even when taking posed photographs. Give your subject a chance to relax and forget about the camera. Talk to him and get him to talk to you. Get his mind off posing and onto anything else.

Take great candids

Spontaneous moments are the basis for many great photos. By keeping a few guidelines in mind you can take even better everyday, candid photos.

- Be ready. While everyone is busy having fun, be sure to have your camera handy and ready.

- Shoot with conviction. Don't belabor the shot. Learn to consider the key points of photo composition quickly (see April, page 60) so that you can snap a candid before the moment is gone.

- Zoom in. Get close to your subject. If you can do this with a zoom lens from far away, all the better, because you'll be less likely to tip her off that a photograph is coming.

- Wait for a second chance. If you miss the shot, wait patiently to see if your subject will return to his activity so you can try again.

CANDID VS. POSED

A wedding is the perfect place to practice candid and posed portraits. For both of these pictures, the photographer used a tripod, 100 ASA film, an exposure of 1/30th of a second, and an F-stop of 1.2.

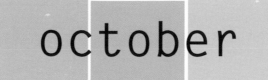

october

The brilliant changing colors of autumn remind us that life is fleeting and every moment is an opportunity to be seized. Amid the hustle of preparing Halloween costumes and shopping for treats for trick-or-treaters, take time to enjoy the season. Put on your jacket and go for a walk in the woods. Set goals for scrapbooking projects to complete by the end of the year—look for ideas and take pictures of nature's beauty while you're outdoors.

MEMORIES TO CAPTURE

As the days become shorter, with a chill in the air, we celebrate autumn's harvest—the bounty of delicious, red apples and big, orange pumpkins. This is also the time for fun and fright as Halloween night comes with its tricks and treats.

AUTUMN GLORY

Leaves

Fall is so spectacular when leaves begin to change colors. Be prepared with your camera to capture this season of color. Collect and press leaves for mounting in your scrapbook.

Pumpkins

No autumn is complete without a trip to a pumpkin patch. Plan an early visit to find the best selection of pumpkins and to get the best photographs. Some pumpkin patches set up bales of hay and stalks of grain along with a few plump pumpkins—a perfect background for snapping photographs. Remember to kneel down to a lower level to take photographs of family members sitting among pumpkins. Here's a sequencing idea for your pumpkin scrapbook page—

SUNFLOWER MASK

This handmade mask says October, Fall . . . and Halloween! **1.** Cut a basic mask from brown cardstock. (We used a clip art mask.) **2.** Cut petals from silk sunflowers. **3.** Glue the petals onto the mask using a hot-glue gun. Begin with the eyes of the mask and work outward. **4.** Use brown ink to stamp a sunflower design onto cream cardstock. **5.** Mount the mask onto the cardstock.

include photographs of the pumpkin you picked to take home with you, photos of your family carving the jack-o-lantern, and photos of the finished product. Add "Before," "During," and "After" captions and journaling (see artwork on next page).

Sunflowers

In many parts of the country, fields of yellow sunflowers are still blooming in October, long after the petals of summer flowers have wilted. Spend some time learning about the macro lens setting on your camera to take close-up shots of flowers. Plan an outing to capture these yellow wildflowers on film. While they are still small, pick a few sunflowers to press and mount with your photos in your scrapbook.

HALLOWEEN

Adult masquerade

We need never outgrow Halloween. The child in all of us still enjoys the thrill of masquerade. Host a spooky celebration for your friends this Halloween. For the perfect ghoulish ambiance for your party, cover your furniture with white sheets, decorate with store-bought cobwebs, fill your house with candles, and serve dips and drinks from bowls hidden in hollowed-out pumpkins and gourds. Of course, encourage your guests to come in costume, and take their photographs as they arrive.

Children's costumes

Create a scrapbook layout over two pages showing each year's Halloween costumes. It is really fun to watch how costumes change over the years as a child grows—from cute little bunnies, clowns, and fairy princesses to ninja warriors, grotesque monsters, and punk rockers. Each year, add a new layout to your memory album featuring a photograph of your child's costume until that final year when he decides he is too old to trick or treat.

PUMPKIN CARVING

Try making lift-up boxes. **1.** Choose photographs, then triple-mat the first and last photographs in the sequence to help draw the eye from the start to the finish. With our four remaining photos, we single-matted two and cut two with a partial silhouette. **2.** Make a lift-up box to go with each step (see instructions below). **3.** Create the title by stamping out letters with pigment ink and foam alphabet stamps. **4.** Arrange and adhere the photographs and boxes sequentially across the page. (That's Anna in #3; her children, Jenna and Jared, in #1; and family friend Elizabeth in #2.)

To make a lift-up box: **1.** Cut a 2½" x 5" rectangle and a 2½" x 2½" square out of orange cardstock. **2.** Cut two 1¼" circles out of cream cardstock, making sure that your circles are large enough for the number stamp. Stamp a 1 onto both circles using evergreen pigment ink and a foam stamp. Cut two circles out of dark green cardstock, making sure that they are ¼" in diameter larger than the cream circles. Mount the cream circles on top of the green circles. **3.** Fold each orange rectangle in half. **4.** Cut a 2" length of green ribbon. **5.** Glue the orange square to the inside of one half of the orange rectangle, sandwiching both ends of the ribbon between the layers to form a tab. **6.** Mount one of the circles to the outside of the folded square. Be sure to adhere it to the side that has the ribbon on it. Mount the other circle to the inside of the folded square, also on the side with the ribbon on it. Make sure both numbers will be right-side-up when the box is adhered to your layout. **7.** Add journaling to the inside of the box. We did ours on the computer, printed it on cream cardstock, cut it out, rounded the corners, and mounted it. Mat the box with green cardstock.

I have to admit that when I was growing up Halloween was one of my favorite times of the year. My sisters and brother would trick-or-treat with large brown grocery bags. And were we stingy with our candy! We would negotiate trades with each other to get rid of the candy we didn't like. My hands-down favorite candy was Milk Duds.

— Debbie

Candy wrappers

Save candy wrappers from your child's treats to use to decorate your Halloween scrapbook page. Since most candy wrappers are not acid-free, consider making color copies or coating the wrappers with an acid-free adhesive (such as Perfect Paper Adhesive).

OTHER NOTABLE EVENTS

National Pasta Month

Fettuccine, spaghetti, tortellini . . . toss your favorite pasta with a delicious, homemade sauce to celebrate National Pasta Month. For an extra treat, make your own pasta. Snap pictures of the whole family pitching in to mix, roll, and shape the dough. Decorate your scrapbook page with photos of the feast along with your favorite pasta recipes.

Another idea is to invite friends over and ask each to bring a pot of his or her favorite homemade pasta or sauce. Have a "taste-off" and give prizes. Include photos and the winning recipes in your scrapbook layout.

State fair

"Our State Fair is a Great State Fair." That's the motto of the largest state fair in the United States, held every year in Texas. The glitzy midway is packed with thrilling rides and games of chance. You can stuff yourself with cotton candy, funnel cakes, Fletcher's corny dogs, and turkey legs. There are barns full of animals and livestock ready to be judged. Colorful jars of jams and homemade jellies sit on shelves with the winners sporting blue ribbons. An outing to the state fair in your great state is a wonderful opportunity to make memories with your family.

TEXAS STATE FAIR

Pop-up dots add dimension to scrapbook pages. **1.** Start with double prints of your focal point photo. Silhouette a strong element in the photo (we chose the Ferris wheel). Mount pop-up dots to the back of the silhouette and position it over the second copy of the photo. **2.** Mat photos in contrasting colors. Use a circle cutter to cut some photos into circles to mount on the layout. **3.** Cut a boot from leather-patterned paper and punch a star in the top of the boot. Punch two stars from silver paper. Layer silver stars to create a stirrup and mount with a pop-up dot on the boot. **4.** Stamp a blue jean pocket design onto cream paper with a rubber stamp. Cut pocket out around the edges. **5.** Mount all elements on royal blue paper matted on tan paper. **6.** Mount blue jean pocket on layout and tuck in a small square of bandanna-print paper and tickets to the state fair. Mount boot on layout.

ALBUM IDEA: GIFT ALBUM

One of the great joys of scrapbooking comes from sharing your art with others. What better gift than one that is crafted with your own hands and steeped in precious memories?

GIFT OCCASIONS

There are any number of occasions for which a gift album can be appropriate—your parent's 50th wedding anniversary, your spouse's 40th birthday, your best friend's wedding, the birth of your sister's baby, Grandparents Day, Christmas. How about making a scrapbook-style alphabet book for your young nephew? Or perhaps an album about your husband's participation in an amateur soccer league?

GIVING STYLES

Work in progress

Often you will want to give your gift album when it's completed. A child's alphabet book should be complete from A to Z (see artwork on page 131). A book about your spouse's first 40 years should include them all. Sometimes, however, you may wish to give a work in progress. Since you will most likely begin your gift album as a secret, it may be difficult to obtain all the photographs and memorabilia that you would like to include. By giving the album partially completed, you can transform your project from a special surprise into a cooperative effort. Your recipient will probably be more than willing to supply you with the additional photographs that you need to complete the project.

Installment plan

This is a variation on the "work in progress" plan. Sometimes, it is appropriate to give one installment at a time for a much larger album. Rather than completing an album, create and give the beginning pages of an album that will eventually hold memories from future years. This is especially fun for grandparents. One year, on Grandparents Day or Christmas, present your children's grandparents with an album containing photographs and memorabilia up to the present day. Pledge to add one or two pages each year to keep their album current as your children grow.

Ready to fill

Another style of gift album is to design a memory book with everything but the photographs. Complete the album pages with fancy borders and titles for all the standard pages (for example, "Coming Home from the Hospital," "First Bath," "First Footsteps")—but leave room for the recipient to add the photographs in a mix of sizes. This style of album makes a great baby gift. When the baby arrives, the proud parents can begin taking pictures to fill in the charming pages you created for the album.

Annual calendar

A scrapbook-style calendar makes a great gift for grandparents. Purchase an "empty calendar" at a craft or stationery store (an "empty calendar" is one-month-per-page; the top half of each page is left blank). Design a page for each month highlighting activities pertinent to the month, such as pool fun and sunglasses for July or August, and Halloween photos and pumpkins for October. Fill in family members' birthdays, anniversaries, and special days, such as Katie's Sweet Sixteen, Bank Street Annual Block Party, or Granny's Annual May Day Lawn Party. This type of calendar will be treasured all year long.

CREATING YOUR GIFT ALBUM

Plan ahead

While a gift album requires many hours of your time to complete, the labor of love will most definitely be appreciated more than any other gift you could give. You can make the job easier, and minimize your effort, with a little planning. For many types of gift albums, such as an anniversary tribute, an 80th birthday album, or a retirement album, it helps to get other people involved.

I have a friend who spent nearly a year clandestinely making an album for her husband about the foot races he had run. She used photographs, brochures, and the racer's numbers he had been assigned over the many years that he had been running. She devoted at least a half-page to each race and decorated it in the theme of the race itself. He was quite surprised and definitely pleased when she presented it to him at Christmas.

— Anna

a word about

using your computer

1. Keep a journal. Use a word processing program to keep a journal of your thoughts, memories, and inspirations on your computer.

2. Make decorative titles. Given the large number of styles and type sizes available, you're sure to find the perfect font for any page (see artwork in April, page 57).

3. Create journal blocks. When you want to write more than a few sentences on a page, nothing beats using your computer. With a word processor, you can format the journaling just the way you want it, choose an appropriate font, and even check your spelling. Just print, cut out, and mount.

4. Print your own photographs. With a photo-quality printer, you can print your own digital photographs—ones you took with a digital camera or ones you had developed and copied to a disk by the photo processor. If you have a scanner, you can scan your own photographs, touch them up (eliminate that annoying red-eye with Adobe PhotoShop), resize and crop them, and print them out yourself.

5. Keep a computer scrapbook. Several computer applications are available that will allow you to make an electronic scrapbook. Scan and include photographs. Add journaling and page embellishments directly on the computer. Then display your virtual scrapbook on your own computer, convert it to a web page, or e-mail it to friends and relatives.

6. Use the Internet. Compare prices and do mail-order shopping on numerous on-line storefronts (see the Resources appendix). Look for scrapbooking "bulletin boards" and chat groups. We invite you to start at our site—www.gracefulbee.com.

Talk up the project, but let friends and family (or colleagues) know that it is a surprise. Ask for photographs and memorabilia to be included in the album. Solicit congratulatory letters. If there are other scrapbookers in your family or office, plan occasions to gather and work on the gift together. As a favor, offer to organize photographs for relatives or family friends, and in the process, you may find special images to include in the album.

Think visually

Plan the design and theme of the album in advance. For example, you may wish to repeat a motif throughout. Choose a few of your favorite techniques, such as papercutting (see November, page 149) or spritzing (see September, page 123) and use them to create repetitive design elements throughout your gift album.

Leave enough time

Don't start a gift album a week before the big day. Make the decision to create a gift album several weeks or even months ahead of time. You'll enjoy the creative process more if you have plenty of time and are not working against the clock.

DESIGN CONCEPT: COLLAGE

By making a collage or by interlocking photographs, you can fit more photographs and memorabilia on a scrapbook page. With a collage, you create an artistic composition of various materials. To interlock is to cut and fit different pieces together, like pieces of a puzzle.

COLLAGE

If you're looking for a new, creative way to showcase your photographs and memories, try making a collage. Snippets of lace or ribbon, cropped portions of photographs, tissue paper, textured paper, and memorabilia can be combined to create a spectacular layout. Begin by gathering all the materials you intend to use, and loosely arrange them on your page. (Make color copies of photographs and memorabilia to try different cropping and cutting techniques before you begin the real thing.) Once you are happy with your planned layout, mount all materials on your scrapbook page, overlapping to impart a sense of depth into your design. Add pressed flowers or scraps of pretty handmade papers to finish your collage. Apply a matte-finish clear-drying adhesive (such as Perfect Paper

ABC GIFT ALBUM

For an ABC album, either include many items for each letter or highlight one word for each. **1.** Cut a 2" high letter (such as "A") from patterned paper and 1" high letters to spell out the word (such as "apple"). **2.** Glue the letters to cardstock and cut around the edge of each, leaving a border of cardstock. **3.** Cut design motifs (such as apples) from patterned paper. **4.** Double mat the photographs. Optional: Mat the photos again, leaving an extra ¾" along the bottom edge. Use a craft punch to punch designs from the lower edge of the mat. Place white paper behind the punched mat to provide contrast for the designs. **5.** Mount photos, letters, and design motifs on the page.

FALL COLLAGE

Use photographs, dried leaves, and different types of papers to create a collage. **1.** Pour strong tea onto cold-pressed watercolor paper in a pan and allow it to sit overnight. **2.** Remove the watercolor paper from the tea and allow it to dry completely. **3.** Create journaling on tan paper and tear it out. **4.** Mount assorted mulberry papers in burgundy, green, and blue on the watercolor paper. **5.** Mount the journaling and photographs atop papers, tearing some photos if you wish. **6.** Mount pressed red maple leaves on the layout with paper adhesive. **7.** Using a dry brush, cover the entire layout with a thin layer of diluted paper adhesive. **8.** Allow the design to dry thoroughly.

Adhesive) to the entire layout, using a sponge brush. Allow the design to dry overnight.

Here are some ideas for great collage pages:

- Create a collage layout for each season—use your best photographs of winter, spring, summer, and fall as focal points. Add collage elements in coordinating colors.

- Create a collage border around the outside of a scrapbook page with paper scraps, candy wrappers, or pieces cut from extra photographs.

- Create a collage as the beginning or title page of one or several albums.

INTERLOCKING PHOTOGRAPHS

Interlocking designs are not as layered and overlapped as collage designs. Photographs are cut to fit next to each other. You can allow photographs to just touch each other or you can leave a gap to allow background paper to show through.

The easiest way to create an interlocking design is to use a template, available in a variety of designs wherever you purchase scrapbooking supplies. You can also make your own template with tracing paper. Draw different shapes onto the tracing paper that "fit" in a design together. Make a photocopy of the design, laminate with a clear plastic, and cut out each shape.

Arrange the photographs that you would like to use under the various laminated shapes. (Don't cut your photographs yet.) When you are pleased

with the overall effect, use the laminated shapes to trace each corresponding design on a photograph using a soft Stabilo pencil. Cut out each photograph, and fit your pieces together into the intended design.

TECHNIQUE TO TRY: TEARING

Despite the availability of elaborate timesaving scrapbooking devices, such as paper trimmers and circle cutters, at times it is rewarding to use low-tech techniques. Paper tearing certainly falls into this category. By tearing papers, you can achieve a unique look for your scrapbook pages. The torn edges give a great rugged look for photographs of a hiking vacation or a trip to a volcano crater. Using lightweight papers, such as mulberry paper, results in a soft and delicate look. Using heavyweight cardstock results in a handmade look resembling the deckle on handmade papers. With care, you can create elaborate scenes by tearing paper and cardstock.

PAPER TEARING

Falling leaves highlight these photographs of covered bridges in New England. **1.** Create a border by inking an oak leaf rubber stamp with brown ink and stamping along the page's edge. (Protect your work surface, as part of each stamped leaf will extend over the edge.) **2.** Using brown ink, stamp leaves of various types on several fall-toned colors of cardstock; heat emboss with clear embossing powder. **3.** Tear instead of cutting out the stamped leaves. **4.** Journal captions for the photographs on a separate piece of cardstock, either by hand or on a computer. Cut out journaling and mat on cardstock. **5.** Arrange and glue the photographs, journaling, and stamped leaves to the page.

TORN PAPER

A formal portrait take.. on a new dimension when mounted on a ragged torn background. **1.** Using a ruler, tear seven diagonal strips of heavy cardstock in four earth-toned colors. **2.** Arrange the strips on the page, creating a series of diagonal stripes. Attach this background to your page with plenty of adhesive. **3.** Mat the portrait on earth-toned cardstock and mount in the center of the page. **4.** Tear two right triangles of cardstock from scrap pieces from step 1. **5.** Glue a pressed flower (see May, page 72) to each triangle using a matte finish adhesive. **6.** Attach the triangles at the upper left and lower right corners of the portrait.

effects you like best. You can also make wavy torn edges using a ruler—just use a hard acrylic wavy-edged ruler instead of a straight ruler. This technique works great when tearing paper for a water scene.

Get it right

When tearing intricate designs or specific angles, draw your design in pencil first. Follow the pencil lines while tearing.

Get it wet

Dampen the area to be torn in advance, especially with lightweight papers, such as mulberry paper. Trace the line to be torn with a wet cotton swab or small wet paintbrush. Your paper will separate very easily at the tear line while it is wet. When tearing dampened mulberry paper, you can actually just pull it apart. Rather than moving one hand towards you and one hand away, pull your left hand to the left and your right hand to the right. This technique allows many of the longer fibers to remain intact, imparting a soft look. With heavier papers, you can use this technique in conjunction with a ruler. Simply draw the wet cotton swab along the edge of the ruler before attempting to tear the paper.

Split the paper

With thicker papers and cardstocks, you can actually expose the inside fibers of the paper when you tear it. You can either hide this effect or use it to your advantage. Begin by positioning the paper right side up. Hold the portion of the paper you will be keeping in your left hand and the portion to be discarded in your right hand. If you move your right hand towards you

TEARING TECHNIQUE

Everyone knows the basic technique for tearing paper—grasp the paper with both hands and push one hand away from you while you pull the other hand towards you. There are additional techniques, however, that can help you achieve more appealing results.

Give yourself room

Don't tear just a sliver or thin selvage from the edge of the paper. You'll get frustrated, and you won't achieve the look you want. When planning your torn edges, leave about 1" to be torn away. An inch is enough to grasp with your fingers but doesn't waste too much cardstock.

Get it straight

When tearing edges that you wish to be straight, such as a strip of cardstock or a mat, use a ruler. Firmly press your ruler against the paper on a hard surface with one hand. (We like to use a metal or acrylic ruler because of its sturdiness.) Pull the excess paper up towards you with the other hand, tearing it at the edge of the ruler. The angle at which you pull the paper will affect its uniformity. Experiment to determine which and your left hand away from you, the rough split edge will be on the front of the portion you want to keep. On the other hand, if you move your right hand away from you and your left hand towards you, the rough edge will be hidden on the back side of the portion you want to keep. Using a rocking motion while tearing helps accentuate the split effect.

TEARING IDEAS

Torn mats

Tear some of your photo mats instead of cutting them with a paper trimmer. When using soft colors, the look can resemble the rough deckle of expensive handmade paper. Use earth-colored cardstock for a rugged look. Tear mats from mulberry papers for a soft, cloudlike appearance (see Creative Lettering in April, page 57).

Torn backgrounds

Tear strips of paper to make a striped background or border for your page. Weave together some torn strips with some straight-cut strips in coordinating colors to make a woven background (see February, page 30).

Torn design elements

Tear specific shapes, such as stars, hearts, leaves, and flowers, in appropriate colors and assemble them into designs on your page.

Torn scenes

Layer torn elements to create a scene (see Ski Memories in January, page 9). Tear the edges of mountains, clouds, trees, or other natural elements and layer them on the page before adding your photographs.

Torn photographs

If you're feeling really bold, try tearing the edges of your photographs. Intersperse untorn photographs mounted on torn mats with torn photos mounted on straight-cut mats.

JOURNALING: GATHERING LETTERS

For some albums, such as a gift album for a retirement, decade anniversary, or significant birthday, you may find yourself representing the good wishes of many people in the album you create. In these situations it is appropriate to include the verbatim expressions and thoughts of others in the special albums.

Send out requests

When you want to incorporate letters from others in a gift album, plan ahead. Begin by deciding from whom you would like to collect letters. Make a list and gather addresses if necessary. Send out plenty of requests so that you'll have plenty of responses to include in the album.

Carefully introduce your request for the letters. A specific request will get more responses than a general one. Instead of "Please write a letter to Jane and Joe for their 50th wedding anniversary party," try "Please write a letter to Jane and Joe for the occasion of their 50th wedding anniversary. I'm sure they would love to hear you reflect on some of your happy times together, or some of the special ways they have touched your heart, or your wishes for the coming years. All letters will be included in a special album to be given to them at their anniversary party."

Make it easy

When packaging your request for a letter, include a piece of plain acid-free stationery that coordinates with the colors you intend to use in the album. First, it provides a safe medium for the letters to be written on

Recently I received a treasure — a packet of letters and cards. Letters, handwritten by my husband's family, expressing their delight at receiving news of the upcoming birth of their first grandchild. There was also a handful of cards sent to celebrate my husband's first birthday. Finally, the packet included a letter written by my husband to his parents while at the Boy Scout Jamboree in Idaho — postmarked July 16, 1969. Receiving letters from the past is as exciting as receiving letters from the here and now. I know I'm going to use these cards and letters in one or more albums. I also like using letters from the past to create a wonderful gift album.

— Debbie

ANNIVERSARY WELL WISHES

This layout was designed for an anniversary memory album. **1.** Mat the letter and photograph in matching colors. **2.** Create your own bouquet or garden using a variety of punched shapes. Hearts and scalloped ovals make good petals. Graduated circles and tiny flowers work well for flower centers. Add a few punched leaves and hand-cut stems. **3.** Arrange and glue matted letter, photograph, and flowers to the page.

so that they will last indefinitely. Second, it gives people an idea of how much to write. Third, it makes it just a little easier for people to respond. If you also include a pre-addressed stamped envelope, your response rate will undoubtedly increase.

Be sure to ask people to write on only one side of the paper. Their letters will be a lot easier to include in the album if they do.

Establish deadlines

Be sure to give clear information on where to send the letters, and include a deadline. Allow people plenty of time to gather their thoughts and to respond—but if you give them too much time, your request may not carry any sense of urgency and could end up on the bottom of everyone's to-do pile.

As the responses begin arriving, keep each letter with the envelope it arrived in until you have placed the letter in the album. You may not know all the people who respond, so you may need the envelope plus your address list to help you translate "Ben" into "Benjamin Ford, Best Man at Jane and Joe's wedding." Even though Jane and Joe will know who Ben is, not everyone else who sees the album will. You'll probably want to add the annotation to the page with Ben's letter.

Put the letters in the album as you receive them. This will save you from staying up until the wee hours at the end of your gift project.

GUESS WHO

Enliven a Halloween layout by using a handmade mask. **1.** Cut a basic mask from black velvet paper. Add long orange ribbon as "ties." **2.** Use a hot-glue gun to mount the mask to orange cardstock, gluing the ribbon to serve as a border. **3.** Mount your Halloween photographs. **4.** Cut letters from plaid, black-patterned paper and mount on small squares of black paper. **5.** Mount letters onto layout.

OUTSIDE THE LINES: MASKS

What is it about the simple act of wearing a mask that brings out the fanciful and playful side in each of us? Decorate your Halloween layouts with hand-fashioned mask designs.

STORE-BOUGHT MASKS

A basic mask can be purchased at costume or craft stores and embellished with a variety of materials, such as flowers, leaves, sequins, ribbon, feathers, and lace. Use a clear-drying adhesive to attach lightweight decorations to the mask with a small paintbrush. Or embellish your mask with decorative paper designs punched with a craft punch. Tie a pretty ribbon to each side of the mask or use a hot-glue gun to attach the mask to a narrow stick or dowel. Wear the mask on Halloween night, then mount it in your scrapbook along with your Halloween photographs.

RUBBER STAMP MASK DESIGNS

Mask designs can also be purchased in the form of a rubber stamp. Usually, these designs are small (intended for decorating instead of wearing). You can find simple mask-design rubber stamps with tiny embellishments or elaborate mask-design rubber stamps adorned with feather designs. There are many ways to use these rubber stamps on your scrapbook pages, for instance, stamping a mask design all over your background paper to create a patterned paper.

Another option is to stamp a mask on a separate piece of cardstock and cut it out to mount on your scrapbook page. Even stamped images of masks can be embellished with other decorations, such as sequins, craft jewels, silk flowers, and feathers.

MASKS FROM CARDSTOCK

Don't overlook creating your own masks from a heavyweight cardstock. Lightly trace a mask design on cardstock using an actual mask as a template. Cut out the mask and decorate it to match your costume. Cutting your own masks allows you to size a mask to fit children—or even your child's favorite stuffed animal. Mask-making is also a great project for a family to do together.

PHOTO TIP: SHADOWS

Some of the most appealing outdoor photographs can be ruined by strong shadows that cause a loss of detail in the darker areas. One of the most common causes of such harsh shadows is strong overhead sunlight. Although there may be times when you can use harsh shadows to achieve an artistic effect, most often such shadows are a nuisance to be avoided.

USE THE SUN TO YOUR ADVANTAGE

One approach to combating strong facial shadows outdoors is to frontlight your subject (see November, page 152). This

FLASH FILL

These before and after photos show the advantage of using a fill flash in certain lighting situations. In the photo on the left, the little girl is backlit by bright sunlight. The photographer did not use a fill flash, so the camera's metering system exposed for that bright area, causing the girl's face to appear in darkness. In the photo on the right, the photographer used a fill flash, which "fills," or compensates for, the shadow, resulting in a properly-lit picture. Note: When shooting in bright sunlight, it is also a good idea to hold a card or place your hand (or someone else's hand) horizontally over the camera lens to cast a purposeful shadow over the lens and prevent the sunlight from hitting the lens directly.

means that you'll want to turn your subject and position yourself so that the sunlight is shining in your subject's face. There is a downside to this however—squinting. It is hard to keep a natural expression when the sun is shining brightly in your eyes. Another downside is that positioning in this fashion may not give you the background that you want for your shot. In order to have the sun shining on your sister's face and still have the Washington Monument in the background, you might have to take a lengthy hike to the opposite side of the monument.

GET A REFLECTION

You can use a reflector to minimize shadows by "bouncing" the light into the darkened areas. Anything that is a light color will do as the reflector—a piece of white paper or a white sheet or even a white wall on a building. Avoid colored items, because they will reflect their color along with the light into those dark areas, thereby distorting the colors in your photograph. The reflector should be as close as possible to the subject without being in the picture. Hold the reflector with the hand not holding the camera, or ask someone else to assist you. Position the reflector so that the light source—for example, the sun—"bounces" off the reflector and fills the dark space by your subject.

ADD A FLASH

The easiest way to combat strong shadows is to use a flash even when you don't think you need one, such as at noon outdoors on a bright day. This technique is called "flash fill." The flash, called a "fill flash" in this situation, gives just enough extra light to illuminate the shadows without overexposing the otherwise light areas. When using a flash in this way, you eliminate squinting, and you'll have better control of your background.

Flash fill is also helpful when the focal point of your photograph is darker than the rest of your scene. A bright background may trick the sensors in your camera into underexposing the shot—remember that your camera sees an average of a medium gray. Add a fill flash to cast additional light on your focal point and the entire scene will be appropriately lit (see photos on previous page).

With "auto-everything" cameras, the flash will not fire automatically in a bright light situation. Read your manual to learn how to force the flash to fire even when the camera thinks there is sufficient light.

AVOIDING SHADOWS

To shoot this simple, quiet scene, the photographer was able to avoid shadows by using 200 ASA film and taking advantage of both ambient light from the window and a regular room lamp. There was no need for a flash.

november

In November, our thoughts turn to home, hearth, and happiness. As the holiday season approaches, contemplate your gratitude for your family and friends. And as you're sitting by the fire planning your holiday feast, take time to plan your holiday photographs as well. As your commitments and plans start to crowd your calendar, make it a point to carve out regular blocks of time, just for you and your scrapbooking projects.

MEMORIES TO CAPTURE

By November we all wonder "where has the year gone?" As you gather with family and friends this month, spend time reminiscing about past good times while making plans for additional quality time in the upcoming year.

THANKSGIVING

We are thankful

As your family gathers for Thanksgiving, take time to think about all of your blessings. Have each family member write what they are most thankful for on a die-cut leaf, acorn, dinner plate, or other appropriate design, using permanent pens. Mount each die cut on a scrapbook page layout. If you used die-cut leaves, glue them on a paper tree; affix die-cut acorns to a beautiful fall wreath. If you have room on your layout, include a picture of each family member.

Welcome wreath

Decorate your front door with a lovely wreath of twisted vines. Make hanging your holiday wreath an annual event. Take pictures to incorporate into a layout for your memory album, using elements from the wreath as a design motif.

DRIED FRUIT

This is the perfect touch for Thanksgiving pages. **1.** Use a hot-glue gun to adhere rust-colored raffia ribbon to sage green cardstock. **2.** Use the glue gun to adhere dried fruit (we used quince and apple) to the raffia ribbon. **3.** Mat the sage green cardstock with rust cardstock. **4.** Mount the design element on a square sheet of olive cardstock and mat with a narrow, rust mat.

Thanksgiving feast

How does your family celebrate Thanksgiving? Does Dad make the gravy while Aunt Cindy makes the fruit salad? Does Mom make her famous, fabulous pumpkin pie? Does Grandpa carve the turkey at the head of the table? Along with the photographs of your family enjoying the Thanksgiving meal, record your Thanksgiving food traditions—including recipes.

Feathered friends

After your Thanksgiving dinner is done, all the dishes are washed, and the snoozers are snoozing, begin the holiday season of giving by decorating outdoor trees with treats for the birds. Attach a ribbon to pine cones, spread them with a thick layer of peanut butter, and roll in birdseed. Hang them outside for birds to enjoy. All the family can join in—take lots of photographs and create a layout with a clear or colored cellophane packet of real bird seed.

ANNIVERSARY

A wedding anniversary is one of those events that we often neglect to photograph. When you exchange gifts and cards and have a fancy dinner out, make it a point to take photographs, too. Since anniversary photos and memorabilia can go into your scrapbook every year, use these layouts to experiment with new techniques, color palettes, or themes, and different approaches to journaling.

The first anniversary

One of the traditions of celebrating a first wedding anniversary is unwrapping and tasting the top layer of your wedding cake. Plan a special dinner for just the two of you. Set up your camera on a tripod with a time release and sit next to each other so that you are both included in the pictures. For fun, restage the classic photographs of the bride and groom feeding each other pieces of wedding cake.

Yearly photograph

A wedding anniversary is a wonderful time to have a professional photograph taken. We like the idea of plac-

I am thankful that some things never change. Just as I sat with my siblings and cousins at the "kids' table" for Thanksgiving dinner, my children now sit with their siblings and cousins. The kids' table — where manners are lax and plates are not fully cleaned — is a fun place for children to relate and form bonds. It makes me almost wish I had not graduated to the "adult table."

— Debbie

ing all of these annual portraits in a special album. Each spouse can write a letter to the other about their special memories of the past year; mount these along with the photograph in the album.

THANKSGIVING DINNER

Capture your family preparing a traditional Thanksgiving dinner. **1.** Mat photographs on a combination of sage cardstock, rust cardstock, and a pear-patterned paper. **2.** Use a computer to journal your memories of Thanksgiving dinner. Print onto cream cardstock and mat with a combination of pear-patterned paper and complementary cardstock. **3.** Mount the matted photographs and journaling onto the layout.

RETIREMENT PARTY

A map makes a clever background for this retirement party page. **1.** Mount map-design cardstock on a sheet of textured green cardstock to create a thin mat around the outside edge. **2.** Mat the photographs with green, yellow, and patterned yellow paper. **3.** Use a computer to journal (we used a font called ScrapMarker). **4.** Mount the journaling and photographs on your layout. **5.** Embellish a tractor die cut by adding black and yellow wheels.

Remembering friends

Create an album of fond farewell for a friend who is retiring. Ask friends of the retiree to create a scrapbook-style page to be included in the album. (We like to use a top loading album so that individual pages can be easily rearranged.) Provide each participant with a packet of supplies, a scrapbook page, and guidelines for creating their page. Encourage each person to include a picture of himself (with the retiree, if possible), a funny story or memories of a special time together, and any parting wishes for the retiree.

OTHER NOTABLE EVENTS

Sadie Hawkins' Day

The tradition of Sadie Hawkins' Day was created in the 1930s in the "Li'l Abner" comic strip. On this popular occasion, observed on November 1, women are encouraged to invite a special man out for a date. So, ladies, invite your favorite someone out for Sadie Hawkins' Day, get your camera ready, and document the date in your scrapbook.

Veterans Day

A day set aside to remember and reflect on all of those women and men who fought in the armed forces, Veterans Day is observed on November 11. For your family heritage album, consider a tribute to all members in your family who served in the military. Record details of their military career, such as service dates, where they were stationed, and any special honors or recognition. If you have a photograph of your family member in uniform, mount the photo as a focal point on this tribute page.

Silver and golden anniversary

These once-in-a-lifetime occasions call for a party! Hire a professional photographer to capture the event on film. Solicit letters and wishes of goodwill from the couples' friends and relatives (see October, page 135). Create for the couple a special album devoted to this event.

RETIREMENT

A job or career is such a big part of our lives that we often celebrate a retirement, especially when someone retires after many years of service with a particular company.

The surprise party

If a good friend is retiring, it is fun to throw a surprise party. Invite fellow workers and friends who have been a part of the retiree's career. Designate a photographer for the evening or place disposable cameras on the tables for guests to use. Be sure to snap photographs of all the gifts as well as the toast—or roast! After the party, put together an album of the event to give to the retiree and his family.

ALBUM IDEA: PET ALBUM

For many single people and couples just starting out, a pet is much like a first-born child—doted upon. And for empty-nesters, a pet can give much-needed companionship. Pets share "member" status in any family who has one. When a pet has such a significant role in a family's life, can photographs be far behind?

PHOTO OPS

The photographs we take of our pets can mimic the ones we take of our family and human friends. Look for opportunities to take photos of your pets all through the year. Here are a few ideas to get you started:

- Bringing a puppy home from the breeder. Get a photo of mom, dad, and the whole litter if you can.

- Adopting a kitten from the animal shelter

- Giving your dog a bath. Who's more sopping wet, you or the dog?

- Formal "portrait" of your pet. Some pet stores regularly have photographers on site for portraits.

- Your pet at play. Try getting your dog to catch a Frisbee, or capture your cat pawing a toy mouse.

TOP DOGS

A special award deserves a special page. **1.** Cut large letters out of stone-colored cardstock and glue them to deep purple cardstock. **2.** Cut around the edge of each letter, leaving a border of deep purple. **3.** Double mat the photograph. Use a wide mat of handmade, cream-colored paper, then add a narrow mat of deep purple. **4.** Create journaling on a computer and print it on stone-colored cardstock. Mat the journaling in forest green. **5.** Cut a wide strip of forest green cardstock and mount it vertically on the page, to the left of center. **6.** Mount the matted photograph, journaling, and title letters on the page. For a different look, right-justify the title.

- Your pet at rest in her favorite chair or on the sun-warmed porch rocker

- Companionship photos—your pet cuddling with (or "kissing"!) family members

- Competitions and awards—show animal competitions, obedience school graduation, and even your local doggy derby

DESIGNING YOUR PET ALBUM

Let your pet's personality inspire the type of album you create. If you have a Persian cat that competes in cat shows, your pet album will be different from an album about your mixed breed dog or your household menagerie of birds, lizards, and hamsters.

Keep it small

Unless you have a large number of pets or lots of photographs, try experimenting with a smaller-sized album than you usually use. An 8"x 10" album is a nice choice for a pet album. You can use an even smaller size if you intend to use only one or two small photographs per page.

Australian Shepherd Club of America

Obedience Trials

Claremore, Oklahoma

Chief and Phoebe, father and daughter, both won High in Trial Obedience at the same competition. Phoebe won on Saturday, competing in the Novice division. Chief won on Sunday, competing in the Open division.

SEA LEGS

This page highlights a pastime enjoyed by both a pet and his owner. **1.** Cut a red circle large enough to serve as a backdrop for a laser-cut sailboat. Glue the sailboat onto the red circle. **2.** Freehand cut strips of navy blue cardstock to make the waves. Be sure to taper the ends of each strip. **3.** Cut two strips out of navy blue cardstock, 1½" wide, to form an "L" for the upper left corner. **4.** Use a large font on your computer to create the title; print it on light gray cardstock. Cut into strips 1" wide. **5.** Double mat the photograph with navy blue and red cardstock. **6.** Mount the navy blue L in the upper left corner, approximately ¼" from the edge of the page. Layer the title over the L, overlapping the strips at the corner. **7.** Mount the matted photograph on the page. **8.** Glue some of the waves randomly onto the page (leave some for step 9). **9.** Mount the circle with the sailboat. Glue the extra waves onto the circle.

Coordinate the color of the outside with the theme of your scrapbook. Choose a deep pine green or a rich burgundy cover for a Christmas album, or a cream-on-cream damask fabric cover for a wedding album. Some album covers have designs and sayings that are appropriate to the contents of your album, such as a school days or baby's album. Another option is to have your album cover stamped with lettering, such as the family's last name, year, child's name, etc. (Many stores that stamp bibles with gold lettering can also stamp album covers.) For a truly personalized touch, decorate your own album cover.

TITLE PAGE

A title page is a wonderful way to introduce the theme of the album. Title pages can be simple or elaborate, contain photographs or just lettering. Here are some ideas for title pages:

- A collage of favorite photographs from the year as a background for the family name and the year (see October, page 130)

- An 8" x 10" baby photograph as a focal point for a baby album title page, with the child's name and the meaning of the name

- A family tree so future generations understand the family relationships of the people in your heritage album

Keep it fun

Capture your pet's spirit in this scrapbook. Is your cat playful or aloof? Reflect her personal style in the way you embellish pages about her. Is your dog "one of the guys" who likes to hunt and fish with Dad and the boys? Choose an outdoors theme to carry throughout his album.

DESIGN CONCEPT: BEGINNINGS

A scrapbook album filled with cherished pages deserves a great beginning. We all know that first impressions often set the stage for what is to come.

THE COVER

Choose an album cover that complements the story that you lovingly tell inside the pages. Depending on the type of album style you use, there are different choices that you can make.

BABY ALBUM COVER

Create a charming cover for your baby's first album. **1.** Mount sticker letters onto a purchased frame. **2.** Position the photograph of your baby into the frame opening. **3.** Mount the frame onto a piece of blue self-adhesive paper. **4.** Tie a pretty, sheer bow to the top of the design with a flat knot (see June, page 82). **5.** Mount the blue self-adhesive paper to the front of the album.

DEDICATIONS

The inside cover opposite the title page is an ideal place for a dedication. A dedication may be a special message to the recipient of the album, such as in an album for your child. A verse that is meaningful to you makes a lovely dedication. Perhaps explain why you created the album, for example, if it is in honor of some special event, such as a silver wedding anniversary or a college graduation.

TECHNIQUE TO TRY: SPONGING

Sponging is a great way to add color and designs to your scrapbook pages. Simply put, sponging involves applying color to your page using a sponge. It is easy to master, and the results can be outstanding.

SUPPLIES

Sponges

Your choice of sponge among the dozens available will directly affect the appearance you achieve on the page. If you choose a kitchen sponge or a sea sponge from an art supply store, you'll get a grainy, rough appearance. A makeup sponge, a sponge paintbrush, or a specially made sponge dauber all yield a much smoother and more delicate look.

We encourage you to experiment with different sponges to determine the effects that appeal to you most. While makeup sponges are inexpensive and readily available, we prefer sponge daubers for applying ink because they have a rounded edge which gives a softer look than the sharper edge of a makeup sponge. Actually, you don't have to use a sponge at all. At times you may want to apply color with a washcloth, crumpled plastic wrap, or even your finger. These and other items can make interesting substitutes for an actual sponge.

Ink or paint

The most common color source for use with a sponge is pigment ink, the same that you use with your rubber stamps. It is readily available and easily applied with a sponge. You can even purchase ink pads in the form of a dauber, which has the sponge built right in. Use these when you want to apply a more intense coloring of ink in the sponging process.

As an alternative to pigment ink, you can use acrylic paint with your sponges. Specially formulated acrylic paints are available for scrapbooking that have a significant advantage—they dry very quickly, allowing you to continue working on the page without having to wait long for the paint to dry. Also, these fast-drying acrylics will not warp your scrapbook pages.

Stencils

Stencils are optional tools for sponging. While you can certainly sponge color onto your page in your own uniform or random patterns, you can also make very elegant designs by masking your page with a stencil and applying the color through the openings in the stencil using a sponge (see artwork on next page).

SPONGED BACKGROUNDS

You can create all-over designs on cardstock that resemble patterned papers. Begin by protecting your work surface with scrap paper—you'll want to be able to sponge all the way to the edge of the paper without worry. With your page in place, cover one surface of your sponge with ink or paint. Press the sponge against the page randomly until you need more color on your sponge. Then repeat the process until you achieve the effect you want. Remember that you can use multiple colors when you sponge. Simply let the first color dry, then sponge with another. Experiment with the sequence in which you apply the colors—different sequences result in different effects.

Shaped sponges

You can create a more detailed background by using a shaped sponge, available in craft stores. You can also cut or punch your own shape from a compressed sponge. Once dampened, you can use it like any other shaped sponge. When using a shaped sponge, apply it to your page and remove it from the page carefully in a straight down-and-up motion to avoid blurring the image.

Sponged borders

You can create borders in a fashion similar to sponged backgrounds. Before beginning, mask the center portion of the page with a scrap piece of cardstock. Then sponge around the edge of the page just as you would a background. When you are finished, remove the mask from the center of the page.

SPONGING WITH STENCILS

You can create detailed borders and designs by applying color with a sponge through a stencil. For this technique, we prefer fine-textured sponges, such as makeup sponges, sponge daubers, or sponge paintbrushes.

SPONGING

An ivy trellis border can enhance almost any outdoors shot. **1.** Using a trellis stencil, sponge white ink through the stencil onto the page around the border. Take care to match the design when turning corners. Allow the white ink to dry. **2.** Using an ivy stencil, sponge evergreen ink through the stencil onto the page over the white trellis. Allow the green ink to dry. **3.** Mat your photograph on green cardstock and mount in the center of the page, overlapping the edge of the sponged trellis.

Position your stencil on the page, then attach it to the page using a temporary adhesive, such as Post-It dots. Cover one surface of the sponge with ink or paint, then dab it over the opening in the stencil. Reposition your stencil when necessary, then repeat the process. Take care when moving the stencil to avoid smudging the design. Avoid turning the stencil over until you are certain that any residual paint or ink has dried (or until you have washed and dried the stencil), as this too will cause smudges.

While most stencils have openings that are intended for the application of the design, some have decorative edges as well. Don't overlook these, and decorative rulers, as templates for applying sponged ink or paint. For instance, with a cloud-edged stencil, you can sponge blue ink on a white page, leaving the clouds white.

JOURNALING: INTERVIEWS

Recording the perceptions, ideas, and memories of others can be an important part of documenting the complete story surrounding your photographs.

The next time you visit with an elderly relative, spend your time listening rather than talking. Prepare three or four thought-provoking questions in advance and get your grand-father or great aunt talking. You'll both enjoy the experience, and you might be surprised at what you learn.

If your relative approves, take along a tape recorder or video camera to capture their words precisely. Otherwise, take plenty of notes. In either scenario, plan time soon afterwards to transcribe your notes, audiotape, or videotape while everything is still fresh in your mind. Prompt transcribing will help you decipher words and phrases that might be difficult to hear or that you abbreviated in your note taking.

BE PREPARED

Before your visit, prepare a list of questions. A little advance preparation will ensure that you don't run out of questions before you run out of time. Instead of questions that can be answered with "Yes" or "No," choose open-ended questions that encourage your relative to offer details about his experiences. Prepare follow-up questions to gather extra information about each topic. Allow your questions to explore areas that will fill in genealogical gaps as well. Here are a few questions to get you started:

- Where were you born? If you moved to another town or country, what prompted the move?
- How did you get your name?
- What do you remember about your parents? Your grandparents?
- What did you do for fun as a child? Tell me about your friends.
- What was life like when you were a child? Tell me about the clothes, cars, customs, pastimes.
- What was school like for you? Were there any special teachers that stand out in your memory?
- How did you meet your spouse? What was your wedding like?
- How is the world different now from when you were young?
- What's the best piece of advice you can give a young person?

BRING PHOTOGRAPHS

Take along photographs that may elicit memories from the person you are interviewing. Who is in the photograph? Do you know when it was taken and on what occasion? If you have old photographs that include people you cannot name, bring them, too. Perhaps you'll find some answers to your questions about the old photos.

My mother is our family historian. At one point she interviewed her father about his youth. One of the most interesting things she learned was the reason he had reacted negatively when she and my father planned a quick wedding shortly before my father went to sea during World War II. It turns out that he himself had been married in a quickly planned ceremony just before he left to serve in World War I. He wanted something better for his daughter.

— Anna

Snap some new photos during your interviews and visits as well. Intergenerational photographs are always special in a family scrapbook or heritage album.

LET THEM RAMBLE

Unlike a job interview, there is no bad answer in a family heritage interview. If you ask about your grandmother's birthplace and she ends up telling you about her husband's parents, don't let it bother you. If you really want to know about her birthplace, ask the question again later after she has had plenty of opportunity to tell you about her in-laws. The most valuable information that you learn will probably be the answers to questions you didn't even ask.

OUTSIDE THE LINES: PAPERCUTTING

Papercutting is the art of cutting a design or picture out of paper. Also called scherenschnitte, wycinanki, or kirigami, papercutting has been a craft for nearly 2,000 years. From simple flowers or leaves to elegant, intricate vines to geometric patterns, this intricate art adds a truly unique look to a scrapbook page.

MATERIALS AND TOOLS

Scissors and craft knife

Papercutting can be done with a pair of scissors or a craft knife. Although you may be able to use a pair of scissors that you already use for scrapbooking, scissors especially designed for cutting small designs is easier to use. A good pair of scissors made of hard steel with long handles and short, sharp blades makes it easy to cut delicate twists and turns. A craft knife can also be used for precision cutting. Use a self-healing mat to protect your work surface as you cut your design.

ELEGANT PAPERCUTTING

Papercut designs are lovely. Intricate designs such as this can also be purchased at most scrapbook stores. **1.** Sparingly apply a spray adhesive to the back of the papercut design. **2.** Carefully align the design onto cardstock. **3.** Mount the photograph on cardstock. **4.** Use a dry brush to apply a thin layer of adhesive to the design.

Paper

Most types of papers are suitable for papercutting. A finer, lightweight paper is good when your design calls for folding, whereas a heavy paper is ideal for open cutting. Parchment paper is an especially good choice for folded designs as it folds and flattens well. Pick a color to complement your theme and design, such as deep pink for a fanciful heart or dark blue for a dramatic silhouette.

BASIC TECHNIQUES

There are two basic techniques for papercutting: (1) folding the paper first and then cutting, and (2) cutting the paper without folding it (also called "open cutting"). Folded papercutting creates symmetrical or repetitive designs. The paper can be folded once, twice, or many times. After cutting, press out the fold with a warm iron or place between the pages of a heavy book.

Transferring designs

Due to the intricate nature of papercutting, it is best to transfer a design to your paper prior to cutting. Use

HERITAGE PAPERCUTTING

Papercutting adds dimension to a heritage page. **1.** Trace through a stencil onto the back of a piece of cardstock. The color of this cardstock should contrast the color of the underlying page. **2.** Use a craft knife to cut through the lines you have drawn (be sure to protect your work surface). Turn the cardstock over and smooth any rough edges with your fingernail. **3.** Use a slot punch to punch the corners of a mat so that the photograph can be held without glue. Mount on a slightly larger mat. **4.** Journal on your computer; print it out and mat on cardstock. **5.** Mount your papercutting on the background page. Mount the photograph and journaling onto the uncut portion of the papercutting.

a sharp, light pencil to draw cutting lines for your design. Copy designs from craft books, using a photocopier to enlarge or reduce the size. Or try your hand at creating your own designs. Other scrapbooking tools that you have on hand, such as plastic stencils with designs or alphabet letters, can also be used. Simply place the stencil design over your paper and dab ink into the design with a small sponge. Then cut the inked area away.

Cutting Tips

- Begin cutting small intricate details in the interior of your design before cutting larger areas.

- Outside edges should be cut last.

- To cut curves, hold the scissors in one place while feeding the paper into the closing blades.

- Don't cut to the end of the scissors' blades (so that the scissors is fully closed), as this will cause ragged edges.

PAPERCUTTING IDEAS

Here are a few ways to use papercutting to embellish scrapbook pages:

- Place a piece of tracing paper over a photograph you are planning to use in a layout. Using a pencil, lightly sketch a design to be overlaid on the photograph. Lines and curves should follow the details in the photograph. Once you are finished marking your design, place the tracing paper on a sheet of cardstock and press firmly with a pencil to transfer the design to the cardstock. Cut out your design on the cardstock and adhere to the front of your photograph. This is an interesting way to create a stained-glass effect without cutting your photograph into small pieces. It is best to adhere the design to your photograph with a spray adhesive.

- Cut an intricate paper border to frame your photographs or an entire scrapbook page.

- Cut a row of charming paper dolls or playful kittens as a border around the edge of a little girl's scrapbook page.

- Mount papers of different colors and patterns behind your papercut design to make it really stand out.

- Use a plastic alphabet stencil to trace the letters of a word (perhaps the title of your page) onto cardstock. Cut out the interior of the letters leaving the outside portion of each letter intact. Cut the cardstock to the desired dimension and mount on your scrapbook page. We sometimes like to mount a patterned paper behind the letters before adhering to the scrapbook page.

- Cut a symmetrical design element, such as a Thanksgiving wreath or Christmas tree, from a folded sheet of paper (much like the way most of us are taught in elementary school to make a perfectly symmetrical heart for valentines). Once you finish cutting the entire design, cut the object into two pieces at the fold. (You'll have a right side and a left side.) On a double-page layout, mount the right side of your design on the left-hand side of the right scrapbook page. Mount the left side of your design on the right-hand side of the left scrapbook page. This is a great way to tie a spread together.

- Use paper punches and hole punches to create additional embellishments in a papercut pattern.

PHOTO TIP: LIGHTING

Have you ever looked at your photographs and wondered why the lighting was better in some than in others? It may have been a matter of luck. A little knowledge of lighting, however, can help you take advantage of light to create more striking and professional-looking photographs.

One of my favorites among the many photographs I have taken through the years is a photo of my son that was taken with natural light streaming through a transom window. The shadows created by the strong directional lighting cast the design of the window across my son for an interesting effect. While you definitely notice the lighting when you look at this photograph, the coloring also stands out. The tones of the winter sunlight, coupled with the navy blue and white outfit he was wearing and the dark cherry hardwood floors, yielded an almost-black-and-white look to the photograph.

— Anna

using the end of a roll of film

As a scrapbooker, chances are that you take a good number of pictures as well. A roll of film probably doesn't last too long. However, there are times when you just have to get those pictures developed to see how they came out, but you haven't finished the roll. Here are some ideas for finishing up that roll.

Celebrate the everyday

Everyday activities are as important to record as special occasions. Take a picture of your husband reading a bedtime story to your child, your children bundled up for a cold winter day's play, your family playing games in front of the fire, or your preschooler struggling to get dressed on his own.

Family treasures

Consider featuring your family "treasures," like a well-worn baseball glove and ball, recital costumes or ballet shoes, handmade clothing, family heirlooms, the contents of a grandmother's trunk, hobby collections, and beloved toys.

Places you go

Take a picture of your house, your children's school, your church or synagogue, your neighborhood park. How about featuring other favorite places, like the farm market, apple orchard, ice cream parlor, and grandma's house?

THE DIRECTION OF LIGHT

Frontlighting

Frontlighting occurs when the sun, or an artificial light source, is directly in front of the subject of a photograph, coming in from behind the photographer (for instance, when the sun is in your subject's eyes). Frontlighting evenly covers the subject with light, eliminating most shadows. With frontlight, colors are richly illuminated and details are easily seen. However, because of the evenness of the lighting, the subject may appear to have less depth and dimension.

Sidelighting

Sidelighting, when the source of light comes in from one or both sides of both subject and photographer, results in a photo with more depth and dimension because it add shadows and texture. The greater the angle of the sidelight, the more dramatic the shadows—and the greater the sense of depth and dimension you will create.

THE COLORS OF DUSK

For many amateur and professional photographers, there is no better place to experiment with the ambient light of nature than the beach. At any time of day, the interplay of light and nature creates endless possibilities for photographs with or without people. Sometimes a beach photograph really benefits from a specific point of focus, as in this photo taken at dusk with the pier as the point of focus. The photographer's camera was set on a tripod and several "bracketed" exposures were taken, according to the light meter reading.

THE COLORS OF MIDDAY

When you take photographs in bright sunlight, experiment with placing your subject under a roof or overhang. For this informal portrait of a brother and sister, the photographer had the children stand under a porch awning to block out direct overhead sunlight and to let the pretty daylight enter the frame from one side.

Backlighting

You can achieve very dramatic effects with a backlit subject, that is, with the light source coming in from behind the subject. Backlighting emphasizes the shape of the subject and can actually create a silhouette or "halo" effect.

CONTRAST

Lighting can produce either high-contrast effects or low-contrast effects. High-contrast lighting is strong and distinctly directional, casting definite shadows. Low-contrast lighting is more diffuse and nondirectional, producing softer shadows and blended color tones.

Bright sunlight (high contrast) is very popular for outdoor photos because the intense sunlight accentuates bright colors and casts interesting shadows. Similarly, the nearly shadowless light found on a cloudy day (low contrast) is flattering for informal portraits because shadows are softened.

High- and low-contrast effects can be duplicated indoors with artificial light. High-contrast lighting can be achieved by using a single strong light source. Depending on where you place the light source, you can create frontlighting, sidelighting, or backlighting. On the other hand, low-contrast lighting can be achieved by using several light sources on different sides of your subject. The varying angles of the light will diffuse shadows and give a softer appearance. Similarly, you can reduce contrast in an otherwise high-contrast setting by using an electronic flash. The flash acts as an additional light source and counteracts some of the shadows created by other light sources (see October, page 138).

THE COLOR OF LIGHT

Just as sunlight changes in intensity from dawn through midday through dusk, it changes in color as well. The soft pastel gold and peach tones of sunrise change many times before becoming the deeper colors of dusk. The color of the light shining on the scene of your photograph can greatly impact the mood. A European castle photographed at twilight might seem dark and foreboding, while the same castle photographed in the clear colors of morning may seem friendly and inviting.

The color of light changes most rapidly at dawn and at dusk. Use patience and take several photographs a few minutes apart during these times of day to get the maximum effect of the natural variations in the color of light.

Here are some places and ideas for thinking about the color of light as you improve your "photographer's eye."

- A backyard or porch dappled with sunlight shining through the trees in early morning

- The beach at dusk when the last little part of the ball of the sun dips under the horizon, creating an ethereal glow in the sky that usually lasts just about five or ten minutes

- An open field just after a storm or thundershower

- The sun's sparkly refection on a waterfall, babbling brook, or still pond

- The *chiaroscuro* effect of a strong shadow across a portion of a bright white surface, such as a barn, house, or fence

- Viewing a scene through the mist or fog

december

In December a special spirit fills us as we celebrate the holiday season with family and friends. Amid the hustle and bustle of shopping, parties, and preparations, be mindful of the memories that you make each day—and those you may wish to record in your memory album. Keep your camera close at hand to capture those memories. Don't forget to put some scrapbooking "toys" on your holiday wish list. Think about ways to use your scrapbooking expertise for handmade gifts.

MEMORIES TO CAPTURE

December is a month of celebration and anticipation—anticipation of the joy and excitement surrounding Christmas, the lighting of the Hanukkah menorah, and for many children, a visit from Santa Claus. Follow this simple recipe for a glorious season: Start with plenty of family and friends, then mix in a generous amount of holiday cheer. The result? Good times, goodwill, and plenty of ideas for scrapbook pages.

CHRISTMAS

Lights of Advent

Many families create centerpiece wreaths from fragrant evergreen boughs and mount within them a pink candle, three purple candles, and a white candle. The white candle is the "Christ candle" and is placed in the center of the wreath. Each week of the Advent season (the four weeks before Christmas) a colored candle is lit and scripture read as families prepare for the birth of the Christ child. On Christmas Eve the Christ candle is lit. Capture this family tradition in your scrapbook with family photographs. A small handmade scrapbook is a lovely way for your children to remember this season of Advent.

ORIGAMI WREATH

This beautiful wreath is easy to create. **1.** Fold small pieces of patterned origami paper. **2.** Cover a piece of cardstock with red metallic paper. **3.** Shape the folded paper into a wreath and mount onto the covered cardstock. **4.** Add a pretty gold bow.

Family and friends

Christmas is a time for catching up with family and friends. Make a point of visiting others and inviting others into your home for informal or formal gatherings. Also, be a friend to those in need. Record your memories with photos and other memorabilia as you begin to put together your holiday scrapbook pages.

All I want for Christmas

Have your child write his annual letter to Santa on acid-free paper with permanent ink. You may want to include pictures from toy catalogs of his most-wanted

While in Vienna, Austria this Christmas season we visited many Christkindlmarkts (Christmasmarkets). Locals gather not only to shop at the evergreen covered buildings but also to visit and warm up over a mug of Glühwein (a hot spiced red wine). Vendors roasted chestnuts and (yummy) potato pancakes in big steaming kettles. The atmosphere was festive and not commercial. We purchased hand-carved wooden toys, hand-made papers, beautiful glass Christmas ornaments, and wonderful pastries.

We visited the Christkindlmarkt in front of Rathaus (town hall). Wiener means Vienna. The large building in the background with neo-Gothic spires is Rathaus. Many of the trees surrounding the Christmasmarket were filled with Christmas ornaments such as these red hearts. The Christmasmarket was especially magical at night with all the ornaments lit up.

Christkindlmarkt

There was a lovely Christmasmarket at Schönbrunn Palace, the summer residence of Empress Maria Teresa. Against the background of the buttercup yellow palace and decorated evergreen tree, we purchased traditional handmade Christmas decorations, wooden toys and Christmas cookies. Our adult church choir stood directly in front of the large evergreen tree and sang. We also enjoyed a mug of Kindepunsch (a children's version of Glühwein).

VIENNESE CHRISTMAS MARKET

Gilded evergreen boughs add elegance to these pages. **1.** Mount photographs with cream paper and pine and burgundy cardstock. **2.** Create journaling on a computer. Print it on patterned cardstock and mat onto plain cardstock. **3.** Adhere gilded evergreen boughs to the page with adhesive and cover with a thin layer of the adhesive to protect the greenery. **4.** Stamp an illuminated C (purchased at the market) with a rubber stamp onto burgundy paper and emboss with gold embossing powder. Mat on deep green cardstock and mount onto the patterned cardstock onto which the titling has been printed.

gifts so that he will remember them in years to come. Save the letters and pictures in a special album that you can show him when he is old enough to appreciate it.

HANUKKAH

Hanukkah is an eight-day celebration of dedication in the Jewish faith. This holiday recounts the story of the Maccabean Revolt and the lighting of the candelabra (menorah) in the Temple.

The Lights of Hanukkah

The menorah is a central part of celebrating Hanukkah. Each night, take a close-up photograph of a different family member lighting one of the candles. Mount each of the eight photographs on a single scrapbook page, or arrange them in a double-page layout along with lines of scripture.

Giving gifts

Children are often given gifts on each of the eight nights of Hanukkah. Capture their excitement in your photographs. Decorate your scrapbook page with brightly decorated "paper boxes" complete with beautiful ribbon bows (see May, page 66).

Spinning dreidels

Another tradition of Hanukkah is spinning the dreidel, a toplike toy marked with four letters from the Hebrew alphabet. Photographs of your children spinning a dreidel, their faces full of concentration, are delightful

We observe a cherished family tradition at Christmas. Early in December we display a ceramic Nativity set made by my mother-in-law — but without the baby Jesus. On Christmas Eve when we retell the Nativity story, we add the small manger with the baby Jesus to our display.

— Debbie

additions to Hanukkah pages. Copy the letters from the dreidel onto your scrapbook page with a calligraphy marker.

OTHER NOTABLE EVENTS

Winter solstice

December also marks the beginning of the first day of winter—which means longer nights. Brighten the season with a picnic dinner in front of your fireplace. Finish off the evening by playing your family's favorite board game. Fashion your scrapbook page around the layout of the board game.

Kwanzaa

Kwanzaa, meaning "first fruit" in Swahili, is observed from December 26 through January 1 by the African-American community. Kwanzaa celebrates the Seven Life Principles: Unity, Self-Determination, Collective Work and Responsibility, Cooperative Economics, Purpose, Creativity, and Faith. Kwanzaa gatherings present a wonderful opportunity to take photographs of extended families. Adorn your scrapbook pages with traditional African colors, symbols, and patterns.

Posada

The Mexican community celebrates this nine-day event in December to restage the search for *posada* (shelter) by Joseph and Mary for the birth of Jesus. During this festive time, a piñata is filled with gifts and goodies and is suspended for blindfolded partygoers to break open. Homemade tamales are often a culinary highlight of Posada. Capture this celebration of heritage and family within the pages of your scrapbook.

ALBUM IDEA: HOLIDAY ALBUM

Keeping an annual holiday album is a wonderful way to follow how your family changes from year to year. By featuring the same day every year in a single album, such as the first night of Hanukkah or Christmas morning, you and your family can savor the joys of holidays past through the pages of that album. You may want to display this album throughout the year, but it can be all the more special if you pack it away with your holiday decorations and take it out annually. Each year you can start your seasonal traditions by enjoying the scrapbook pages about the holiday from years past.

FAMILY TRADITIONS

December is filled with special family traditions—perfect material for your holiday album. What kind of tree does your family like at Christmas? Do you take a trek to a Christmas tree farm and cut it down yourself? When do you decorate it? Who lights the candles each night of Hanukkah? When do you open gifts? What is the menu for your holiday dinner? Be sure to include any special recipes, especially those served only at this time (see Passover in April, page 50).

HANUKKAH

Create a unique backdrop by mounting a pretty napkin onto blue cardstock using an acid-free glue stick.
1. Apply a thin layer of adhesive across the entire surface of the napkin and the blue cardstock.
2. Mat the photographs using blue cardstock and gold paper. **3.** Use a computer to create the title HANUKKAH. Print the title onto blue paper.
4. Trace the lettering with a clear embossing pen, then heat emboss with thick gold embossing powder. **5.** Stamp dreidels with a rubber stamp onto cream cardstock. Heat emboss with thick gold embossing powder. **6.** Cut out the dreidels and adhere to a piece of thin gold thread. **7.** Mount photos, title, and dreidels to the layout.

My father used to make his own Christmas cards. He would come up with a design, then arrange a scene, photograph it, and develop and print the photographs. Everyone saved the cards that my dad made. Over the years, many of those cards — some of them 40 to 50 years old — have come home. Family friends realize what a treasure they are and return them to my mom. She is collecting the cards in hopes of having a complete original set for each of us children. I can't wait to make a small scrapbook just for those precious cards.

— Anna

SAME POSE, DIFFERENT YEAR

Include photographs of the same activities in similar poses year after year in your holiday album. When decorating your Christmas tree, photograph your children hanging ornaments or your spouse putting the star on top. Other annual photo ops include hanging your holiday wreath on the door, making latkes (potato pancakes), leaving cookies and milk out for Santa, and opening presents while sitting amidst piles of torn wrapping paper.

HOLIDAY DECORATIONS

Much of the joy of the holiday season is inspired by the decorations that have been made or collected over the years. Take photographs of your cherished decorations and write about their history. Each year, as you acquire new ornaments or holiday decorations, take a close-up or "macro" photograph. Use journaling to tell about where the item came from, who gave it to you, and why it is special.

SEASONS GREETINGS

Greetings sent and received

You can also make a home in your holiday album for the cards that you have sent and received. A pocket page works well because you can still remove the

TRIMMING THE TREE

A custom-made tree is the focal point of this layout. **1.** Cut a piece of scrap cardstock the shape of the planned Christmas tree, but slightly smaller in size. This will form the base on which you "build" your tree before mounting it on the page. **2.** Using the technique of paper tearing (see October, page 133), tear several heart shapes in various sizes. **3.** Attach the hearts upside down on the tree base to create the branches. Begin at the bottom with larger hearts and work towards the top of the tree with smaller hearts, overlapping as you go. **4.** Glue round, glittery spangles to the branches, tucking them slightly under the edge of individual branches. **5.** Add a faux jewel star at the top, mounted over a punched metallic star shape. **6.** Create journaling and a title on your computer. (We used a font called Xmas, which automatically prints capital letters inside a Christmas bulb.) **7.** Mat the journaling and photographs. **8.** Attach all of the elements to the page, overlapping to create an appealing layout.

cards to read the message inside (see September, page 120). If you exchange holiday photographs and newsletters with your friends, include those in the pocket page as well. At a glance you'll be able to see all the holiday cards that you have sent through the

HOLIDAY CARD POCKET PAGE

Store precious cards in a pocket page in your holiday album. **1.** Cut three strips of cardstock 3½" wide and long enough to span the page. **2.** Trace the edge of two strips with an embossing pen. Sprinkle on gold embossing powder and heat emboss. **3.** Arrange the strips on the page, ensuring that the top of each hides the bottom of the strip above and behind it. **4.** Attach pockets at the bottom and sides using double-sided tape. **5.** Use a craft punch to make ⅛" holes around the edge of the page. Lace ribbon through the holes. **6.** Punch two ⅛" holes in the front pocket and tie another piece of gold ribbon into a bow.

years. Try using your scrapbooking skills to make your own holiday card (see Not Just Albums, page 166).

Photos of families you know

Instead of putting these treasures in your regular holiday album, dedicate another album just for holiday family photos. Organize the album into sections—one for each family. At the beginning of each section, journal about the family and their relationship to you. Then mount their photographs and newsletters in chronological order.

DESIGN CONCEPT: FINISHINGS

Just as an artist signs his masterpiece, we like the idea of signing memory albums. An album represents your inspired endeavor of telling a story through photographs, mementos, and journaling. Future generations will want to know who created such priceless treasures for their family. The final page of your album or the inside back cover is a perfect place to sign your scrapbook. Always include your full name and the date the album was completed. Here are some more ideas for what to include:

- A brief personal history (your birth date and city of birth, your parents' names, your wedding date and spouse's name, names and birth dates of your children, where you live)

FINISHING TOUCHES

A perfect way to end an album is with a bookplate containing your signature and the date. **1.** Print a favorite verse (perhaps one you have written) onto a pretty, imprintable card. To do this, print the verse onto plain, white paper first. Apply a temporary adhesive to the back of the imprintable card. Using a light box or a bright window (see April, page 54) hold the imprintable card over the white paper, lining up the text on the white paper with where you want it to appear on the imprintable card. Press the card over the text to adhere to the white paper. Then run the white paper and card—as one piece—through the printer to print the text on your card. Remove the card from the paper. **2.** Mat the card with complementary colors and mount on an album page.

- A photograph of yourself (perhaps snapped while signing the very album the photo will be mounted in)

- Your special memories of the time frame represented in the album

- Photographs of your scrapbooking workspace

- A message to future generations, perhaps encouraging them to continue the tradition of documenting your family's history

TECHNIQUE TO TRY: PAPER FOLDING

Although paper folding is best known as "origami"—a name reflecting its Japanese roots—this delicate art is enjoyed worldwide. Folded paper designs can be either three-dimensional or flat. Flat paper designs are ideal for

Moments like these are given to treasure as memories.

This album was handmade with love by

MaryBeth Johnson

2-99

人 金閣舍利殿御守護

開運招福

家内安全

京都北山

鹿苑寺

Kinkakuji Temple
Kyoto, Japan

PAPER FOLDING

Folded kimonos are the perfect way to combine the traditional art of paper folding with contemporary photographs of Japan. **1.** Fold three kimonos out of Japanese washi paper or wrapping paper. (Check your local library or art and crafts store for books about paper folding.) **2.** Mount the kimonos on black cardstock and silhouette by cutting the cardstock approximately ⅛" from the edge of each kimono. **3.** Use calligraphy or a Japanese-style font on your computer for the journaling. Journal on light-colored paper and mat with black cardstock to match the matting of the kimonos. **4.** Arrange and glue the photographs, memorabilia, journaling, and kimonos onto your layout.

scrapbooking. Paper folding designs and patterns can be found in books and crafting magazines, and you can even find patterns on the Internet. Once you have mastered basic patterns, you may want to create some designs of your own. Consider the themes, motifs, and design elements you are using in your scrapbook layouts to inspire you.

KEYS TO SUCCESS

Follow a pattern exactly

Paper folding patterns outline a series of steps. Follow the steps in sequence, and don't skip any of them. Pay attention to all the instructions, including the direction of the fold and whether or not it will be opened again.

Choose a suitable paper

Most flat paper folding designs are best made with light- to medium-weight paper. Heavy cardstock will not usually work for flat designs.

Fold paper precisely

Work on a hard surface, and take care to fold your paper completely and cleanly. Make crisp, precise corners. Run your thumbnail along the folds to make them smooth.

Practice

Before attempting a new design with expensive or one-of-a-kind paper, practice your folding on scrap paper of a similar weight. Practicing also helps you judge the actual size of paper needed to accomplish a completed design in the dimensions you want.

CHOOSING PAPER

Origami paper

Found in craft stores, packaged origami paper is convenient for paper folding because it comes already cut into squares, the starting shape for many paper folding designs. The paper is white on one side and either patterned, a solid color, or foil on the other. The contrast between front and back makes appealing designs when the paper is folded in a way that allows both sides to be seen at once.

Japanese washi paper

Washi paper is a high-quality, handmade paper from Japan. Most washi paper bears elegant, fabriclike designs. Washi paper is expensive and can be hard to find, although some art supply stores carry it. If you have trouble finding washi paper, ask the manager of your local art supply store to order some, or see the contact information in the Resources appendix for the Ichiyo Art Center.

Patterned scrapbooking paper

Almost any patterned scrapbooking paper can be used for paper folding. Not only is the weight appropriate, but scrapbooking paper is usually patterned only on one side, lending it the visual appeal of origami paper. Lightweight metallic papers also work well. You can easily use your paper trimmer to cut scrapbooking paper to the proper size and shape for your design.

Wrapping paper

Many wrapping papers are the ideal weight for paper folding. The patterns available are nearly limitless, and you can cut the paper to any size you wish. Some wrapping papers are printed with a complementary design on the reverse side, giving an incredible effect when folded.

Other paper

Any lightweight paper can be used for paper folding, as long as it is acid-free. Consider decorative stationery, magazine pages or covers, pretty shopping bags, and maps. Let your imagination guide you for the perfect paper to finish your page.

JOURNALING: CUTE QUOTATIONS

As a parent, aunt, or godparent, you quickly realize how many cute and funny things children say. A certain two-year-old we know ended his prayers with "Oh, man" instead of "Amen." It probably seems like you will never forget some of the things your child comes up with, but, regrettably, you often do. Let those precious quotations live forever in your scrapbooks.

WRITE IT DOWN—FAST

The key to remembering adorable kid-isms is to write them down as soon as your child utters them. You might find it helpful to jot quotations on your kitchen calendar on the date they were said and later transcribe the notes into files for future scrapbook pages.

Another idea is keeping a special treasure box just for these quotations. Keep your box in a part of your house where you spend lots of time, because that's where the cute experiences are bound to happen. A decorative cookie jar in the kitchen works well; so does a small, handcrafted box on the coffee table in your family room. Place a small pad of paper and a pen in the box. Whenever you are recording a quotation, remember to include the context in which it was spoken and the date. Whenever you are looking for a "kid quote" for an album page, check the box.

USING CUTE QUOTATIONS

As a scrapbooker and family photo historian, you will often find yourself with single photographs that don't fit into a particular layout or theme album. You can combine a "just because" photograph of your child with a cute utterance to create an endearing page in a family album. Be sure to use a photograph that was taken around the same time the quotation was spoken.

Another way to immortalize those adorable sayings is to create an annual page of journaling in your child's album. On a single page, include all the precious snippets that you have recorded during the year. Write each down on a separate square (or circle) of cardstock and mat each one. Arrange the quotations on the page, overlapping as needed. If you have room for a photograph, include that as well. Be sure to journal the time span represented by the quotations, such as "Summer 1999."

OUTSIDE THE LINES: 3-D ELEMENTS

Three-dimensional elements, such as shells, feathers, artificial flowers, and flat holiday ornaments, add depth to your scrapbook pages. You'll find a surprising number of ways in which to incorporate such elements to create unique and lasting layouts.

CHOOSING 3-D ELEMENTS

Size

Obviously, the size of a three-dimensional element is a factor to consider. Choose small items for your scrapbook that will enhance your photographs, not overshadow them.

Bulk and texture

How bulky is the item that you want to mount in your scrapbook? Keep in mind that an element that is too large will keep the album from shutting properly. Also examine the surface and edges of any three-dimensional objects. Avoid items with sharp or hard edges or protrusions as they may tear your scrapbook pages.

Safety

Take care not to mount items in your scrapbook that will harm your photographs. Do not place three-dimensional items that are not

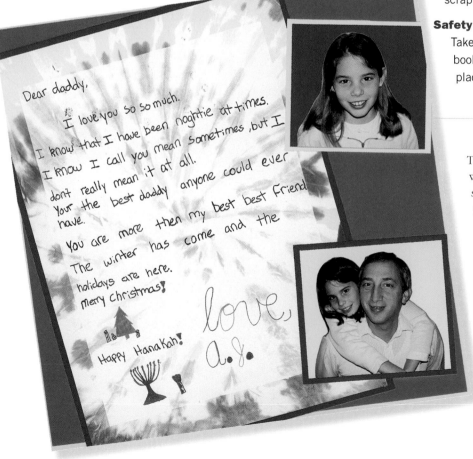

DEAR DADDY

This layout began with a letter a young girl wrote to her father—on tie-dyed-patterned stationery. **1.** Make a color photocopy of your letter (or use the original). Reduce or enlarge the size if you wish. Mat with deep pink cardstock. **2.** Use scissors to silhouette the people in the photographs. **3.** Mount one photograph on deep pink cardstock and mat with yellow. Mount the other photograph on yellow cardstock and mat with deep pink. **4.** Arrange and mount the letter and photographs on the page. If you choose to have part of the letter or photographs "bleed" over the edge of the page, use a paper cutter to trim the edges flush with your background page.

3-D ELEMENTS

A three-dimensional Christmas ornament complements this page. **1.** Mount a photograph on cream paper, patterned dollhouse wallpaper, and purple cardstock. **2.** Mount sticker letters to spell NUTCRACKER onto purple cardstock. **3.** Mount the photographs and lettering onto tan cardstock matted with purple cardstock. **4.** Mount a ballet tutu Christmas ornament with a pretty pink ribbon.

a word about

changing photographers

In many families, one person emerges as the photographer. On occasion, have someone else take pictures, if for no other reason than to get some shots of the family's regular photographer. The newly appointed photographer may not be as accomplished behind the lens, but you may be surprised at how good the pictures turn out.

Another reason to have someone else take pictures is to get a different point of view. One person may see the "big picture" and take photographs accordingly; another may notice detail and take close-ups that reveal the subtle nuances of a scene.

Don't overlook your children as budding photographers. Their pictures will certainly have a point of view different from yours—it will be about two feet lower. Children love cameras and taking pictures. Get them started using a simple, auto-focus camera with an automatic flash. The camera should be light enough to hold steady and small enough to fit comfortably in little hands. Disposable cameras work well as starter cameras, especially for children.

acid-free close to your photographs. And make sure that the three-dimensional item itself is protected. For instance, the small knit hat that your newborn son wore in the hospital can be safely displayed in a sealed plastic sleeve (see Baptism in February, page 26).

MOUNTING 3-D ELEMENTS

Mounting three-dimensional items in your scrapbook can be a challenge. Flat items made of paper or fabric can be affixed with adhesive or sewn directly onto the page with a sharp needle and embroidery thread. Use a low-temperature glue gun to attach items such as small plastic toys, pieces from game boards, or flat, polished stones to your scrapbook page.

3-D ELEMENT IDEAS

Ideas for three-dimensional items to decorate your scrapbook pages are everywhere. Here are a few to get you started:

- A tiny pair of hand-knit mittens
- Infant socks. Mount your child's first pair.
- Buttons. Small decorative buttons can be sewn onto your page with embroidery thread (see May, page 63).
- T-shirts. Purchase an extra-small T-shirt on your vacation to color photocopy and use as a background.
- Hand-cast paper molds. Paper casts made in clay molds are great for scrapbook pages (see April, page 48).
- Seed packets. Mount empty flower or vegetable seed packets onto your gardening pages.

PHOTO TIP: WINTER PHOTOGRAPHY

Wintertime is a magical but challenging season in which to shoot outdoor photographs. Knowing how to meet those challenges will enhance the quality of your winter photos.

BABY, IT'S COLD OUTSIDE

The photographer

When taking outdoor photographs in the winter, be sure to keep yourself warm. A shivering photographer translates into blurry photos. And, if you're cold, you're likely to be in a hurry to return indoors where it's warmer—and you may miss some dynamite shots. Wear lightweight gloves inside thicker, warmer mittens. When you're ready to shoot, slip off the mittens but leave the gloves on. If you still find it difficult to use your camera with the lightweight gloves on, consider fingerless gloves to increase your dexterity.

The camera

Cold weather can sap the energy of batteries or cause your camera to malfunction. Always keep your camera inside its case when not in use to keep it warm and to preserve the batteries. Carry spare batteries in an interior pocket near your body so that they'll stay warm. Switch batteries when those in your camera seem to be sluggish.

Film

Cold film can be brittle. Take special care when loading, advancing, or removing film in cold weather.

Moisture

Condensation can form on your camera when it warms up after being extremely cold. Condensation on the exterior of the camera can be wiped off, but condensation on the interior can cause significant damage. You can minimize the chance of condensation forming on and in your camera by sealing the camera in a plastic bag while still in the cold air, then letting it warm up gradually within the plastic bag. Since the cold air trapped in the bag is drier than the warm air indoors, any condensation will form on the exterior of the plastic bag instead of on the camera itself.

THE COLOR OF WINTER

If you're lucky enough to have a terrific snowstorm, bundle up and capture the color of winter. These photographs were taken the day after a blizzard at a stone mansion tucked away in the country.

THE COLOR OF WINTER

Gray skies can make a photo look dreary. Minimize the amount of gray sky in your photographs by carefully choosing the angle at which you shoot. However, bright or stark subjects photographed against a bleak, gray sky can yield dramatic, high-contrast photos.

Cameras see gray

The electronic circuitry in modern cameras is calibrated in such a way that the average of all of the colors and intensities the camera "sees" will be a medium gray. This can be a problem when a large portion of your photograph is snow or ice. The camera reacts to the large expanse of white, translates it to gray, and ends up underexposing the darker elements of your photograph. Check your camera's manual to see how you can adjust the exposure to compensate for this. If you have a fully manual camera, you should be able to set your light meter reading based on a neutral object, such as a purchased "gray card" or the palm of your hand. If you have an automatic camera, you may still be able to adjust the light meter reading—check your manual. Although your camera will probably not indicate the need to use a flash while outdoors, using a fill flash can help illuminate the darker elements of your photograph, allowing for better overall exposure (see October, page 138).

Special effects

Drab skies, leafless trees, and snowy ground can give an almost-black-and-white effect. For a change of pace, instead of compensating for the exposure challenges, take advantage of them to accentuate the contrast of the scene. The loss of detail due to underexposure of darker subjects can yield a striking silhouette effect. Try shooting such scenes with black-and-white film, like the famous nature photography of Ansel Adams.

not just albums

While the term "creative scrapbooking" implies scrapbook pages in an album, you can use scrapbooking techniques for countless projects. Rather than confining your scrapbooking art to the pages between the front and back covers of your albums, expand your skills into new territory. The tools and techniques you use for scrapbooking can easily be translated into practical uses: greeting cards, lovely gifts, party invitations, everyday remembrances, and children's projects.

GREETING CARDS

A natural extension of scrapbooking is creating your own greeting cards. In addition to rubber stamps, inks, and embossing powders, you can use photographs, decorative scissors, pigment pens, die cuts, and stickers to design a personalized greeting card for any occasion. Begin with a prefolded blank note card, or make your own blank card from colored cardstock. Embellish and personalize to your heart's content. You can even make your own envelopes—or plan the size of your cards to fit into available envelopes. Don't forget to add a personal touch or design element from the card to your envelope as well.

A store-bought card may someday be thrown aside, but a handmade card will always be a treasured keepsake. Use archival-quality materials so that the card's recipient can place it in her own album or other display. (A party invitation and birthday card are shown in this section; also, see March, page 35, June, page 76, and September, page 115.) For inspiration for greeting card designs, take a look at the art shown on the first page of every chapter of this book—each one shows a design element, geared towards a particular month of the year, that is perfectly suited for greeting cards, invitations, or thank you notes.

PARTY INVITATION

Here's a whimsical invitation to fellow scrapbookers for a cropping party. **1.** Stamp a cow onto white cardstock with black ink and heat emboss with clear embossing powder. Cut out around the outside of the cow design. **2.** Create an invitation postcard with your computer (we used a font called DJ Inkers MOO). **3.** Mount the cow onto the invitation. **4.** Glue a strip of cow-design patterned paper onto the reverse side of the postcard.

Birthday cards

A great way to embellish a handmade birthday card is to mount a picture of yourself with the card's recipient. As an alternative, stage a fun photograph expressly for the card. One idea is to gather your family holding a "Happy Birthday" banner and take a photograph. Use the photo as the focal point for a birthday card for a beloved grandparent.

Thank you notes

A handwritten thank you note is always appreciated, but a handmade thank you is especially meaningful. Take a picture with your thank you card in mind—your husband wearing the shirt his mother sent, your children playing with the toys from Aunt Kay.

Christmas cards

Next year, make your own Christmas cards. Your card can be as simple as a photograph matted and mounted on the front, with a rubber-stamped message inside—or it can be a showcase of advanced scrapbooking techniques. For a change from the traditional newsy Christmas letter, create a scrapbook page using photos and journaling. Make color copies, fold, and include them in your cards.

Get well cards

Anyone suffering from an extended illness appreciates get well wishes. What better way to show how much you care than to make the get well card yourself? Choose a theme and photographs that will make the recipient smile.

Party invitations

A handmade invitation is an ideal way to draw people to your party. A scrapbook-style invitation to a morning tea or a 50th anniversary celebration brings back memories of days gone by when such niceties were commonplace. Include a small photo of your child to personalize the invitation to his or her birthday party.

"I Love You" cards

The next time you are at a loss for what to give your sweetheart for Valentine's Day or an anniversary, make a card that comes straight from the heart. The time you spend on this expression of love will tell more than any store-bought gift could.

BIRTHDAY CARD

A handmade birthday card says "I'm thinking of you today" in the most sincere way. **1.** Use blue cardstock to make the base for your card. Our finished card is 4½" x 6¼", so we started with a piece of cardstock that measured 6¼" x 9". **2.** Fold your card in half. **3.** Cut a piece of white cardstock 4¼" x 6" (¼" smaller than your card in both dimensions). Mount it in the center of the front of the card. **4.** Tear a piece of blue mulberry paper approximately 3½" x 5½" (see October, page 133). **5.** Glue the mulberry paper to the center of the front of the card. **6.** Use a circle cutter to cut a ring of white cardstock. (First cut a circle about 2½" in diameter. Without lifting the circle cutter, read just the measurement to cut a smaller circle, about 2" in diameter. Cut again, and you'll have a perfect ring.) **7.** Use the circle cutter to cut a picture of a flower to fit behind the ring you cut in step 6. **8.** Mount the flower in the upper center of your card. **9.** Use calligraphy or a fancy computer font to create your greeting. Print it on white cardstock. **10.** Cut out your greeting. Use a scallop-edged scissors to gently round the corners of the greeting block. Mat in yellow and use the same scissors to round the corners of the mat. **11.** Mount the greeting in the lower center of the card front.

Wishing You a Beautiful Birthday

SHOW-OFFS

We believe that the best photographs are meant to be displayed and shared—not just within the bounds of our photo albums. Any photograph that you decorate and display we call a "show-off." You may display your show-off at your place of work, or slip it into a simple picture frame for your spouse to display in his office. A show-off can be a gift—rather than just giving your friend the double prints from your families' trip to the zoo together, turn the best photograph into a show-off and give that as well.

SHOW-OFF

Highlight the special relationship between brothers with a show-off. **1.** Mat the photograph with a narrow white mat. **2.** Mat it again with a ½" mat in yellow. **3.** Use embroidery floss to sew a blanket stitch around the edge of the yellow mat. **4.** Mat it again with a ⅜" mat in red. **5.** Mount it on a blue background. **6.** Draw the words "Brothers" and "Buddies" on separate scraps of yellow cardstock (or use your computer to print a fancy font). Cut out the captions. **7.** Double mat the captions in red and yellow. Attach to the corners of the mounted photograph.

Just as the portraits on your mantle are eventually replaced with more recent photographs, your show-offs may eventually be replaced with newer ones. But your show-off can have a permanent home—just mount it on a page in one of your scrapbooks and create a border to tie the page together.

MEMORY BOXES

We all have special items of memorabilia that won't fit in an album—your daughter's first tap shoes, the candle from your son's baptism, a packet of love letters, a special item of clothing, such as the outfit your baby wore home from the hospital. These items deserve a special home. Rather than storing them in a shoe box under your bed, why not make a special memory box for them?

Any box with a cover can become a memory box, although we recommend choosing a sturdy, acid-free, lignin-free cardboard box or a PVC-free plastic box. Begin by decorating your box. You might cover it with a layer of fabric or acid-free paper. You can stamp or paint an elegant design, or for

I'll never forget the joy I saw in my daughter's face when she looked through my husband's treasure box for the first time. She was fascinated by the numerous small items he had saved — ticket stubs, foreign currency, bowling league patches from years gone by. For everything she found, she had a question. I watched and listened as father and daughter sat together pondering the wonders of the little things in life.

—Anna

a more personal touch, add extra photographs. After gluing them down, seal the surface with a non-tacky adhesive, such as Perfect Paper Adhesive. Inside your memory box, include a small written index of what is in your box and what makes the item or items special.

BULLETIN BOARDS AND POSTERS

When you think about it, bulletin boards and posters are really just giant scrapbook pages. It makes sense to use the tools, supplies, and techniques that you use for scrapbooking for these projects, too.

SPECIAL OCCASIONS

A wonderful addition to a wedding reception is a poster featuring baby photos of the bride and groom. Expand this concept to exhibit a larger number of family photos. Decorate each photo as a show-off and display it on a poster or bulletin board. Alternatively, create a collage of childhood photographs with captions or journaling (see October, page 130).

For a 25th or 50th wedding anniversary party, collect and display photographs from the couple's wedding and many years together. For a retirement party, gather photos of the honoree through the years, but also include memorabilia about the company from which he or she is retiring.

GROUP BULLETIN BOARDS

Churches and schools use bulletin boards to announce upcoming events, as well as photos from recent ones. If you are in charge of such a bulletin board, use your scrapbooking skills to dazzle everyone. Instead of putting up a poster with photos glued to it or pinning original photos directly to the corkboard, compile the photos into scrapbook pages and temporarily display them on the bulletin board. When it's

SPECIAL EVENT POSTER

Create eye-catching posters to advertise your next event. **1.** Cut lettering from pine tree-patterned paper. **2.** Mat the photographs using complementary cardstock and patterned papers. **3.** Use an L-square ruler and a brown colored pencil to draw a border around a piece of tan cardstock. **4.** Create copy for the posted event using your computer. We used a circle paper punch to create the "labeling" for the poster.

People always assumed that David and I met at work — we were both working for Texas Instruments at the time. Not so. Here's how it all began.

A friend of mine, Trina, heard about a trip to San Francisco that a church singles group was taking. She knew one person in the group and decided to go. She asked me to go along. Initially, I declined. About a week before the trip, however, I decided I needed to get away. There was still a slot available on the group trip, so I went. I knew no one except Trina.

The night before the trip, we all met at a bar called San Francisco Rose on Lower Greenville Avenue in Dallas for a send-off. I met David then, but just in passing. As it turned out, Trina and David were second cousins by marriage, but didn't even know each other.

The trip was a low-budget one -- we stayed in youth hostels and camped at Yosemite National Park. We had plenty of time to get to know each other that week without the stresses of first dates. I also got to know many of David's friends during the week.

When we returned to Dallas, another friend was getting tickets to see Simon and Garfunkel at the Cotton Bowl. I called some of my new friends, including David, and invited them. Once the ice was broken, David asked me out – for an outdoor Kenny Loggins concert. Unfortunately, the concert was sold out, so we went to see a movie instead – The Twilight Zone. And the rest is history.

HOW WE MET

Some stories can't be told in just a few sentences. This page tells an entire story, emphasizing the words rather than the photograph. **1.** Leave room for an illuminated letter in the upper left-hand corner and a photograph in the lower right-hand corner of the page. **2.** Journal on the computer. Choose your font size to allow the story to fit on a single page. **3.** Print the story on light green, parchment-style cardstock. **4.** Print an illuminated letter (P) in black ink. (We used the computer, but you could also use a rubber stamp.) Color in using metallic opaque markers. We embedded the illuminated letter into the story using a word processor, but you could add the letter as a separate layer. Mount the illuminated letter on the page, if necessary. **5.** Double mat a small photograph that goes with the story and mount it in the space reserved. (This is Anna and her husband David.)

often leave behind a legacy of property and family heirlooms, but we neglect to pass down a piece of ourselves.

Start a journal—handwritten (using acid-free paper and permanent ink pens, of course) or typed on a computer. The thoughts, dreams, and ideas you record are more important than the medium in which they are set down. Remember, however, that while future generations would love to see your words written in your own handwriting, it will be useless to them if it is illegible.

Include photographs and memorabilia wherever appropriate. Photographs and memorabilia often act as triggers to help us remember specific events and times in our lives. Or draw in your journal—perhaps a sketch of your garden, or the layout and furniture of your favorite room. Here are some additional ideas:

- Date and sign each entry in your journal.

- Carry a common design element throughout your journal to tie all the pages together.

- Use an illuminated letter design for the first letter of the first word in each journal entry.

- Mount memorabilia in your journal.

- Keep it fun by decorating your journal pages with scrapbooking elements, such as colored papers, stickers, and die cuts.

time for a change, preserve those pages in the organization's scrapbook and post new ones.

PERSONAL BULLETIN BOARDS

An easy way to enjoy your favorite photographs as soon as they come back from the developer is to put up a personal bulletin board in a place where you spend a lot of time—your office, your kitchen, even your dressing area. Choose a pin-free design to avoid putting holes in your precious photos.

JOURNALS

Future generations will cherish your scrapbooks—especially if the story behind your photographs is told. But don't neglect telling future generations about yourself. We

My scrapbooking tools and supplies are a virtual treasure chest when my children have school projects to complete. Science fair projects, Student of the Week posters, and any assignments needing visual aids are made easier with scrapbooking tools. And a nice side benefit is that the artwork is "archival and safe" to put in their School Days album.

— Debbie

SCRAPBOOKING WITH CHILDREN

The keys to working with children on a scrapbooking project are guidance and patience. Demanding perfection will be frustrating for both you and the child. Focus on the process and enjoyment of the art, not the finished product. (It will be charming, no matter what.) Demonstrate the required steps to complete a task but allow the child to bring her own creative ideas to the project.

ACTIVITY BOOKS

Activity books are small scrapbooks devoted to capturing a specific activity, such as planting a garden, baking cookies, getting a puppy, or going to the dentist. These books have a two-fold benefit: spending time with your child photographing all the steps involved in completing an activity and creating the actual activity book. Small albums (spiral bound or 3-ring binders) are ideal for this type of scrapbook. Mount photographs in a sequence to chronicle the activity. If your child can write, let her add a caption to each page.

BOOKMARKS

Most children love to make gifts. Using your scrapbook supplies and a few good photographs, you can help your child to create a unique bookmark for a grandparent, friend, or teacher. Simply cut a strip of cardstock; add photographs (you may wish to reduce their size on a color copier), decorative elements, and creative lettering. Cover the bookmark with a clear plastic, acid-free laminate. (Do not use a heat lamination process, as this will damage photographs.) Punch

CHILD'S BOOKMARK

A bookmark is a small project that you and your child can do together. **1.** Cut a strip of green paper to use as a flower stem. **2.** Using a large circle paper punch, punch a circle from a photograph for the middle of the flower. **3.** On a precut bookmark, adhere a flowerpot die cut. **4.** Create lettering with your computer and print onto plain white paper. Using a temporary adhesive, adhere the bookmark over the white paper aligning the text to the bottom of the bookmark. Run the white paper with the bookmark through your printer to print the text at the bottom of the bookmark. **5.** Mount the green stem into the flowerpot. **6.** Mount a flower die cut to the top of the green stem. Mount the photograph into the center of the flower. **7.** Cover the bookmark with an acid-free, non-heat laminate to protect it and to make it sturdy.

a hole and add a tassel to the top of the cardstock strip and the bookmark is complete.

OTHER IDEAS

Here are some more projects that will instill a love of scrapbooking in your children:

- Handmade valentines
- ABC books (see October, page 131)
- Greeting cards
- Party invitations
- School projects
- Photo album featuring photographs taken by your child

glossary

Acid. A chemical substance that weakens paper and cloth, causing it to brown and become brittle. Look for scrapbooking supplies that are labeled "acid-free" (see Acid-free).

Acid migration. The transfer of acid from an acidic material to a less acidic or pH neutral material. This may occur when an acidic material comes into contact with another material.

Acid-free. Materials that have a pH of 7.0 or higher.

Anchor. To add visual weight to an element (such as a sticker or die cut) so that it doesn't appear to float on the page.

Archival. A non-technical term suggesting that a material is permanent, durable, or chemically stable. Usually means that the material can safely be used for preservation purposes, although there are no quantifiable standards as to how long an "archivally sound" material must last.

Asymmetrical balance. Balance that is achieved by assembling dissimilar elements.

Backlighting. When the sun or an artificial light source shines directly behind a photographic subject. Backlighting emphasizes the shape of the subject; extreme backlighting creates a silhouette.

Balance. The visual equilibrium achieved by handling proportions and arranging elements on a scrapbook page in an aesthetically pleasing way. A balanced layout is neither top-heavy nor bottom-heavy.

Buffered. The result of adding alkaline substances to materials to counteract acids that may form in the future. The most common buffers used are magnesium carbonate and calcium carbonate.

Circle cutter. A device used to cut perfect circles in various diameters; usually used to cut photographs or cardstock. Circle cutters work like a pencil and compass—a blade swings around a central pivotal post.

Complementary colors. The pairs of colors directly opposite each other on the color wheel, such as red-orange and blue-green.

Corner punch. A craft punch that can be aligned to the corner of a photograph or mat to punch a decorative design into the corner.

Corner rounder. A craft punch that can be aligned at the corner of a photograph or mat to cut off a precisely-shaped portion of the photograph or mat, leaving, for example, a rounded corner rather than the original squared one.

Cornering. Any technique, such as punching or rounding, that adds emphasis and/or decoration to the corners of a photograph or mat.

Cornering scissors. A type of decorative scissors that cuts designs into the corner of a photograph or mat. Cornering scissors have guides that allow the user to line up the scissors with the corner of the photo or mat to produce consistent results.

Corrugator. A handheld device, also known as a crimper, that creases paper or cardstock, resulting in corrugation. A corrugator works by forcing the cardstock between two interlocking spindles.

Craft punch. A small device that cuts, or punches, designs from cardstock or paper. The specially-shaped design can be glued to a scrapbook page. Craft punches come in a wide variety of sizes and shapes, including flowers, small stars, and even large handprints.

Creative lettering. A writing technique in which one hand-draws or creates on the computer fancy letters to make titles and captions for scrapbook pages.

Crimper. See Corrugator.

Crop. To reduce the size or shape of a photograph by cutting. Cropping can be as simple as trimming the edge of a rectangular photograph to create a square image, or as elaborate as tracing a shape onto a photograph and cutting the photograph into that shape.

Cutting mat. A rubber-like mat used to protect the work surface when cutting with a craft knife.

Deckle edge. A jagged edge that resembles the border on old-fashioned black-and-white photographs or parchment stationery. A deckle edge can be achieved by cutting with a pair of deckle-edged scissors.

Depth. The perception of distance from one part of a scrapbook page (or photograph) to another. Depth can be created by mounting photographs and design elements on the page in layers.

Die cut. A store-bought shape or letter cut from paper by a die-cutting machine.

Dry embossing. Creating a raised design on cardstock through the use of a stencil and a stylus. The resulting impression is similar to a raised monogram on fancy notepaper. See Stylus.

Echo print. A design created by stamping more than once before reinking a rubber stamp. After the first impression, all subsequent impressions become fainter and fainter until the stamp is reinked.

Embossing pen. A pen that writes with colored or near-invisible ink, used in conjunction with embossing powder and heat to create a raised, shiny design. See Embossing powder; Heat embossing.

Embossing powder. A powdered plastic that adheres to wet ink and melts when heated. See Heat embossing.

Encapsulate. To place a paper document between two sheets of transparent polyester film and then to seal the sheets together. Encapsulating protects documents from damage caused by handling, moisture, and contact with acidic materials and harmful chemicals.

Fill flash. An electronic camera flash used to create just enough extra light to illuminate shadows, but not so much as to overexpose the otherwise adequately-lit areas.

Flex-hinge album. An album style that uses a set of plastic straps threaded through holes on the edge of blank scrapbook pages to create its binding. Flex-hinge albums can be expanded by adding additional scrapbook pages to the strap binding.

Flower press. A device for flattening flowers and leaves. A flower press is usually made from two pieces of wood with several layers of cardboard in between. Flowers are laid between paper towels or blotter sheets and placed between the cardboard layers. The cardboard is then placed between the two pieces of wood and pressure applied for a period of days or weeks. Pressure may be created by tightening long screws that connect the wood, or by tightening a belt around the flower press.

Focal point. A particular photograph or group of photographs being emphasized on a scrapbook page; the subject of a photograph.

Frontlighting. When the sun or an artificial light source comes from directly behind the photographer and falls directly in front of the subject of a photograph. Frontlighting evenly covers the subject with light, eliminating most shadows.

Graphite paper. A sheet of paper covered on one side with a pencil lead-like substance called graphite, and which is used as a transfer medium. Used for tracing images, letters, or shapes to an underlying page.

Harmony. The selection and use of design elements that share a common characteristic, such as shape, color, texture material, or size.

Heat embossing. The process of enhancing a rubber stamped or other inked image by covering the still-wet image with embossing powder, and then heating the underside of the image. As the embossing powder melts and then hardens, the image becomes raised and shiny.

Hue. The identifying name for a specific color, such as navy blue, hot pink, or apple green.

Illuminated letter. A large, intricately drawn initial letter of a paragraph. An illuminated letter is usually placed so that several lines of text are aligned to the right edge of it.

Journaling. Written information; the act of writing information.

Laser cut. A decorative element, similar to a die cut, that is cut out using a laser rather than a metal die. Laser-cut designs are typically more elaborate than die-cut designs.

Light box. A box with one transparent or translucent side and a light source such as a light bulb inside. The light from a light box is used to trace decorative designs onto scrapbook pages or to view photographic slides. Sometimes called a light table.

Lignin. A substance found naturally in the cell walls of plants. Lignin is largely responsible for the strength and rigidity of plants, but its presence in paper is believed to contribute to chemical degradation.

Mask. To temporarily cover a portion of an element or page so that color (paint or ink) can be applied to a selective portion of the page, leaving the masked portion untouched.

Memorabilia. Any memento other than a photograph, such as a lock of hair, theater ticket, or award ribbon, that you have saved because it has special meaning to you. Some memorabilia is flat and can be used on scrapbook pages. Larger memorabilia can be saved in a memory box.

Memory box. A decorated box for storing memorabilia that will not fit in an album.

Metal Quilting. The process of imprinting a design into a paper-thin sheet of metal, using a stylus. The resulting effect bears similarity to designs quilted in fabric using a needle and thread. See Stylus.

Monochromatic. A color scheme comprised of various shades and tints of the same hue.

Mulberry paper. A slightly translucent, handmade paper made from the inner bark of the mulberry tree. Mulberry paper is well-suited to decorative tearing. It is available at art supply stores in a wide variety of colors.

Opaque pen. A marker containing opaque ink. The ink is often metallic, white, or a light color. Opaque pens are used for writing on dark paper.

Oval cutter. A device, similar to a circle cutter, that cuts perfect ovals in various sizes. Some oval cutters can also cut circles. See Circle cutter.

Page protector. A plastic sleeve for a finished scrapbook page. Page protectors are usually made from polyethylene, which is an archivally-safe plastic.

Paper folding. The art of folding paper into decorative shapes. The term "paper folding" encompasses traditional origami as well as contemporary techniques, such as tea-bag folding.

Paper mold. A decorative clay mold for making three-dimensional ornamental paper decorations.

Paper piercing. A technique that adds texture and design to paper by piercing it in a pattern with a sharp needle or corsage pin.

Paper tearing. A technique that employs the tearing of paper or cardstock for a decorative effect.

Paper trimmer. A paper cutter. Some paper trimmers cut by means of a long, sharp handle that is pulled down and through the paper. Others use a sliding blade that cuts like a craft knife or razor blade along a guide.

Papercutting. The art of cutting a design out of paper. Papercutting may be done with sharp scissors or a craft knife.

Penstitching. A technique which simulates the look of embroidery by drawing "stitches" on the page or on a die cut.

pH. A measure of acidity or alkalinity. The scale runs from 0 to 14, with 0 being highly acidic and 14 being highly alkaline. Scrapbooking materials should have a pH of 7 or higher.

pH neutral. Having a pH of 7; neither acidic nor alkaline.

pH testing pen. A pen that can be used to test for acid content in paper. When used to mark on the paper, the mark will change color according to the acid content of the paper. The colors vary based on the brand of pen.

Photo corners. Adhesive triangular pockets used to hold photographs to a page. Since the adhesive does not touch the photograph, this method is considered safe for irreplaceable photographs.

Photo map. A line drawing representing the subjects in a photograph and on which the subjects' names have been written.

Piercing. See Paper piercing.

Pigment ink. A high-quality ink that is permanent, fade-resistant, and waterproof. Pigment ink is preferred for pens or ink pads used to journal in or decorate scrapbook layouts.

Pocket page. A scrapbook page that contains a pocket or slot for holding memorabilia. Since the memorabilia is slipped into a pocket, it can be removed for viewing if desired.

Pop-up page. A scrapbook page that becomes three-dimensional when the book is opened to that page. Most pop-ups are created by joining two adjacent pages in the book with an additional piece of cardstock embellished with a decorative element and glued on at an angle, allowing the cardstock to remain flat when the book is closed but to stand up between the pages when the book is opened.

Post-bound album. An album style in which the front and back covers are connected with a series of posts (usually 2, 3, or 4) that fit together like tiny screws. Scrapbook pages for these albums have prepunched holes that fit onto the posts much like a three-ring binder. Post-bound albums can be expanded by adding additional pages and even post "extenders."

Primary colors. Red, blue, and yellow—pure hues that are not mixed from other colors.

Proportion. The relationship of the parts of a layout to one another and to the page as a whole.

Punch art. Decorative elements created by combining pieces of cardstock punched out of various craft punches. See Craft punch.

Quilting. See Metal Quilting.

Radial balance. A circular arrangement of elements around a central point.

Red-eye pen. A marker, typically with light blue-green ink, used to draw over and neutralize bright red pupils when they appear in photographs.

Rhythm. A design principle based upon repeating a design element in such a manner as to lead the viewer's eyes across a scrapbook layout.

Rotary trimmer. A paper cutter that uses an interchangeable round blade to cut through paper or photographs. The round blade gives a continuous clean cut. The interchangeable blades, which come in plain and decorative styles, give a variety of looks.

Rule of Thirds. A design principle that refers to dividing a photograph with imaginary lines into three equal sections horizontally and three equal sections vertically. In visually-pleasing photographs the subject appears at one of the four intersections of the imaginary grid.

Sanwa tissue. An ultra-sheer Japanese paper that is used for covering delicate pressed botanicals when used on a scrapbook page.

Secondary colors. Orange, green, and violet—created by mixing equal parts of two primary colors. For instance, mixing red paint with blue paint results in violet paint.

Shade. A dark tone of a color created when mixed with black. For instance, burgundy is a shade of red.

Shadowing. A technique for adding the illusion of depth to a scrapbook page. Shadowing can be accomplished by adding a contrasting colored mat or line offset to one or two sides of a photograph or design element.

Sidelighting. When the sun or an artificial light source shines on the subject in a photograph from one side. Sidelighting gives a 3-D effect because it adds shadows and shows off the texture of the photographic subject.

Silhouette. To remove the background from a photograph by using a pair of sharp, straight scissors or craft knife to trim very close to the edge of the photograph's subject.

Slot punch. A craft punch that can be aligned at the corner of a mat to punch two diagonal slots in the corner of the mat. A photograph can then be slipped into the slots for mounting on the page. Since no adhesive is required on the photograph, this is an example of an adhesiveless mounting technique.

Spiral-bound album. An album style that has a fixed number of pages permanently bound together with a spiral binding much like a spiral notebook.

Splicing. A technique for merging one or more photographs by cutting and pasting them together to create a new image.

Sponge dauber. A rounded, fine-grain sponge with a small handle. See Sponging.

Sponging. A technique for adding color to a page by using a sponge or sponge dauber to apply pigment ink or acrylic paper paint. The color may be pressed through a stencil or sponged freeform onto the page.

Spritzing. The use of an airbrush tool to add flecks of color to a page.

Stylus. A pen-shaped device with a rounded metal tip used to press an image into cardstock or thin sheet metal. See Dry embossing; Quilting.

Symmetrical balance. The balanced arrangement of similar elements around a dominant element.

Tactile texture. Texture created by layering different materials, fabrics, and other elements for a three-dimensional look. See also Visual texture.

Tearing. See Paper tearing.

Template. A large stencil used to trace designs onto photographs for the purpose of creative cropping.

Tertiary colors. The six colors that are produced by mixing a primary color with its adjacent secondary. For instance, mixing red and violet yields red-violet.

Tint. The resultant light tone of a color when mixed with white. For instance, pink is a tint of red.

Tone. The darkness or lightness of a color.

Triadic colors. Any three colors at equal distance from one another on the color wheel.

Two-way glue. A liquid glue that can create either a temporary bond or a permanent bond. If used immediately, the bond will be permanent. If allowed to dry slightly before use, the bond will be temporary.

Unity. The repetition of common traits and elements to tie together several scrapbook pages or several elements on a page. Unity may be created with color, texture, or design.

Vellum. A type of transparent paper. Historically, vellum was made from fine-grained lambskin, kidskin, or calfskin. While true vellum is highly acidic and unsafe for scrapbooking, safer synthetic alternatives are now available.

Visual texture. Texture that can be seen but not felt. Visual texture can be created by using ink, paint, or patterned papers to fool the eye with the impression of texture when none actually exists.

Visual weight. The amount of attention a photograph or design element attracts in the overall page design.

Warp. The vertical strips in a woven item.

Watercolor pencils. Pencils that contain dry watercolor paint instead of lead. Watercolor pencils are applied to the page dry, then a wet brush is lightly applied to blend the color. Color can also be applied by scribbling with the pencils on a scrap piece of paper, then drawing a wet brush into the color and applying the color from the brush to the page.

Weft. The horizontal strips in a woven item.

White space. The unused portion or background of a page.

resources

Here is a listing of special supplies used to create the scrapbooking layouts in the book. You'll find contact information for the companies following this section.

THE ART OF SCRAPBOOKING

Page 2: **Four Seasons.** *Leaves rubber stamp:* Personal Stamp Exchange. *Tree rubber stamp:* Posh Impressions (Stamp-A-Scene). *Cork paper:* Magenta. *Verdigris embossing powder:* Personal Stamp Exchange.

Page 3: **Cousins Make the Finest Friends.** Satin ribbon: Offray. Font: Modeled after Curlz MT.

Page 5: **Arizona Cactus.** All materials used are available wherever scrapbooking supplies are sold.

Page 6: **Paris by Night.** *Font:* Modeled after French Script MT.

Page 7: **Day at the Art Museum.** *Tassel:* JudiKins

JANUARY

Page 8: **Pine Cones.** *Rubber stamp:* Personal Stamp Exchange (F-2379). *Snowy paper:* MPR Associates (Paperbilities).

Page 9: **Ski Memories.** *Small dots plastic template:* Printworks. *Rubber stamp:* Printworks (F1513). *Snowy paper:* MPR Associates (Paperbilities). *Alphabet stencil:* Frances Meyer (Fat Caps). *Iridescent embossing powder:* Personal Stamp Exchange.

Page 11: **Tea Party.** *Acid-free paper doily:* Printworks. *Rubber stamp:* D.O.T.S.

Page 12: **Plano Balloon Festival.** *Font:* Modeled after Jokerman.

Page 13: **Focal Point.** *Paper crimper:* Fiskars.

Page 15: **Metal "Quilting."** *Rubber stamp:* Embossing Arts Company (Gentle Zebra—287-JJ). *Copper metal:* Comotion.

Page 17: **First Impressions.** Patterned paper: Frances Meyer. Decorative scissors: Westrim Crafts (Memories Forever). Satin ribbon: Offray. Font: Modeled after Parsons Technology (PT Lullaby).

Page 18: **Paper Piercing.** *Decorative scissors:* Fiskars (Scallop).

Page 19: **Baby's First Haircut.** All materials used are available wherever scrapbooking supplies are sold.

Page 20: **Old-Fashioned Wedding.** *Decorative scissors:* Fiskars (Deckle). *Stencil:* Stampendous.

FEBRUARY

Page 22: **Woven Valentine.** All materials used are available wherever scrapbooking supplies are sold.

Page 23: **Send Roses.** *Flower bouquet card:* The Gifted Line. *Font:* DJ Inkers (DJ Fancy). *Elegant border rubber stamp:* Stampendous (Brush Swirl—QN015). *Peg rubber stamps:* Hero Arts (Tiny Backgrounds).

Page 25: **Handmade Baby Announcement.** *Tissue paper:* Marvel Exquisitely Elegant Tissue Wrap. *Font:* Modeled after Harrington.

Page 26: **Baptism.** *Cross rubber stamp:* JudiKins (2071G). *Border stickers:* Hallmark. *Dove rubber stamp:* Printworks (F1549). *Teal ribbon (¼"):* Available wherever scrapbooking or sewing supplies are sold. *Font:* DJ Inkers (DJ Script).

Page 28: **Matting Examples.** *Patterned paper:* The Paper Patch.

Page 29: **Friendship Frame.** *"I'm so glad you're my friend!" rubber stamp:* Darcie's. *"True friends" rubber stamp:* Hero Arts (C 326). *Heart with dots rubber stamp:* Hero Arts (A 1293). *Swirl heart rubber stamp:* Personal Stamp Exchange (B-1896).

Page 30: **Letters from Friends.** *Background paper:* NRN Designs. *Love letters (left to right):* Hot Off the Press (Pink Stencil—10035), Building a Better Scrapbook, Hot Off the Press (Pink Moire—10030). *Pierced design:* Gick (Super Colossal Iron On Transfer Book). *Font:* Parsons Technology (PT Tassel).

Page 31: **Woven Heart and Border.** All materials used are available wherever scrapbooking supplies are sold.

Page 32: **Smiles.** *Interlocking design template:* PuzzleMates (Heart set).

MARCH

Page 34: **Gold-Dusted Shamrock.** *Gold rub-on:* Craf-T Products (Earth Tones Kit).

Page 35: **First Birthday.** *Border stickers:* Hallmark. *Font:* Inspire Graphics (Scrap Swirl). *Balloon stickers:* Frances Meyer. *Die cut:* Accu-Cut.

Page 36: **Happy Birthday.** *Accordion book kit:* Papers by Catherine. *Rubber stamp:* All Night Media (Happy Birthday Swirl—244H). *Patterned vellum paper:* Papers by Catherine.

Page 38: **Birthday Best Wishes.** *Rubber stamp:* Personal Stamp Exchange (F-318). *Pressed pansy flower:* Nature's Pressed.

Page 39: **Czech Wedding Play.** *Border and medallion stickers:* Hallmark. *Calligraphy pen:* Sakura (1.8 Black).

Page 40: **Heritage Album.** *Deckle edge:* Fiskars Rotary Cutter. *Title font:* Parsons Technology (PT Impressive Bold).

Page 42: **Adding Color.** All materials used are available wherever scrapbooking supplies are sold.

Page 43: **Cornering.** (Top) *Cornering scissors:* Fiskars Corner Edgers (Art Deco). (Middle) *Corner punches:* Family Treasures Lace Edge (Teardrop & Corner Frame). (Bottom) *Heritage photograph photo corners:* Gina Bear (9001—Rose).

Page 44: **In Stitches.** *Rubber stamp:* JudiKins (9001F). *Letter template:* Bemiss-Jason Corp (Fadeless Art Board 2" Letters). *Font:* Parsons Technology (PT Hand Label).

Page 46: **Tactile Texture.** *Embossing powder:* Personal Stamp Exchange (Desert Tapestry).

APRIL

Page 48: **Paper Cast Rabbit.** *Ceramic mold:* Brown Bag Paper Art.

Page 49: **Bluebonnets.** *Deckle edge:* Fiskars Rotary Cutter. *Font:* Modeled after Inspire Graphics (Scrap Flower).

Page 50: **Easter Egg Hunt.** *Font:* Inspire Graphics (Scrap Swirl).

Page 51: **Passover.** *"Grape Vitis" square rubber stamp:* Personal Stamp Exchange (G-1302). *Leaf and grape border rubber stamp:* Hero Arts (F378). *Cork paper:* Magenta. *Metallic pen:* Marvy.

Page 52: **Arbor Day.** *Alphabet stencil:* Frances Meyer (Fat Caps). *Leaf-print vellum paper:* Papers by Catherine. *Font:* Inspire Graphics (Scrap Swirl).

Page 53: **Lullaby Album.** *Rubber stamp:* Hot Potatoes. *Font:* Parsons Technology (PT Saigon).

Page 55: **Dry Embossing.** *Stencil:* Stampendous (ET03—Butterfly Circle).

Page 57: **Creative Lettering.** *Angel wings:* Saint Louis Trimming (Wings!). *Font:* DJ Inkers (DJ Calli).

Page 59: **Victorian Ribbon Embroidery.** *Micro hole punch:* McGill (Size: 1/16). *Embroidery stitch instructions and patterns:* Bucilla. *Green stems straight stitch:* DMC Cotton Embroidery Floss (937). *Pink buds French knot:* silk ribbon (7mm). *Purple buds French knot:* silk ribbon (7mm). *Yellow daisies' centers French knots:* silk ribbon (4mm). *Green leaves Japanese ribbon stitch:* silk ribbon (7mm). *Daisy petals Japanese ribbon pistil stitch:* silk ribbon (7mm). *Spider web rose:* silk ribbon (7mm). Silk ribbon is available wherever scrapbooking or sewing supplies are sold.

MAY

Page 62: **Pressed Botanicals.** *Pressed flowers and leaves:* Nature's Pressed. *Adhesive:* Perfect Paper Adhesive by USArt Quest Inc.

Page 63: **Mother's Pearls.** *Pink plaid patterned paper:* Northern Spy. *Black velvet paper:* Papers by Catherine. *Pink embroidery ribbon (¼"):* Available wherever scrapbooking or sewing supplies are sold.

Page 64: **Prom Night.** *Marble-design paper:* Hot Off the Press. *Harlequin-style ivory paper:* Hallmark (Wedding Memories kit). *Raspberry cardstock:* Creative Memories. *Font:* CompuWorks (Flower Caps).

Page 66: **Bridal Shower.** *Patterned paper (packages):* Sally Foster Gift Wrap. *Patterned paper (mat):* Papers by Catherine. *Font:* Bookman Old Style.

Page 67: **Wedding Portrait.** *Stencil:* StenSource (W6003—Rambling Roses).

Page 68: **Kara at Disneyland.** *Blue-striped cardstock:* Hallmark. *Rubber stamp:* Rubber Stampede (Mickey Balloon—A393C).

Page 69: **Garden Glory.** *Basket rubber stamp:* River City Rubber Works (1066 N—Round Basket). *Hibiscus flower rubber stamp:* Similar to rubber stamp by Stamp Oasis (Hibiscus—G448)

Page 71: **Butterfly in Motion.** *Rubber stamp:* Rubber Stamps of America.

Page 72: **Flower Show.** *Handmade paper:* Printworks (Dancing Colors). *Pressed flowers and leaves:* Nature's Pressed.

Page 73: **Wedding Invitation.** *Invitation:* Hallmark. *Pressed flowers:* Nature's Pressed

Page 75: **Grand Canyon.** *Alphabet rubber stamps:* Stampendous! (SS121—Jungle Alpha). *Hand rubber stamp:* Rubber Stamps of America. *Star rubber stamp:* Personal Stamp Exchange (B-1933). *Spiral rubber stamp:* JudiKins (6560H).

JUNE

Page 76: **Summer Solstice.** *Rubber stamp:* JudiKins (2124H). *Gold metal:* Commotion.

Page 77: **Father's Day Box.** *Non-heat laminate:* Therm O Web. *Rubber stamp:* Hero Arts (Wordprints—S1251 Love).

Page 79: **Take Me Out to the Ballgame.** *Font:* Inspire Graphics (Scrap Marker). *Baseball stickers:* Frances Meyer. *Patterned paper:* Northern Spy.

Page 80: **All My Sports.** *Alphabet template:* C Thru Ruler (Helvetica Bold). *Rubber stamps:* Hero Arts (Sports Stamps set). *Patterned paper:* Hot Off The Press.

Page 81: **Capture Your Hobby.** *Title font:* Parsons Technology (PT Cozy Outline).

Page 82: **Anchoring.** *Font:* French Script MT.

Page 84: **Tinting.** *Rubber stamps:* Rubber Stampede (Posh Impressions). *Background paper:* Indian silkscreen paper. *Font:* Imprint MT Shadow. *Colored pencils:* Berol (Prismacolor).

Page 85: **Identifying Groups.** *Font:* Modeled after Harrington.

Page 86: **Patterned Paper.** *Font:* DJ Inkers (DJ Fat Chat). *Rubber stamp:* Hero Arts (Sports Stamps set). *Bike clip art:* Inspire Graphics.

JULY

Page 88: **Summer Watermelon.** *Chunky stamp:* Back Street, Inc. *Paper paint:* Delta (Cherished Memories). *Patterned paper:* Creative Memories.

Page 89: **July 4th Bike Parade.** *Star bunting punch:* McGill. *Patterned paper:* Northern Spy.

Page 90: **Picking Blueberries.** *Rubber stamp:* Stampouri. *Font:* DJ Inkers (DJ Fat Chat). *Patterned paper:* Creative Memories.

Page 92: **Vacation Album I.** *Rubber stamp:* Hot Potatoes. *Font:* Modeled after Bookman Old Style.

Page 93: **Vacation Album II.** *Rubber stamp:* Tin Can Mail (Small Suitcase—59289E). *Marble paper:* Papercuts. *Clear photo corners:* Creative Memories. *Black photo corners:* Canson. *Font:* Franklin Gothic Book.

Page 94: **Capturing Motion.** *Alphabet stencil:* Frances Meyer (Fat Caps). *Stickers:* Mrs. Grossman's (Design Lines).

Page 95: **Die Cuts.** *Umbrella die cut:* Remember When by Colorbök. *All other die cuts:* Creative Memories.

Page 97: **Sequencing.** *Font:* Copperplate Gothic.

AUGUST

Page 100: **Seashells.** *Rubber stamp:* Peddler's Pack Stampworks. *Peach paper:* Fascinating Folds. *Cork paper:* Embossing Arts.

Page 101: **Near the Sea.** *Seashell rubber stamp:* Stampworks. *Cork paper:* Embossing Arts. *"Near the Sea" rubber stamp:* Personal Stamp Exchange (G-1481). *Embossing powder:* Personal Stamp Exchange (Turquoise Tapestry).

Page 102: **Summer Camp.** *Paper:* Hallmark. *Font:* Inspire Graphics (ScrapWood). *Font:* Kidprint.

Page 104: **Collector's Album I.** *Background paper:* Indian silkscreen paper. *Font:* Harrington.

Page 105: **Collector's Album II.** All materials used are available wherever scrapbooking supplies are sold.

Page 106: **Creating Depth.** *Tall tree stencil:* Provo Craft. *Patterned paper:* Hallmark. *Small tree stencil:* Pebbles in My Pocket.

Page 107: **Pop-up Page.** *Deckle edge:* Fiskars Rotary Cutter (Deckle Blade). *Die cuts:* Ellison (Shapes©™). *Pop-up base pattern:* "The Scrap Happy Guide to Pop-ups," by Suzanne McNeill, Design Originals, Fort Worth, 1998.

Page 109: **Buddies.** *Alphabet stickers:* Creative Memories. *Red patterned paper:* Frances Meyer (5006-60—Red Gingham). *Blue patterned paper:* Creative Memories. *Font:* Parsons Technology (PT Hand Label).

Page 111: **Watercolor.** *Rubber stamp:* Printworks (D1456).

SEPTEMBER

Page 114: **Orchard Apple.** *Rubber stamp:* A Stamp in the Hand Company.

Page 115: **Grandparents' Photocard.** *Rubber Stamp:* JudiKins (2233J). *Gold powder:* Jacquard Products.

Page 116: **School Portrait.** *Alphabet template:* Pebbles in My Pocket (Block Letter Tracer). *Background patterned paper:* Northern Spy (318—Woven). *Apple patterned paper:* Provo Craft (Apple for the Teacher).

Page 117: **Back to School.** *Rubber stamp:* A Stamp in the Hand Company. *"Kindergarten" paper:* Canson. *"Kindergarten" font:* Kidsprint. *Alphabet stencils:* Pebbles in My Pocket (Block 1¼"). *"High School" font:* Phyllis (Script). *"High School" letters:* Expert Software (3D Font Creator).

Page 119: **A Child's Artwork.** *Alphabet template:* C-Thru Ruler (Helvetica Bold). *Patterned paper:* Creative Memories. *Cork paper:* Magenta.

Page 120: **Double-Page Layout.** All materials used are available wherever scrapbooking supplies are sold.

Page 121: **Pocket Page.** *Patterned paper:* Sonburn. *Font:* Parsons Technology (PT Mercury).

Page 123: **I Love to Dance.** *Font:* Modeled after DanceStep.

Page 124: **Spritzing and Colored Pencils.** *Air Gun:* E. K. Success (Inkworx). *Rubber stamp:* Stamps Happen, Inc. (Keeper of the Lighthouse—80199).

OCTOBER

Page 126: **Sunflower Mask.** *Clip art mask:* Inspire Graphics.

Page 127: **Pumpkin Carving.** *Alphabet and number rubber stamps:* Crafty Productions (Memory Blocks). *Patterned paper:* The Paper Patch. *Satin ribbon:* Offray.

Page 128: **Texas State Fair.** *Leather-patterned paper:* Fascinating Folds. *Rubber stamp:* JudiKins.

Page 131: **ABC Gift Album.** *Alphabet template:* C-Thru Ruler (Helvetica Bold). *Apple-patterned paper:* Provo Craft (Apple for the Teacher). *Apple cutouts:* Frances Meyer patterned paper (5001-303—Apple Bob). *Rabbit-patterned paper:* Similar to paper by Current, Inc.

Page 132: **Fall Collage.** *Dried maple leaves:* Nature's Pressed. *Font:* CompuWorks (Country).

Page 133: **Paper Tearing.** *Rubber stamp:* JudiKins (5557 H—Fall Leaves).

Page 134: **Torn Paper.** *Pressed flowers:* Nature's Pressed.

Page 136: **Anniversary Well Wishes.** All materials used are available wherever scrapbooking supplies are sold.

Page 137: **Guess Who.** *Black velvet paper:* Papers by Catherine. *Plaid- patterned paper:* The Paper Patch. *Alphabet stencils:* Pebbles in My Pocket (Hollywood ¾").

NOVEMBER

Page 140: **Dried Fruit.** All materials used are available wherever scrapbooking supplies are sold.

Page 141: **Thanksgiving Dinner.** *Pear-patterned paper:* Provo Craft.

Page 142: **Retirement Party.** *Map-design cardstock:* Hallmark. *Textured green and yellow cardstock:* Canson. *Font:* Inspire Graphics (ScrapMarker).

Page 143: **Top Dogs.** *Mat paper:* Inkadinkado. *Font:* Cloister Black BT.

Page 144: **Sea Legs.** *Sailboat:* Gina Bear (6035—Sailboat). *Font:* Tristan.

Page 145: **Baby Album Cover.** *Spiral Album:* Canson. *Frame:* K & Company. *Sticker letters:* K & Company. *Blue self-adhesive paper:* Canson.

Page 147: **Sponging.** *Stencils:* StenSource (W6044—Lattice and W6000—Ivy).

Page 149: **Elegant Papercutting.** *Papercut frame:* Gina Bear.

Page 150: **Heritage Papercutting.** *Stencil:* StenSource (W6006—Periwinkle). *Corner punch:* Family Treasures (Slot Punch—921).

DECEMBER

Page 154: **Origami Wreath.** *Red foil paper:* Loose Ends. *Patterned paper:* Hot Off the Press (10012—Holly).

Page 155: **Viennese Christmas Market.** *Adhesive:* Perfect Paper Adhesive by USArt Quest.

Page 156: **Hanukkah.** *Adhesive:* Perfect Paper Adhesive by USArt Quest. *Thick gold embossing powder:* Suze Weinberg. *Rubber stamp:* Personal Stamp Exchange (B-085).

Page 157: **Trimming the Tree.** *Faux jewel star:* The Beadery. *Colored spangles:* Sulyn Industries. *Iridescent spangles:* Westrim Crafts. *Font:* Christmas Tree.

Page 158: **Holiday Card Pocket Page.** *Gold wire-edged ribbon:* Ribbon Textiles. *Gold embossing powder:* Mark Enterprises (Stamp-n Stuff Embossing Tinsel, Gold Opaque—TII-102).

Page 159: **Finishing Touches.** *Imprintable card:* Colors by Design (Artist: Victoria Cole—BL3043).

Page 160: **Paper Folding.** *Patterned paper:* Wrapping paper. *Font:* Matura MT Script Capitals.

Page 162: **Dear Daddy.** *Patterned paper:* GeoGraphics (GeoPaper—GeoTyeDie).

Page 163: **3-D Elements.** *Patterned dollhouse paper:* MiniGraphics. *Sticker letters:* K & Company.

NOT JUST ALBUMS

Page 166: **Party Invitation.** *Rubber stamp:* Mostly Animals (Betsy—291S6). *Font:* DJ Inkers (DJ Scrap Moo). *Patterned paper:* Provo Craft. *Grass sticker:* Mrs. Grossman's.

Page 167: **Birthday Card.** *Font:* Parsons Technology (PT Impressive Bold).

Page 168: **Show-Off.** *Font:* DJ Inkers (DJ Cross Stitch).

Page 169: **Special Event Poster.** *Pine tree-patterned paper:* Hallmark. *Alphabet stencil:* Pebbles in My Pocket (Block 1¼"). *Die cuts:* Hallmark.

Page 170: **How We Met.** *Illuminated letter:* Parsons Technology (PT Letterbook).

Page 171: **Child's Bookmark.** *Precut acid-free bookmark:* Hero Arts. *Flowerpot die cut:* Creative Memories. *Font:* Inspire Graphics (Scrap Kids).

COMPANIES

A Stamp in the Hand Company
562-403-7137
Carson, CA

Accu-Cut
800-288-1670
www.accucut.com

All Night Media
415-459-3013
www.allnightmedia.com

Back Street, Inc.
678-206-7373

Beadery, The
401-539-2432
105 Canonchet Road
Hope Valley, RI 02832

Bemiss-Jason Corp.
800-544-0093
www.bemiss-jason.com

Berol
www.berol.com

Brown Bag Paper Art
77 Regional Drive
Concord, NH 03301

Bucilla
717-384-2525
www.bucilla.com

C-Thru Ruler Company
800-243-8419
www.cthruruler.com

Canson-Talens, Inc.
413-538-9250
www.canson-us.com

Colorbök
734-426-5300
www.colorbok.com

Colors by Design
800-832-8436
www.colorsbydesign.com

Comotion
800-257-1288
www.comotion.com

CompuWorks
The Wizardworks Group
Minneapolis, MN 55447

Craf-T Products
507-235-3996
PO Box 83
Fairmont, MN 56031

Crafty Productions
800-925-6838
681 Encinitas Boulevard
Encinitas, CA 92024

Creative Memories
800-341-5275
www.creative-memories.com

Current, Inc.
800-848-2848
www.currentcatalog.com

DJ Inkers
800-325-4890
www.djinkers.com

DMC
201-589-0606
www.dmc-usa.com

D.O.T.S./Close to My Heart
888-655-6552
738 East Quality Drive
American Fork, UT 84033

Darcie's
800-453-1527 www.darcie.com

Delta
213-686-0678
www.deltacrafts.com

E.K. Success
973-458-0090
www.eksuccess.com

Ellison
800-253-2238
www.ellison.com

Embossing Arts Company
800-662-7955
www.embossingarts.com

Expert Software
305-567-9990
www.expertsoftware.com

Family Treasures
800-413-2645
www.familytreasures.com

Fascinating Folds
800-968-2418
www.fascinating-folds.com

Fiskars
www.fiskars.com

Frances Meyer
www.francesmeyer.com

GeoGraphics
800-426-5923
www.geographics.com

Gick Publishing, Inc.
949-581-5830
9 Studebaker Drive
Irvine, CA 92718

Gifted Line, The
999 Canal Boulevard
Point Richmond, CA 94804

Gina Bear
888-888-4453
www.ginabear.com

Hallmark
www.hallmark.com

Hero Arts
800-822-HERO
www.heroarts.com

Hot Off the Press
503-266-9102
www.hotp.com

Hot Potatoes
615-269-8002
www.hotpotatoes.com

Ichiyo Art Center
494-233-1846
www.ichiyoart.com

Inkadinkado
617-938-6100
www.inkadinkado.com

Inspire Graphics
877-472-3427
www.inspiregraphics.com

Jacquard Products
800-442-0455
www.jacquardproducts.com

JudiKins
310-515-1115
www.judi-kins.com

K & Company
913-685-1458
7441 W. 161st Street
Stilwell, KS 66085

Loose Ends
503-390-7457
www.4loosends.com

MPR Associates
High Point, NC 27264

Magenta
450-446-5253
351 Blain
Mont Saint-Hilaire
Qc, Canada J3H 3B4

Mark Enterprises
800-443-3430
www.markenterprises.com

Marvel Products, Inc.
203-255-3511
P.O. Box 763
Fairfield, CT 06430

Marvy Uchida
800-541-5877
www.uchida.com

McGill
800-982-9884
PO Box 177
Marengo, IL 60152

Microfleur Microwave Flower
Press
888-883-5387
1281 Kimmerling Road
Gardnerville, NV 89410

MiniGraphics
800-442-7935
www.minigraphics.com

Mostly Animals
209-848-2552
PO Box 2355
Oakdale, CA 95361

Mrs. Grossman's
800-429-4549
www.mrsgrossmans.com

Nature's Pressed
801-225-1169
www.naturespressed.com

Northern Spy
916-620-7430
www.northernspy.com

NRN Designs
800-421-6958
5362 Bolsa Avenue
Huntington Beach, CA 92649

Offray
908-879-4700
www.offray.com

Paper Adventures
800-727-0699
www.paperadventures.com

Papercuts
800-661-4399
www.papercuts.com

Paper Patch, The
801-253-3018
PO Box 414
Riverton, UT 84065

Paper Reflections
www.dmdind.com
DMD Industries
Springdale, AR 72764

Papers by Catherine
713-723-3334
11328 S. Post Oak Road
#108
Houston, TX 77035

Parsons Technology
800-973-5111
www.parsonstechnology.com

Pebbles in My Pocket
800-438-8153
www.pebblesinmypocket.com

Peddler's Pack Stampworks
800-29STAMP
www.peddlerspack.com

Personal Stamp Exchange
(PSX)
707-588-8058
www.psxstamps.com

Posh Impressions
800-421-7674
www.poshimpressions.com

Printworks
310-696-4562
E-mail: PrntWorks@aol.com

Provo Craft
800-937-7686
285 East 900 South
Provo, UT 84606

PuzzleMates
714-671-9438
www.puzzlemates.com

Ribbon Textiles, Inc.
800-327-6444
205 Industrial Drive
Boone, NC 28607

River City Rubber Works
316-262-5318
1018 West Maple Street
Wichita, KS 67213

Rubber Stampede
800-632-8386
www.rstampede.com

Rubber Stamps of America
800-553-5031
www.stampusa.com

Saint Louis Trimming
314-771-8388
5040 Arsenal Street
St. Louis, MO 63139

Sakura of America
800-776-6257
www.gellyroll.com

Sally Foster Gift Wrap, Inc.
619-554-1090
San Diego, CA 92121

Sonburn Inc.
800-527-7505
PO Box 167
Addison, TX 75001

Stamp Oasis
702-878-6474
www.stampoasis.com

Stampendous!
714-563-9501
www.stampendous.com

Stampourri
888-80-STAMP
www.localmall.com/stampourri

Stamps Happen, Inc.
714-879-9894
369 S. Acacia Avenue
Fullerton, CA 92631

Stampworks
818-761-8757
www.stampworks.com

StenSource International, Inc.
209-536-1148
www.stensource.com

Stickopotamus
PO Box 6507
Carlsdadt, NJ 07072

Sulyn Industries, Inc.
954-755-2311
www.sulyn.com

Suze Weinberg
908-364-3136
www.schmoozewithsuze.com

Therm O Web
847-520-5200
www.thermoweb.com

Tin Can Mail
800-546-5982
PO Box 5748
Redwood City, CA 94063

USArt Quest Inc.
800-200-7848
www.usartquest.com

Westrim Crafts
800-727-2727
www.westrimcrafts.com

index

about
the authors

Debbie Janasak and Anna Swinney are the creators of www.gracefulbee.com—a web-zine providing techniques, ideas, tips, and inspirations to fellow scrapbookers. When a friend invited Anna to an introductory scrapbooking class in 1994, she thought it was just going to be a night out with the girls. She ended up loving it and immediately stocked up on scrapbooking "toys," including albums and supplies. Anna showed Debbie the family album she had made and described her plans for a heritage album featuring antique photos of her family and photos her father had taken during the 1940s. Debbie was hooked. She jumped on the scrapbooking bandwagon, accompanying Anna to a class in 1996. Debbie had dabbled in arts and crafts, cross-stitch, watercolor, oil painting, and photography. Now, scrapbooking provides her the opportunity to meld all these passions. She also loves journaling directly onto scrapbook pages and is a self-described "pen fanatic."

As their mutual love of scrapbooking deepened their friendship, Debbie and Anna quickly began developing many techniques of their own, drawing their inspiration from mixed media, as well as nature, magazines, and even children's storybooks. In 1997, Debbie and Anna combined their love of scrapbooking with their computer training to start their web-zine, which is viewed by thousands of visitors weekly.

Anna is married and has two children, Jenna and Jared. Debbie is married and has two children, Kara and Nathan. The Swinneys and the Janasaks both live in Plano, Texas—and always carry a camera with them wherever they go.